FAVORITE BRAND NAME
Best-Loved
HOLIDAY
RECIPES

Publications International, Ltd.

Microwave Cooking: Microwave ovens vary in wattage. Use the cooking times as guidelines and check for doneness before adding more time.

Contents

BLACK BEAN SPIRALS

4 ounces PHILADELPHIA® Cream Cheese, softened
½ cup (2 ounces) KRAFT® Mexican Style Finely Shredded
Cheddar and Monterey Jack Cheese with Jalapeño Peppers*
¼ cup BREAKSTONE'S® or KNUDSEN® Sour Cream
¼ teaspoon onion salt
1 cup canned black beans, rinsed, drained
3 (10-inch) flour tortillas
Salsa

*May also use KRAFT Shredded Monterey Jack Cheese.

MIX cheeses, sour cream and onion salt with electric mixer on medium speed until well blended.

PLACE beans in food processor container fitted with steel blade or blender container; cover. Process until smooth. Spread thin layer of beans on each tortilla; spread cheese mixture over beans.

ROLL tortillas up tightly. Refrigerate 30 minutes. Cut into ½-inch slices. Serve with salsa.   *Makes 10 servings*

Prep Time: 15 minutes plus refrigerating

Black Bean Spirals

EAST MEETS WEST
COCKTAIL FRANKS

1 cup prepared sweet and sour sauce
1½ tablespoons rice vinegar or cider vinegar
1 tablespoon grated fresh ginger *or*
1 teaspoon dried ginger
1 tablespoon dark sesame oil
½ teaspoon chile oil (optional)
1 package (12 ounces) HEBREW
NATIONAL® Cocktail Beef Franks
2 tablespoons chopped cilantro or chives

Combine sweet and sour sauce, vinegar, ginger, sesame oil and chile oil in medium saucepan. Bring to a boil over medium heat. Cook 5 minutes or until thickened. Add cocktail franks; cover and cook until heated through. Transfer to chafing dish; sprinkle with cilantro. Serve with frilled wooden picks.
Makes 12 appetizer servings
(2 cocktail franks per serving)

ORIGINAL BUFFALO
CHICKEN WINGS

Zesty Blue Cheese Dip (recipe follows)
2½ pounds chicken wings, split and tips
discarded
½ cup FRANK'S® REDHOT® Hot Sauce
(or to taste)
⅓ cup butter or margarine, melted
Celery sticks

1. Prepare Zesty Blue Cheese Dip.

2. Deep fry* wings at 400°F 12 minutes or until crisp and no longer pink; drain.

3. Combine REDHOT sauce and butter in large bowl. Add wings to sauce; toss to coat evenly. Serve with Zesty Blue Cheese Dip and celery.
Makes 24 to 30 individual pieces

*Or, prepare wings using one of the cooking methods below. Add wings to sauce; toss well to coat completely.

To Bake: Place wings in a single layer on rack in foil-lined roasting pan. Bake at 425°F 1 hour or until crisp and no longer pink, turning halfway through baking time.

To Broil: Place wings in a single layer on rack in foil-lined roasting pan. Broil 6 inches from heat 15 to 20 minutes or until crisp and no longer pink, turning once.

To Grill: Place wings on an oiled grid. Grill, over medium heat, 30 to 40 minutes or until crisp and no longer pink, turning often.

Prep Time: 10 minutes
Cook Time: 15 minutes

ZESTY BLUE CHEESE DIP

½ cup blue cheese salad dressing
¼ cup sour cream
2 teaspoons FRANK'S® REDHOT® Hot
Sauce

Combine all ingredients in medium serving bowl; mix well. Garnish with crumbled blue cheese, if desired.

East Meets West Cocktail Franks

OREGON HOT APPLE CIDER

    8 cups apple cider
    ½ cup dried cherries
    ½ cup dried cranberries
    3 cinnamon sticks, broken in half
    8 whole cloves
    1 pear, quartered, cored, sliced

1. Combine cider, cherries, cranberries, cinnamon and cloves in large saucepan. Heat just to a simmer; do not boil.

2. Add pear before serving.

Makes 8 servings

PEPPERIDGE FARM®
SPINACH-CHEESE SWIRLS

    ½ package (17¼-ounce size) PEPPERIDGE
        FARM® Frozen Puff Pastry Sheets
        (1 sheet)
    1 egg
    1 tablespoon water
    ½ cup shredded Muenster *or* Monterey Jack
        cheese (2 ounces)
    ¼ cup grated Parmesan cheese
    1 green onion, chopped (about
        2 tablespoons)
    ⅛ teaspoon garlic powder
    1 package (about 10 ounces) frozen
        chopped spinach, thawed and well
        drained

1. Thaw pastry sheet at room temperature 30 minutes. Preheat oven to 400°F. Mix egg and water and set aside. Mix Muenster cheese, Parmesan cheese, onion and garlic powder. Set aside.

2. Unfold pastry on lightly floured surface. Brush with egg mixture. Top with cheese mixture and spinach. Starting at one side, roll up like a jelly roll. Cut into 20 (½-inch) slices. Place 2 inches apart on baking sheet. Brush tops with egg mixture.

3. Bake 15 minutes or until golden.

Makes 20 appetizers

Tip: To thaw spinach, microwave on HIGH 3 minutes, breaking apart with fork halfway through heating.

Thaw Time: 30 minutes
Prep Time: 20 minutes
Cook Time: 15 minutes

PHILLY® GARLIC & HERB DIP

    1 package (8 ounces) PHILADELPHIA®
        Cream Cheese, softened
    3 tablespoons milk
    3 tablespoons finely chopped fresh basil
    3 tablespoons finely chopped fresh parsley
    2 tablespoons chopped fresh chives
    1 clove garlic, minced

MIX cream cheese and milk with electric mixer on medium speed until smooth.

BLEND in remaining ingredients. Refrigerate. Serve with assorted cut-up vegetables, breadsticks or chips.

Makes 1 cup

Prep Time: 10 minutes plus refrigerating

Oregon Hot Apple Cider

CRUDITÉS WITH CREAMY CHEESE DIP

CREAMY CHEESE DIP

**12 ounces (2 cartons) ALPINE LACE®
  Reduced Fat Cream Cheese with
  Garlic & Herbs**
⅔ cup nonfat mayonnaise dressing
⅓ cup finely chopped red onion
1 tablespoon whole-grain Dijon mustard
½ teaspoon freshly ground black pepper
¼ teaspoon curry powder
  Red onion rings (optional)

CRUDITÉS

  **Assorted fresh vegetables (your choices!):
  bell pepper strips (green, red and
  yellow), broccoli florets, peeled baby
  carrots, celery sticks, whole green
  beans, mushroom slices, snow peas,
  yellow squash circles, zucchini circles,
  unpeeled red potato chunks, cherry
  tomatoes, cucumber rounds**

1. To make the Creamy Cheese Dip: In a medium-size bowl, using an electric mixer set on high speed, beat the cream cheese until smooth. Stir in the remaining dip ingredients except onion rings. Place in a small serving bowl, cover with plastic wrap and chill.

2. To prepare the Crudités: Half-fill a large saucepan with water and bring to a boil over high heat. Add the bell pepper, broccoli, carrots, celery, beans, mushrooms, peas, yellow squash and zucchini, one at a time, and blanch for 15 to 30 seconds or just until their color brightens. (Do not overcook!)

Remove the vegetables with a slotted spoon, immediately plunge them into cold water, then drain well. Cook the potatoes in the same water for 15 minutes or until tender.

3. Arrange the blanched vegetables, potatoes, tomatoes and cucumbers in a circle on a large platter, leaving space in the center for the bowl of dip. Cover with plastic wrap and chill. To serve: Uncover, garnish with the onion rings and place the bowl of dip in the center.

Makes 2 cups dip

CALIFORNIA MARINATED MUSHROOMS

1 pound small fresh mushrooms, cleaned
1 small cucumber, peeled and sliced
**1 jar (4 ounces) chopped pimiento,
  drained**
**1 bottle (8 ounces) LAWRY'S® Classic Red
  Wine Vinaigrette with Cabernet
  Sauvignon Dressing**
½ teaspoon LAWRY'S® Garlic Salt

In large resealable plastic bag or medium glass bowl, combine all ingredients; seal bag or cover dish. Refrigerate at least 1 hour, turning bag over or stirring occasionally.

Makes 8 appetizer servings

Serving Suggestion: Serve in lettuce cup made with layers of curly lettuce, red cabbage and radicchio.

Crudités with Creamy Cheese Dip

PARTY CHEESE WREATH

2 packages (8 ounces each)
  PHILADELPHIA® Cream Cheese,
  softened
1 package (8 ounces) KRAFT® Shredded
  Sharp Cheddar Cheese
1 tablespoon chopped red bell pepper
1 tablespoon finely chopped onion
2 teaspoons Worcestershire sauce
1 teaspoon lemon juice
  Dash ground red pepper

MIX cream cheese and cheddar cheese with electric mixer on medium speed until well blended.

BLEND in remaining ingredients. Refrigerate several hours or overnight.

PLACE drinking glass in center of serving platter. Drop round tablespoonfuls of mixture around glass, just touching outer edge of glass to form ring; smooth with spatula. Remove glass. Garnish with chopped fresh parsley and chopped red pepper. Serve with crackers.

Makes 12 servings

Variation: Substitute 2 packages (8 ounces each) PHILADELPHIA® Neufchâtel Cheese, 1/3 Less Fat than Cream Cheese for cream cheese.

Mini Cheeseballs: Shape cream cheese mixture into 1-inch balls. Roll in light rye bread crumbs or dark pumpernickel bread crumbs.

Prep Time: 15 minutes plus refrigerating

Cream cheese was developed over 100 years ago and was first produced commercially by an ambitious, hard-working farmer in upstate New York. It was primarily used as a flavorful spread for bread, toast or crackers. This fresh, delicate cheese was not used as a recipe ingredient until the mid-1920s. One of the first recipes developed was the "Kraft Philadelphia Cream Cake," which was later retitled "Supreme Cheesecake." This recipe became an instant favorite and what began as a novel idea—cooking with cream cheese—has become a universally accepted concept. Today, Philadelphia Cream Cheese is an indispensable ingredient used by great American cooks like you.

Party Cheese Wreath

TORTELLINI WITH ROASTED GARLIC SAUCE

1 large bulb garlic
1 package (9 ounces) fresh tortellini pasta
2 to 3 tablespoons olive oil
½ cup reduced-fat mayonnaise
½ cup nonfat sour cream
⅓ cup grated Parmesan cheese
2 tablespoons FRANK'S® REDHOT® Hot Sauce

1. Preheat oven to 350°F. Cut ½-inch off top of garlic, discard. Remove papery outer skin, leaving cloves intact. Wrap garlic in foil; bake 1 hour or until tender when pierced with sharp knife. Let stand until cool enough to handle.

2. Cook tortellini according to package directions. Rinse under cold water; drain well on paper towels. Heat 2 tablespoons oil in large nonstick skillet over medium heat. Add tortellini in batches to oil, cook and stir 3 to 5 minutes or until lightly golden. Add more oil, if necessary. Drain on paper towels.

3. Separate cooled garlic into cloves; pinch each clove so roasted flesh comes out. Place cloves in blender or food processor. Add mayonnaise, sour cream, Parmesan cheese and REDHOT sauce. Cover; process until puréed and very smooth. Spoon into small saucepan; cook and stir over low heat until hot and bubbly. Transfer to small serving bowl.

4. To serve, arrange tortellini on serving platter. Dip into Roasted Garlic Sauce.

Makes 12 servings
(about 1¼ cups sauce)

Tip: Roasted Garlic Sauce can be tossed with your favorite hot cooked pasta.

Prep Time: 35 minutes
Cook Time: about 1 hour

CELEBRATION PUNCH

1 can (46 fluid ounces) DEL MONTE® Pineapple Juice, chilled
1 can (46 fluid ounces) apricot nectar, chilled
1 cup orange juice
¼ cup fresh lime juice
2 tablespoons grenadine
1 cup rum (optional)
Ice cubes

1. Combine all ingredients in punch bowl.

2. Garnish with pineapple wedges and lime slices, if desired.

Makes 16 (6-ounce) servings

Tortellini with Roasted Garlic Sauce

The mustard business, founded by an Englishman named Grey, flourished in the same French community for two centuries.

PESTO BRIE

2 tablespoons GREY POUPON® Dijon
    Mustard
2 tablespoons prepared pesto sauce
1 (8-ounce) wheel Brie cheese
2 tablespoons PLANTERS® Walnuts, finely
    chopped
  Chopped tomatoes and fresh basil leaves,
    for garnish
  Assorted crackers or breadsticks

In small bowl, blend mustard and pesto; set aside. Cut cheese in half horizontally. Place bottom half on greased baking sheet, cut-side up; spread with half the pesto mixture. Replace top of Brie, cut-side down; spread with remaining pesto mixture and sprinkle with nuts.

Bake at 350°F for 3 to 4 minutes or until cheese is slightly softened. Do not overbake. Transfer to serving dish. Garnish with chopped tomatoes and basil leaves. Serve with assorted crackers or breadsticks.

Makes 6 to 8 appetizer servings

HOLIDAY VEGETABLE NIBBLES

½ pound (8 ounces) VELVEETA® Pasteurized
    Cheese Product, cut up
¼ cup sour cream
¼ cup finely chopped green or red pepper
1 tablespoon chopped green onion
½ teaspoon dried tarragon leaves, crushed

• Beat all ingredients at medium speed with electric mixer until well blended. Pipe or spread onto assorted vegetable dippers or serve with crackers.   *Makes 1 cup*

Suggested Vegetable Dippers: Pea pods, cherry tomatoes, cucumber slices, jicama slices, carrot sticks, celery sticks or Belgian endive.

Prep Time: 10 minutes

Pesto Brie

CRANBERRY SANGRÍA

**1 bottle (750 ml) Beaujolais or dry red
   wine**
1 cup cranberry juice cocktail
1 cup orange juice
½ cup cranberry-flavored liqueur (optional)
1 orange,* thinly sliced
1 lime,* thinly sliced

*Orange and lime may be scored before slicing to add a special touch. To score, make a lengthwise groove in fruit with citrus stripper. Continue to make grooves ¼ to ½ inch apart until entire fruit has been grooved.

Combine wine, cranberry juice cocktail, orange juice, liqueur, orange slices and lime slices in large glass pitcher. Chill 2 to 8 hours before serving.

Pour into glasses; add orange and/or lime slices from sangría to each glass.
   Makes about 7 cups, 10 to 12 servings

Sparkling Sangría: Just before serving, tilt pitcher and slowly add 2 cups well-chilled sparkling water or club soda. Pour into glasses; add orange and/or lime slices from sangría to each glass.
   Makes about 9 cups, 12 to 15 servings

SHRIMP AND SNOW PEA APPETIZERS WITH CURRANT MUSTARD SAUCE

6 ounces fresh snow peas (about 36)
**1½ pounds medium shrimp, cooked and
   peeled**

CURRANT MUSTARD SAUCE

¾ cup SMUCKER'S® Currant Jelly
¼ cup Dijon mustard

Blanch snow peas in boiling salted water for 45 seconds. Immediately drain and run under cold water.

Wrap 1 blanched pea pod around each shrimp and secure with toothpick.

Combine jelly and mustard; beat with a fork or wire whisk until smooth. (Jelly will dissolve in about 5 minutes.) Serve sauce with appetizers.
   Makes 36 appetizers

Try serving sangria from a punch bowl with a festive fruit ice ring. Place a layer of crushed ice in a 6-cup ring mold; arrange cranberries and orange slices over the ice. Top with cranberry juice and freeze until firm. Run warm water over the mold to release the ice ring.

Cranberry Sangría

SMOKY EGGPLANT DIP

1 large eggplant (about 1 pound)
¼ cup olive oil
3 tablespoons FRANK'S® REDHOT® Hot
    Sauce
2 tablespoons peanut butter or tahini paste
1 tablespoon lemon juice
2 cloves garlic, minced
¾ teaspoon salt
½ teaspoon ground cumin
    Spicy Pita Chips (recipe follows)

1. Prepare grill. Place eggplant on oiled grid.
Grill, over hot coals, 15 minutes or until soft
and skin is charred, turning often. Remove
from grill; cool until easy enough to handle.

2. Peel skin from eggplant with paring knife;
discard. Coarsely chop eggplant. Place in
strainer or kitchen towel. Press out excess
liquid.

3. Place eggplant in food processor; add oil,
REDHOT sauce, peanut butter, lemon juice,
garlic, salt and cumin. Cover; process until
mixture is very smooth. Spread eggplant
mixture on serving platter. Cover; refrigerate
until chilled. Serve with Spicy Pita Chips.

Makes 1½ cups dip

Spicy Pita Chips: Split 4 pita bread rounds
in half lengthwise. Combine ½ cup olive oil,
¼ cup FRANK'S® REDHOT® Hot Sauce and
1 tablespoon minced garlic in small bowl.
Brush mixture on both sides of pitas. Place
pitas on grid. Grill, over medium coals, about
5 minutes or until crispy, turning once. Cut
pitas into triangles.

Prep Time: 30 minutes
Cook Time: 20 minutes
Chill Time: 30 minutes

PEPPER CHEESE COCKTAIL PUFFS

½ package (17¼ ounces) frozen puff pastry,
    thawed
1 tablespoon Dijon mustard
½ cup (2 ounces) finely shredded Cheddar
    cheese
1 teaspoon cracked black pepper
1 egg

1. Preheat oven to 400°F. Grease baking
sheets.

2. Roll out 1 sheet puff pastry dough on well
floured surface to 14×10-inch rectangle.
Spread half of dough (from 10-inch side) with
mustard. Sprinkle with cheese and pepper.
Fold dough over filling; roll gently to seal
edges.

3. Cut lengthwise into 3 strips; cut each strip
diagonally into 1½-inch pieces. Place on
prepared baking sheets. Beat egg and 1
tablespoon water in small bowl; brush on
appetizers.

4. Bake appetizers 12 to 15 minutes or until
puffed and deep golden brown. Remove from
baking sheet to wire rack to cool.

Makes about 20 appetizers

Tip: Work quickly and efficiently when using
puff pastry. The colder puff pastry is, the better
it will puff in the hot oven. Also, this recipe
can be easily doubled.

Prep and Bake Time: 30 minutes

Smoky Eggplant Dip

MUSHROOM PARMESAN CROSTINI

1 tablespoon olive or vegetable oil
1 clove garlic, finely chopped
1 cup chopped mushrooms
1 loaf Italian or French bread (about
    12 inches long), cut into 12 slices and
    toasted
¾ cup RAGÚ® Pizza Quick® Sauce
¼ cup grated Parmesan cheese
1 tablespoon finely chopped fresh basil
    leaves or 1 teaspoon dried basil leaves

Preheat oven to 375°F. In 8-inch nonstick skillet, heat oil over medium heat and cook garlic 30 seconds. Add mushrooms and cook, stirring occasionally, 2 minutes or until liquid evaporates.

On baking sheet, arrange bread slices. Evenly spread Ragú® Pizza Quick Sauce on bread slices, then top with mushroom mixture, cheese and basil. Bake 15 minutes or until heated through.   *Makes 12 crostini*

Recipe Tip: Many varieties of mushrooms are available in supermarkets and specialty grocery stores. Shiitake, portobello and cremini mushrooms all have excellent flavor.

HOLIDAY MEATBALLS

1½ pounds lean ground beef
 ⅔ cup dry bread crumbs
 1 egg, slightly beaten
 ¼ cup water
 3 tablespoons minced onion
 1 clove garlic, minced
 ½ teaspoon salt
 ¼ teaspoon pepper
 1 tablespoon vegetable oil
 1 cup HEINZ® Chili Sauce
 1 cup grape jelly

Combine first 8 ingredients. Form into 60 bite-sized meatballs using rounded teaspoon for each. Place in shallow baking pan or jelly roll pan brushed with oil. Bake in 450°F oven 15 minutes or until cooked through. Meanwhile, in small saucepan, combine chili sauce and grape jelly. Heat until jelly is melted. Place well-drained meatballs in serving dish. Pour chili sauce mixture over; stir gently to coat. Serve warm.

Makes 60 appetizers

Tip: For a zestier sauce, substitute hot jalapeño jelly for grape jelly.

Mushroom Parmesan Crostini

SALMON-WRAPPED MOUSSE

1 can (10¾ ounces) reduced-fat condensed cream of celery soup, divided
2 pounds deboned and skinned halibut or other firm white fish, cut into 1-inch cubes
¼ cup chopped onion
1 clove garlic
¼ teaspoon dried thyme leaves
⅛ teaspoon ground nutmeg
6 ounces smoked salmon (lox), thinly sliced
¼ cup fat-free (skim) milk
1½ tablespoons lemon juice

Preheat oven to 350°F. Combine half the soup, fish, onion, garlic, thyme and nutmeg in food processor. Process 30 seconds or until mixture resembles thick pudding. Generously spray 1-quart ring mold with nonstick cooking spray. Press salmon slices into bottom and side of mold. Carefully spoon mousse into ring mold without moving salmon slices. Gently bang mold on flat surface to remove any air bubbles.

Cover mold with wax paper sprayed with vegetable cooking spray; cover waxed paper with flat lid. Place ring mold in roasting pan. Pour hot water into pan to reach two-thirds up side of mold. Bake 1 hour or until mousse is springy to the touch and shrinks from side of mold. Let stand 10 minutes to cool before unmolding.

Combine remaining soup, milk and lemon juice in small saucepan; mix well. Simmer until heated through. Unmold ring onto serving platter. Fill center of ring with favorite green vegetable or salad. Spoon sauce around outside of mousse ring. Serve with toasted bread rounds or crackers.

Makes 12 servings

Holiday entertaining can be an enjoyable experience. Here are a few tips to make your life as a host or hostess a little easier:

• Chafing dishes are easy to rent and will keep your food hot and fresh (without you having to stay in the kitchen).

• Disposable plates and flatware are now available in many festive styles and colors, and they make cleanup a breeze!

• Candles are a simple and elegant way to dress up both the buffet and dining tables. Storing them in the refrigerator will help them burn longer and drip less.

Salmon-Wrapped Mousse

SOUTH-OF-THE-BORDER QUICHE SQUARES

1 (8-ounce) package refrigerated crescent
    dinner roll dough
1½ cups shredded Monterey Jack and Colby
    cheese blend (6 ounces)
½ cup diced green chiles
½ cup chopped onion
4 eggs, beaten
1 cup milk
⅓ cup GREY POUPON® COUNTRY
    DIJON® Mustard
1 tablespoon chopped cilantro or parsley
½ teaspoon chili powder
    Chopped tomato and yellow and green
    bell peppers, for garnish

Unroll dough and press perforations together.
Press dough on bottom and 1 inch up sides of
greased 13×9×2-inch baking pan. Bake crust
at 375°F for 5 to 8 minutes or until lightly
golden. Remove from oven; sprinkle with half
the cheese. Top with chiles, onion and
remaining cheese.

In medium bowl, blend eggs, milk, mustard,
cilantro or parsley and chili powder. Pour
mixture evenly over cheese layer. Bake at
375°F for 25 to 30 minutes or until set. Cool
5 minutes. Garnish with tomato and bell
peppers; cut into 2-inch squares. Serve hot.

Makes 24 appetizers

FIESTA FRUIT PUNCH

2 cans (12 ounces each) banana-pineapple
    nectar, chilled *or* 2½ cups chilled
    pineapple juice and 1 large banana,
    mixed in blender
3 cups lemon-lime flavored soda, chilled
1½ cups fresh squeezed grapefruit juice
    (2 SUNKIST® grapefruits)
2 tablespoons grenadine syrup
    Ice
    Grapefruit Shells (recipe follows,
    optional)
    Mint leaves (optional)
    Garnish: unpeeled grapefruit wedges or
    quarter-slices, banana or pineapple
    chunks
    Maraschino cherries (optional)

In large pitcher, combine nectar, soda,
grapefruit juice and grenadine. Serve over
ice in grapefruit shells garnished with mint or
in 8-ounce glasses garnished with fruit
threaded on short wooden skewers.

Makes about 7½ cups
(ten 6-ounce servings)

Grapefruit Shells: Cut off about ⅓ of each
(small to medium) grapefruit at stem end.
Squeeze juice from both halves, preferably
with electric juicer. With spoon, scrape out
pulp from larger halves. Chill shells and use as
beverage containers. Discard smaller shell
halves.

South-of-the-Border Quiche Squares

Spinach Cheese Triangles

1 package (8 ounces) PHILADELPHIA®
    Cream Cheese, softened
1 package (10 ounces) frozen chopped
    spinach, thawed, well drained
⅓ cup chopped drained roasted red
    peppers
¼ teaspoon garlic salt
6 sheets frozen phyllo, thawed
½ cup (1 stick) butter or margarine, melted

MIX cream cheese, spinach, red peppers and garlic salt with electric mixer on medium speed until well blended.

LAY 1 phyllo sheet on flat surface. Brush with some of the melted butter. Cut lengthwise into 4 (18×3½-inch) strips.

SPOON about 1 tablespoon filling about 1 inch from one end of each strip. Fold the end over the filling at a 45-degree angle. Continue folding as you would fold a flag to form a triangle that encloses filling. Repeat procedure with remaining phyllo sheets. Place triangles on cookie sheet. Brush with melted butter.

BAKE at 375°F for 12 to 15 minutes or until golden brown.   *Makes 3 dozen appetizers*

Tip: Unfold phyllo sheets; cover with wax paper and damp towel to prevent drying until ready to use.

Prep Time: 30 minutes
Baking Time: 15 minutes

Holiday Meat and Vegetable Kabobs

1 cup fresh pearl onions
⅓ cup olive oil
2 tablespoons balsamic vinegar
1 tablespoon TABASCO® brand Pepper
    Sauce
1 tablespoon dried basil leaves
2 large cloves garlic, crushed
1 teaspoon salt
1 pound boneless skinless chicken breasts
1 pound boneless beef sirloin
2 large red peppers, cored, seeded and cut
    into ¾-inch-pieces
1 large green pepper, cored, seeded and
    cut into ¾-inch-pieces
1 large zucchini, cut into ¾-inch-pieces

Soak 3 dozen 4-inch-long wooden skewers in water overnight. Bring pearl onions and enough water to cover in 1-quart saucepan over high heat to a boil. Reduce heat to low. Cover and simmer 3 minutes or until tender. Drain. When cool enough to handle, peel away outer layer of skin from onions.

Combine oil, vinegar, TABASCO® Sauce, basil, garlic and salt in medium bowl. Pour half of mixture into another bowl. Cut chicken and beef into ¾-inch pieces and place in bowl with TABASCO® Sauce mixture, tossing well to coat. In remaining bowl of TABASCO® Sauce mixture, toss pearl onions, red and green peppers and zucchini. Let stand at least 30 minutes, tossing occasionally.

Preheat broiler. Skewer 1 piece of chicken or beef and 1 piece each of red pepper, green pepper, onion and zucchini onto each skewer. Broil 4 to 6 minutes, turning occasionally.
Makes 3 dozen hors d'oeuvres

In Los Angeles in 1938, Lawrence Frank opened a restaurant like one he had heard of in London, where prime rib was carved and served at the table. He wanted to call it Larry's but decided Lawry's sounded more English. From salad greens tossed tableside to valet parking, the successful eatery brought many firsts to the U.S. restaurant scene. Frank also turned his kitchen into a lab to create the world's largest spice blend, Lawry's® Seasoned Salt.

POTPOURRI PARTY MIX

½ cup butter, melted
2 teaspoons Worcestershire sauce
½ to 1 teaspoon LAWRY'S® Seasoned Salt
¼ to ½ teaspoon LAWRY'S® Garlic Powder
 with Parsley
1 quart cubed sourdough bread
1 jar (8½ ounces) dry roasted peanuts
¾ cup diced cheddar cheese
8 bacon strips, cooked and crumbled

In small bowl, combine butter, Worcestershire sauce and seasonings; mix well. On jelly-roll or oblong cake pan, toss bread cubes with seasoned butter. Bake, uncovered, in 350°F oven 20 minutes, stirring occasionally. Cool thoroughly; combine with remaining ingredients.   *Makes about 1½ quarts*

Serving Suggestion: Serve in attractive serving bowls or napkin-lined baskets.

SPICY TOASTED NUTS

2 tablespoons vegetable oil
1 tablespoon HEINZ® Worcestershire Sauce
1 cup pecan or walnut halves

In bowl, combine oil and Worcestershire sauce; add nuts and toss to coat. Spread nuts in shallow baking pan; drizzle with any remaining oil mixture. Bake in 325°F oven, 15 minutes, stirring occasionally. Sprinkle with salt or garlic salt, if desired.   *Makes 1 cup*

ARTICHOKE-PEPPER CHEESECAKE

2½ cups chopped bagels (about 2 bagels)
2 tablespoons olive oil
3 teaspoons dried chives, divided
2 (8-ounce) packages reduced-fat cream cheese, softened
1 (15-ounce) container part-skim ricotta cheese
1 can (10¾ ounces) condensed broccoli and cheese soup
1 (4-ounce) container egg substitute (equivalent to 2 eggs)
1 tablespoon Italian seasoning
1 teaspoon garlic salt
1 (8.5-ounce) can artichoke hearts, drained and chopped
1 (15-ounce) jar roasted red bell peppers, drained and chopped
1 cup chopped fresh basil

Preheat oven to 375°F. Combine bagels, oil and 1 teaspoon chives in medium bowl; mix well. Spray 9×2½-inch springform baking pan with nonstick cooking spray. Press bagel mixture into bottom of springform pan. Bake 15 minutes; let cool.

With electric mixer, combine cheeses, soup, egg substitute, herbs, garlic salt and remaining 2 teaspoons chives; mix well. Spread half the cheese mixture over bagel crust. Top with artichokes and half each of peppers and basil.

Spread remaining cheese filling over basil; top with remaining peppers. Bake 1 hour 15 minutes to 1 hour 30 minutes or until completely set; cool. Refrigerate 6 to 8 hours or overnight. Run knife around edge of torte; remove side of pan. Top with remaining basil. Slice thinly and serve with crackers.

Makes 20 servings

HIDDEN VALLEY BOURSIN CHEESE

2 packages (8 ounces each) cream cheese, softened
½ cup butter or margarine, softened
1 package (1 ounce) HIDDEN VALLEY® Milk Recipe Original Ranch® salad dressing mix
1 tablespoon Dijon mustard
1 teaspoon minced garlic
Round French bread

In large bowl, beat all ingredients except bread with electric mixer until thoroughly blended. Spoon into 3-cup serving bowl. Cover tightly and refrigerate overnight. Let stand at room temperature 30 minutes before serving. To serve, slice off top of French bread. Remove inside, leaving ¼-inch-thick shell. Spoon cheese mixture into bread shell. Garnish with parsley and serve with additional French bread and fresh vegetables, as desired.

Makes about 2 cups

Artichoke-Pepper Cheesecake

CHAMPAGNE PUNCH

1 orange
1 lemon
¼ cup cranberry-flavored liqueur or cognac
¼ cup orange-flavored liqueur or triple sec
1 bottle (750 mL) pink or regular champagne or sparkling white wine, well chilled
Fresh cranberries (optional)
Citrus strips for garnish

Remove colored peel, not white pith, from orange and lemon in long thin strips with citrus peeler. Refrigerate orange and lemon for another use. Combine peels and cranberry- and orange-flavored liqueurs in glass pitcher. Cover and refrigerate 2 to 6 hours.

Just before serving, tilt pitcher to one side and slowly pour in champagne. Leave peels in pitcher for added flavor. Place a cranberry in bottom of each glass. Pour into champagne glasses. Garnish with citrus strips tied in knots, if desired. *Makes 4 cups, 6 to 8 servings*

Nonalcoholic Cranberry Punch: Pour 3 cups well-chilled club soda into ⅔ cup (6 ounces) cranberry cocktail concentrate, thawed. *Makes 3½ cups, 6 servings*

EASY SPAM™ TRIANGLES

1 (7-ounce) can SPAM® Luncheon Meat, cut into small cubes
¾ cup (3 ounces) shredded Gouda cheese
½ cup diced peeled apple
2 tablespoons onion sour cream dip
1 (15-ounce) package refrigerated pie crusts
1 egg white, beaten
Nonstick cooking spray
¼ teaspoon poppy seeds

Heat oven to 425°F. In medium bowl, combine SPAM®, cheese, apple and dip. Cut one pie crust sheet into 8 wedges. Place ¼ cup SPAM™ mixture in center of each wedge, spreading to within ½ inch of each edge. Moisten edges of pastry with egg white. Cut remaining pie crust sheet into 8 wedges. Place over filling. Press edges of filled pastry firmly together using fork. Place on baking sheet coated with nonstick cooking spray. Brush with remaining egg white and sprinkle with poppy seeds. Bake 15 to 20 minutes or until lightly browned. *Makes 8 servings*

Champagne Punch

Fresh Garden Dip

1½ cups fat free or reduced fat mayonnaise
1½ cups shredded DOLE® Carrots
  1 cup finely chopped DOLE® Broccoli
    Florets
  ⅓ cup finely chopped green onions
  2 teaspoons dried dill weed
  ¼ teaspoon garlic powder
    DOLE® Broccoli Florets, Cauliflower
    Florets or Peeled Mini Carrots

• Stir together mayonnaise, shredded carrots, broccoli, green onions, dill and garlic powder in medium bowl until blended.

• Spoon into serving bowl. Cover and chill 1 hour or overnight. Serve with assorted fresh vegetables. Refrigerate any leftovers in airtight container. *Makes 3½ cups*

Fiesta Quesadillas with Fruit Salsa

  1 can (11 ounces) DOLE® Mandarin
    Oranges, drained and finely chopped
  1 tablespoon chopped fresh cilantro or
    fresh parsley
  1 tablespoon lime juice
  4 (8-inch) whole wheat or flour tortillas
  ¾ cup shredded low fat Monterey Jack,
    mozzarella or Cheddar cheese
  ⅔ cup finely chopped DOLE® Pitted Dates
    or Chopped Dates or finely chopped
    Pitted Prunes
  ⅓ cup crumbled feta cheese
  2 tablespoons chopped green onion

• Combine mandarin oranges, cilantro and lime juice in small bowl for salsa; set aside.

• Place two tortillas on large baking sheet. Sprinkle half of shredded cheese, dates, feta and green onion over each tortilla to within ½ inch of edge.

• Brush outer ½-inch edge of each tortilla with water. Top with remaining tortillas; press down edges gently to seal.

• Bake at 375°F 5 to 8 minutes or until hot. Cut each quesadilla into 6 wedges.

• Drain salsa just before serving, if desired; serve over warm quesadillas.

Makes 6 servings

Dole Food Company is the world's largest grower and supplier of fresh fruit and vegetables and sells over 170 different food products. Dole is also a leader in nutrition education for children, using personalities such as Bobby Banana, Pamela Pineapple, Anthony Apple and Juanita Watermelon to teach the benefits of proper nutrition.

Top to bottom: Fresh Garden Dip and
Fiesta Quesadillas with Fruit Salsa

CHEESY CRAB MOUSSE

2 cups fresh shelled crab meat or 2 cans
   (6 ounces each) canned crab meat
1½ cups (6 ounces) shredded ALPINE LACE®
   Reduced Fat Colby Cheese
½ cup finely chopped celery
½ cup finely chopped green onions
½ cup finely chopped red bell pepper
1 cup sour half-and-half
½ cup reduced fat mayonnaise
¼ cup bottled chili sauce
2 tablespoons fresh lemon juice
3 tablespoons cold water
1 tablespoon unflavored gelatin

1. Lightly oil a 1-quart fish-shaped or other shaped mold.

2. Rinse the crab meat, drain well and pick through for shells. Place in a large bowl. Toss with the cheese, celery, green onions and bell pepper.

3. In a small bowl, blend together the half-and-half, mayonnaise, chili sauce and lemon juice. Into a small saucepan, pour the cold water and stir in the gelatin. Heat over low heat, stirring constantly, until thoroughly dissolved. Stir quickly into the half-and-half mixture.

4. Fold half-and-half mixture into the crab mixture and spoon into the mold. Cover with plastic wrap and refrigerate for 3 hours or until set. Unmold onto a serving platter. Garnish with the cucumber slices and sprigs of dill, if you wish.   *Makes 32 appetizer servings*
(2 tablespoons each)

LITTLE TURKEY TRAVELERS

2 pounds BUTTERBALL® Peppered Turkey
   Breast, sliced thin in the deli
1 jar (16 ounces) mild pepper rings,
   drained
1 can (14 ounces) artichoke hearts,
   drained and quartered
1 jar (8 ounces) mild giardiniera,
   undrained
1 jar (7 ounces) roasted red peppers,
   drained and cut into wide strips
2 packages (8 ounces each) soft cream
   cheese with chives and onion
1 package (17 ounces) soft cracker bread
   (three 16-inch round flat breads)
½ pound thinly sliced provolone cheese

Combine mild peppers, artichoke hearts, giardiniera and roasted peppers in medium bowl. Spread cream cheese on each flat bread. Place turkey and cheese slices on each bread; top each with 1½ cups vegetable mixture.* Roll tightly, jelly-roll style, beginning at the filled end. Wrap each roll in plastic wrap. Chill 2 hours. Cut each roll into 16 slices.
Makes 48 appetizers

*For better roll sealing, leave 4 inches across top of each bread covered with cream cheese only.

Preparation Time: 30 minutes plus chilling time

Cheesy Crab Mousse

HOT ARTICHOKE DIP

1 package (8 ounces) PHILADELPHIA®
   Cream Cheese, softened
1 can (14 ounces) artichoke hearts,
   drained, chopped
1/2 cup KRAFT® Real Mayonnaise
1/2 cup (2 ounces) KRAFT® 100% Grated
   Parmesan Cheese
2 tablespoons finely chopped fresh basil
   or 1 teaspoon dried basil leaves
2 tablespoons finely chopped red onion
1 clove garlic, minced
1/2 cup chopped tomato

MIX cream cheese and all remaining
ingredients except tomato with electric mixer
on medium speed until well blended.

SPOON into 9-inch pie plate.

BAKE at 350°F for 25 minutes. Sprinkle with
tomato. Serve with assorted cut-up vegetables
or baked pita bread wedges.

Makes 3 1/4 cups

Note: To make baked pita bread wedges, cut
3 split pita breads each into 8 triangles. Place
on cookie sheet. Bake at 350°F for 10 to 12
minutes or until crisp.

Prep Time: 15 minutes
Baking Time: 25 minutes

COCKTAIL WRAPS

16 thin strips Cheddar cheese*
16 HILLSHIRE FARM® Lit'l Smokies, scored
   lengthwise into halves
 1 can (8 ounces) refrigerated crescent roll
   dough
 1 egg, beaten *or* 1 tablespoon milk
   Mustard

*Or substitute Swiss, taco-flavored or other variety
of cheese.

Preheat oven to 400°F.

Place 1 strip cheese inside score of each Lit'l
Smokie. Separate dough into 8 triangles; cut
each lengthwise into halves to make 16
triangles. Place 1 link on wide end of 1 dough
triangle; roll up. Repeat with remaining links
and dough triangles. Place links on baking
sheet. Brush dough with egg. Bake 10 to 15
minutes.

Serve hot with mustard.

Makes 16 hors d'oeuvres

Hot Artichoke Dip

FESTIVE CRAB TOASTS

1 can (10¾ ounces) reduced-fat condensed
    cream of celery soup
12 ounces crabmeat or surimi seafood,
    flaked
¼ cup chopped celery
¼ cup sliced green onions
1 tablespoon lemon juice
1 clove garlic, minced
½ teaspoon salt
⅛ teaspoon grated lemon peel
1 French bread baguette
⅓ cup fat free shredded Parmesan cheese
    Paprika

Preheat broiler. Combine soup, crabmeat, celery, onions, lemon juice, garlic, salt and lemon peel in medium bowl; mix well. Cut baguette diagonally into ½-inch slices; arrange slices on 2 cookie sheets. Broil 5 inches from heat 2 minutes until toasted, turning once.

Spread 1 tablespoon crab mixture on each baguette slice. Top with Parmesan cheese; sprinkle with paprika. Broil 5 inches from heat 2 minutes or until lightly browned.

Makes about 30 appetizers

STUFFED MUSHROOMS

1 package (6 ounces) STOVE TOP® Chicken
    Flavor Stuffing Mix
24 large mushrooms (about 1½ pounds)
¼ cup (½ stick) butter or margarine
¼ cup each finely chopped red and green
    pepper
3 tablespoons butter or margarine, melted

Prepare stuffing mix as directed on package, omitting butter. Remove stems from mushrooms; chop stems. Melt ¼ cup butter in skillet. Add mushroom caps; cook and stir until lightly browned. Arrange in shallow baking pan. Cook and stir chopped mushroom stems and peppers in skillet until tender; stir into prepared stuffing. Spoon onto mushroom caps; drizzle with 3 tablespoons butter. Place under preheated broiler for 5 minutes to heat through. *Makes 12 appetizer servings*

CREAMY FLORENTINE DIP

2 cups dairy sour cream
1¾ cups mayonnaise
2½ tablespoons lemon juice
1¼ teaspoons LAWRY'S® Seasoned Salt
½ teaspoon LAWRY'S® Garlic Powder with
    Parsley
½ teaspoon dried oregano leaves
½ teaspoon dried basil leaves
½ teaspoon dry mustard
½ teaspoon LAWRY'S® Seasoned Pepper
1 package (10 ounces) frozen chopped
    spinach, thawed and well drained

In large bowl, combine all ingredients except spinach. Squeeze excess moisture from spinach; add and mix thoroughly. Chill several hours to blend flavors.

Makes about 4 cups

Serving Suggestion: Serve with assorted crisp, raw vegetables as dippers.

Festive Crab Toasts

Spam™ Pinwheels

1 (1-pound) loaf frozen bread dough, thawed
¼ cup pizza sauce
1 (7-ounce) can SPAM® Luncheon Meat, cubed
2 cups (8 ounces) shredded mozzarella cheese
2 tablespoons chopped pepperoncini
Additional pizza sauce

Roll bread dough out onto lightly floured surface to 12-inch square. Brush pizza sauce over bread dough. Sprinkle SPAM®, cheese and pepperoncini over dough. Roll dough, jelly-roll fashion; pinch seam to seal (do not seal ends). Cut roll into 16 slices. Place slices, cut side down, on greased baking sheet. Cover and let rise in warm place 45 minutes. Heat oven to 350°F. Bake 20 to 25 minutes or until golden brown. Serve immediately with additional pizza sauce.

Makes 16 appetizer servings

Pepperidge Farm® Parmesan Cheese Crisps

½ package (17¼-ounce size) PEPPERIDGE FARM® Frozen Puff Pastry Sheets (1 sheet)
1 egg
1 tablespoon water
¼ cup grated Parmesan cheese
1 tablespoon chopped fresh parsley *or*
    1 teaspoon dried parsley flakes
½ teaspoon dried oregano leaves, crushed

1. Thaw pastry sheet at room temperature 30 minutes. Preheat oven to 400°F. Mix egg and water and set aside. Mix cheese, parsley and oregano and set aside.

2. Unfold pastry on lightly floured surface. Roll into 14- by 10-inch rectangle. Cut in half lengthwise. Brush both halves with egg mixture. Top 1 rectangle with cheese mixture. Place remaining rectangle over cheese-topped rectangle, egg-side down. Roll gently with rolling pin to seal.

3. Cut crosswise into 28 (½-inch) strips. Twist strips and place 2 inches apart on greased baking sheet, pressing down ends. Brush with egg mixture.

4. Bake 10 minutes or until golden. Serve warm or at room temperature.

Makes 28 appetizers

Tip: To make ahead, twist strips. Place on baking sheet and brush with egg mixture. Freeze. When frozen, store in plastic bag for up to 1 month. To bake, preheat oven to 400°F. Place frozen strips on greased baking sheet. Bake 15 minutes or until golden.

Thaw Time: 30 minutes
Prep Time: 20 minutes
Cook Time: 10 minutes

Spam™ Pinwheels

Bountiful Breads

BOUNTIFUL BREADS

CINNAMON BUBBLE RING

¼ cup sugar
½ teaspoon ground cinnamon
1 can (11 ounces) refrigerated French bread dough
1½ tablespoons margarine or butter, melted

1. Preheat oven to 350°F. Grease 9-inch tube pan. Combine sugar and cinnamon in small bowl.

2. Cut dough into 16 slices; roll into balls. Arrange 12 balls evenly spaced against outer wall of pan. Arrange remaining 4 balls evenly spaced against tube of pan. Brush with margarine. Sprinkle sugar mixture evenly over balls.

3. Bake 20 to 25 minutes or until golden brown. Serve warm.

Makes 8 servings

Tip: For a fast start to your morning, prepare the cinnamon buns in the pan, cover and refrigerate overnight. All you have to do in the morning is bake them for a quick, delicious treat.

Prep and Cook Time: 30 minutes

Cinnamon Bubble Ring

CRANBERRY CHEESECAKE MUFFINS

1 package (3 ounces) cream cheese, softened
$\frac{1}{4}$ cup sugar, divided
1 cup reduced-fat (2%) milk
$\frac{1}{3}$ cup vegetable oil
1 egg
1 package (15.6 ounces) cranberry quick bread mix

1. Preheat oven to 400°F. Grease 12 muffin cups.

2. Beat cream cheese and 2 tablespoons sugar in small bowl until well blended. Combine milk, oil and egg in large bowl; beat with fork until blended. Stir in quick bread mix just until dry ingredients are moistened.

3. Fill muffin cups $\frac{1}{4}$ full with batter. Drop 1 teaspoon cream cheese mixture into center of each cup. Spoon remaining batter over cream cheese mixture.

4. Sprinkle batter with remaining 2 tablespoons sugar. Bake 17 to 22 minutes or until golden brown. Cool 5 minutes. Remove from muffin cups to wire rack to cool.

Makes 12 muffins

Prep and Bake Time: 30 minutes

ONION DILL BREAD

2 cups bread flour
1 cup whole wheat flour
$\frac{1}{2}$ cup instant non-fat dry milk
$\frac{1}{2}$ teaspoon salt
1 package active dry yeast
2 tablespoons sugar
$1\frac{1}{4}$ cups water (110° to 115°F)
1 cup KELLOGG'S® ALL-BRAN® cereal
2 egg whites
$\frac{1}{4}$ cup reduced-calorie margarine
$\frac{1}{4}$ cup chopped green onions
$\frac{1}{4}$ cup chopped red onion
1 tablespoon dill weed
1 tablespoon skim milk
2 tablespoons finely chopped onion

1. Stir together flours, dry milk and salt.

2. In large bowl, combine yeast, sugar and water. Stir in Kellogg's® All-Bran® cereal; let stand 2 minutes or until cereal is soft. Add egg whites, margarine and $\frac{1}{2}$ of flour mixture. Beat at medium speed for 2 minutes or about 200 strokes by hand.

3. Mix in green onions, red onion and dill. Stir in remaining flour mixture by hand to form stiff, sticky dough. Cover lightly. Let rise in warm place until double in volume.

4. Stir down dough to original volume. Spoon into 2-quart round casserole dish or $9\frac{1}{4} \times 5\frac{1}{4} \times 2\frac{3}{4}$-inch loaf pan coated with nonstick cooking spray. Brush with milk and sprinkle with 2 tablespoons chopped onion.

5. Bake at 350°F for 55 minutes or until loaf is golden brown and sounds hollow when tapped. Cool on wire rack.   *Makes 1 loaf*

Cranberry Cheesecake Muffins

HOLIDAY STOLLEN

1½ **cups unsalted butter, softened**
 4 **egg yolks**
 ½ **cup granulated sugar**
 1 **teaspoon salt**
   Grated peel from 1 lemon
   Grated peel from 1 orange
 1 **teaspoon vanilla**
2½ **cups hot milk (120° to 130°F)**
 8 **to 8½ cups all-purpose flour, divided**
 2 **packages active dry yeast**
 ½ **cup golden raisins**
 ½ **cup candied orange peel**
 ½ **cup candied lemon peel**
 ½ **cup chopped red candied cherries**
 ½ **cup chopped green candied cherries**
 ½ **cup chopped almonds**
 1 **egg, beaten**
   Powdered sugar

Beat butter, egg yolks, granulated sugar, salt, lemon peel, orange peel and vanilla in large bowl until light and fluffy. Slowly add milk; mix thoroughly. Add 2 cups flour and yeast; mix well. When mixture is smooth, add enough remaining flour, ½ cup at a time, until dough forms and can be lifted out of bowl. Lightly flour work surface; knead dough until smooth and elastic, about 10 minutes. Mix raisins, candied orange and lemon peels, cherries and almonds in medium bowl; knead fruit mixture into dough.

Place dough in greased bowl, cover with plastic wrap and let rise in warm place about 1 hour or until doubled in bulk.

Grease 2 large baking sheets. Turn dough out onto floured work surface. Divide dough in half. Place one half back in bowl; cover and set aside. Cut remaining half into thirds. Roll each third into 12-inch rope. Place on prepared baking sheet. Braid ropes together. Repeat procedure with remaining dough.

Brush beaten egg on braids. Let braids stand at room temperature about 1 hour or until doubled in bulk.

Preheat oven to 350°F. Bake braids about 45 minutes or until golden brown and sound hollow when tapped. Remove to wire rack to cool. Sprinkle with powdered sugar before serving.   *Makes 2 braided loaves*

CHEESE PULL-APART BREAD

 3 **packages frozen bread dough dinner**
   rolls, thawed to room temperature
 ⅓ **cup melted butter**
 1 **cup freshly grated BELGIOIOSO®**
   Parmesan
 1 **cup shredded BELGIOIOSO® Provolone**

Roll each dinner roll in melted butter, and then roll in BelGioioso® Parmesan to coat. Arrange half of rolls in well-greased fluted tube pan. Sprinkle with BelGioioso® Provolone. Top with remaining half of coated rolls. Sprinkle with any remaining Parmesan. Let rise until doubled in size, about 1 hour. Bake in preheated 375°F oven 35 to 45 minutes or until golden brown. Use table knife to loosen edge of bread; remove from pan. Serve warm.   *Makes 12 servings*

Holiday Stollen

APPLE CHEDDAR MUFFINS

2 cups sifted all-purpose flour
1 tablespoon baking powder
1/3 cup sugar
1/2 teaspoon salt
1/4 teaspoon ground nutmeg
1/2 cup egg substitute or 2 large eggs
3/4 cup 2% low fat milk
1/4 cup unsalted butter, melted
1 cup grated, cored, peeled baking apples, such as Granny Smith, Rome Beauty or Winesap
3/4 cup (3 ounces) shredded ALPINE LACE® Fat Free Pasteurized Process Skim Milk Cheese Product—For Cheddar Lovers

1. Preheat the oven to 400°F. Spray 12 regular-size muffin cups with nonstick cooking spray.

2. In a large bowl, sift together the flour, baking powder, sugar, salt and nutmeg. In a small bowl, whisk the egg substitute (or the whole eggs) with the milk and butter until blended.

3. Using a wooden spoon, make a hole in the center of the flour mixture, then pour in the egg mixture all at once. Stir just until the flour disappears. (Avoid overmixing!) Fold in the apples and cheese. Spoon the batter into the muffin cups until three-fourths full.

4. Bake the muffins for 20 to 25 minutes or until golden brown. Cool the muffins in the pan on a wire rack for 5 minutes, then lift them out with a spatula. They're delicious when served hot with honey!

Makes 12 muffins

APRICOT CARROT BREAD

1 3/4 cups all-purpose flour
1 teaspoon baking powder
1/4 teaspoon baking soda
1/4 teaspoon salt
1/2 cup granulated sugar
1/2 cup finely shredded carrots
1/2 cup MOTT'S® Natural Apple Sauce
1 egg, beaten lightly
2 tablespoons vegetable oil
1/3 cup dried apricots, snipped into small bits
1/2 cup powdered sugar
2 teaspoons MOTT'S® Apple Juice

1. Preheat oven to 350°F. Spray 8×4-inch loaf pan with nonstick cooking spray.

2. In large bowl, combine flour, baking powder, baking soda and salt.

3. In small bowl, combine granulated sugar, carrots, apple sauce, egg and oil.

4. Stir apple sauce mixture into flour mixture just until moistened. (Batter will be thick.) Fold in apricots. Spread batter into prepared pan.

5. Bake 45 to 50 minutes or until toothpick inserted in center comes out clean. Cool in pan 10 minutes. Invert onto wire rack; turn right side up. Cool completely. For best flavor, wrap loaf in plastic wrap or foil; store at room temperature overnight.

6. Just before serving, in small bowl, combine powdered sugar and apple juice until smooth. Drizzle over top of loaf. Cut into 12 slices.

Makes 12 servings

Apple Cheddar Muffins

SWEET POTATO BISCUITS

2½ cups all-purpose flour
¼ cup packed brown sugar
1 tablespoon baking powder
¾ teaspoon salt
¾ teaspoon ground cinnamon
¼ teaspoon ground ginger
¼ teaspoon ground allspice
½ cup vegetable shortening
½ cup chopped pecans
¾ cup mashed canned sweet potatoes
½ cup milk

Preheat oven to 450°F.

Combine flour, sugar, baking powder, salt, cinnamon, ginger and allspice in medium bowl. Cut in shortening with pastry blender or 2 knives until mixture resembles coarse crumbs. Stir in pecans.

Combine sweet potatoes and milk in separate medium bowl with wire whisk until smooth.

Make well in center of flour mixture. Add sweet potato mixture; stir until mixture forms soft dough that clings together and forms a ball.

Turn out dough onto well-floured surface. Knead dough gently 10 to 12 times.

Roll or pat dough to ½-inch thickness. Cut out dough with floured 2½-inch biscuit cutter.

Place biscuits 2 inches apart on ungreased large baking sheet. Bake 12 to 14 minutes or until tops and bottoms are golden brown. Serve warm.   *Makes about 12 biscuits*

ORANGE MARMALADE BREAD

3 cups all-purpose flour
4 teaspoons baking powder
1 teaspoon salt
½ cup chopped walnuts
¾ cup milk
¾ cup SMUCKER'S® Sweet Orange
    Marmalade
2 eggs, lightly beaten
¼ cup honey
2 tablespoons oil

Grease 9×5×3-inch loaf pan. Combine flour, baking powder and salt into large bowl. Stir in nuts. Combine milk, marmalade, eggs, honey and oil; blend well. Add to flour mixture; stir only until dry ingredients are moistened (batter will be lumpy). Turn into prepared pan.

Bake at 350°F for 65 to 70 minutes or until lightly browned and toothpick inserted in center comes out clean.

Makes 8 to 10 servings

A loaf of homemade bread makes a great holiday gift—especially when it's given in a new loaf pan. Just add a wooden spoon and the recipe, wrap it all up in a festive towel and tie it with ribbon.

Sweet Potato Biscuits

SAVORY ONION FOCACCIA

1 pound frozen pizza or bread dough*
1 tablespoon olive oil
1 clove garlic, minced
1⅓ cups FRENCH'S® French Fried Onions, divided
1 cup (4 ounces) shredded mozzarella cheese
½ pound plum tomatoes (4 small), thinly sliced
2 teaspoons fresh chopped rosemary *or* ½ teaspoon dried rosemary
3 tablespoons grated Parmesan cheese

*Pizza dough may be found in frozen section of supermarket. Thaw in refrigerator before using.

Bring pizza dough to room temperature. Grease 15×10-inch jelly-roll pan. Roll or pat dough into rectangle same size as pan on floured board.** Transfer dough to pan.

Combine oil and garlic in small bowl; brush onto surface of dough. Cover loosely with kitchen towel. Let dough rise at room temperature 25 minutes. Prick dough with fork.

Preheat oven to 450°F. Bake dough 20 minutes or until edges and bottom of crust are golden. Sprinkle *1 cup* French Fried Onions and mozzarella cheese over dough. Arrange tomatoes over cheese; sprinkle with rosemary. Bake 5 minutes or until cheese melts.

Sprinkle with remaining ⅓ *cup* onions and Parmesan cheese. Bake 2 minutes or until onions are golden. To serve cut into rectangles.
Makes 8 appetizer servings

**If dough is too hard to roll, allow to rest on floured board.

CHEDDAR OLIVE SCONES

2 cups all-purpose flour
1½ cups (6 ounces) shredded sharp Cheddar cheese
1 tablespoon sugar
2 teaspoons baking powder
1½ teaspoons cumin seed
¾ cup sour cream
¼ cup salad oil
1 large egg
½ cup pitted California ripe olives, cut into wedges

Mix flour, cheese, sugar, baking powder and cumin in large bowl. Beat sour cream, oil and egg in small bowl. Add egg mixture to flour mixture; stir just enough to moisten evenly. Gently stir in olives. Scrape dough onto lightly greased 15×10-inch baking sheet. Lightly flour hands; pat dough into 1-inch-thick round with lightly floured fingers. Cut round into 8 wedges with knife. Bake in 375°F oven 30 to 35 minutes or until well browned. Serve warm or at room temperature. Cut or break scones into wedges. *Makes 8 servings*

Favorite recipe from **California Olive Industry**

Savory Onion Focaccia

APPLE SAUCE COFFEE RING

BREAD

1 package active dry yeast
$\frac{1}{3}$ cup plus 1 teaspoon granulated sugar, divided
$\frac{1}{4}$ cup warm water (105° to 115°F)
$\frac{1}{2}$ cup skim milk
$\frac{1}{2}$ cup MOTT'S® Natural Apple Sauce
1 egg
2 tablespoons margarine, melted and cooled
1 teaspoon salt
1 teaspoon grated lemon peel
5 cups all-purpose flour
1 teaspoon skim milk

FILLING

1$\frac{1}{2}$ cups MOTT'S® Chunky Apple Sauce
$\frac{1}{2}$ cup raisins
$\frac{1}{3}$ cup firmly packed light brown sugar
1 teaspoon ground cinnamon

GLAZE

1 cup powdered sugar
2 tablespoons skim milk
1 teaspoon vanilla extract

1. To prepare Bread, in large bowl, sprinkle yeast and 1 teaspoon granulated sugar over warm water; stir until yeast dissolves. Let stand 5 minutes or until mixture is bubbly. Stir in $\frac{1}{2}$ cup milk, $\frac{1}{2}$ cup apple sauce, remaining $\frac{1}{3}$ cup granulated sugar, egg, margarine, salt and lemon peel.

2. Stir in flour, 1 cup at a time, until soft dough forms. Turn out dough onto floured surface; flatten slightly. Knead 5 minutes or until smooth and elastic, adding any remaining flour to prevent sticking if necessary. Shape dough into ball; place in large bowl sprayed with nonstick cooking spray. Turn dough over so that top is greased. Cover with damp towel; let rise in warm place 1 hour or until doubled in bulk.

3. Punch down dough. Roll out dough on floured surface into 15-inch square. Spray baking sheet with nonstick cooking spray.

4. To prepare Filling, in small bowl, combine 1$\frac{1}{2}$ cups chunky apple sauce, raisins, brown sugar and cinnamon. Spread filling over dough, to within $\frac{1}{2}$ inch of edges. Roll up dough jelly-roll style. Moisten edge with water; pinch to seal seam. Moisten ends of dough with water; bring together to form ring. Pinch to seal seam. Place on prepared baking sheet. Make $\frac{1}{8}$-inch-deep cuts across width of dough at 2-inch intervals around ring.

5. Let dough rise in warm place, uncovered, 30 minutes.

6. Preheat oven to 350°F. Brush top lightly with 1 teaspoon milk.

7. Bake 45 to 50 minutes or until lightly browned and ring sounds hollow when tapped. Remove from baking sheet; cool completely on wire rack.

8. To prepare Glaze, in small bowl, combine powdered sugar, 2 tablespoons milk and vanilla until smooth. Drizzle over top of ring. Cut into 24 slices.   *Makes 24 servings*

Apple Sauce Coffee Ring

CRANBERRY POPPY SEED LOAF

2½ cups all-purpose flour
¾ cup granulated sugar
2 tablespoons poppy seed
1 tablespoon baking powder
1 cup skim milk
⅓ cup FLEISCHMANN'S® Original Margarine, melted
¼ cup EGG BEATERS® Healthy Real Egg Substitute
1 teaspoon vanilla extract
2 teaspoons grated lemon peel
1 cup fresh or frozen cranberries, chopped Powdered Sugar Glaze, optional (recipe follows)

In large bowl, combine flour, granulated sugar, poppy seed and baking powder; set aside.

In small bowl, combine milk, margarine, Egg Beaters®, vanilla and lemon peel. Stir milk mixture into flour mixture just until moistened. Stir in cranberries. Spread batter into greased 8½×4½×2¼-inch loaf pan. Bake at 350°F for 60 to 70 minutes or until toothpick inserted in center comes out clean. Cool in pan on wire rack. Drizzle with Powdered Sugar Glaze if desired.   *Makes 12 servings*

Powdered Sugar Glaze: In small bowl, combine 1 cup powdered sugar and 5 to 6 teaspoons water until smooth.

GOOD OLD AMERICAN WHITE ROLLS

5 to 5½ cups all-purpose flour
2 packages RED STAR® Active Dry Yeast or QUICK•RISE™ Yeast
4 tablespoons nonfat dry milk
2 tablespoons sugar
2 teaspoons salt
1½ cups water
1 tablespoon shortening (or oil)
3 tablespoons melted butter
2 teaspoons honey

In large mixer bowl, combine 2½ cups flour, yeast, milk, sugar and salt; mix well. In saucepan, heat water and shortening until very warm (120° to 130°F; shortening does not need to melt). Add to flour mixture. Blend at low speed until moistened; beat 3 minutes at medium speed. By hand, gradually stir in enough remaining flour to make firm dough. Knead on floured surface until smooth and elastic, 5 to 8 minutes. Place in greased bowl, turning to grease top. Cover; let rise in warm place until doubled, about 45 minutes (30 minutes for QUICK•RISE Yeast). Punch down dough. Divide dough into 2 parts. Divide each part into 6 to 12 equal pieces (for 2- or 1-ounce rolls). Shape into smooth balls. Place on greased cookie sheet. Cover; let rise in warm place until about doubled, 25 to 30 minutes (15 to 20 minutes for QUICK•RISE Yeast). Bake at 400°F for 10 to 12 minutes until golden brown. Mix melted butter and honey together; brush rolls with mixture. Remove from cookie sheet and cool.   *Makes 12 to 24 rolls*

Cranberry Poppy Seed Loaf

CHEDDAR PEPPER BREAD

Basic Yeast Bread (recipe follows)
$\frac{2}{3}$ **cup chopped red bell pepper**
$\frac{2}{3}$ **cup chopped green bell pepper**
$\frac{1}{2}$ **cup chopped onion**
 2 **cups cubed sharp Cheddar cheese**
2 **eggs**
Coarse salt (optional)

1. Prepare Basic Yeast Bread through Step 4. Grease baking sheets; set aside. Turn out dough onto lightly oiled work surface; divide in half.

2. Combine bell peppers, onion and cheese in medium bowl; divide in half. Knead half the pepper mixture into half the dough. Knead remaining half of pepper mixture into remaining half of dough. Cover with towel on work surface; let rest 5 minutes.

3. Round each half of dough into a ball. Place on prepared baking sheets. Flatten each round of dough to about 2 inches thick. Cover with towel; let rise in warm place 45 minutes.

4. Beat eggs with 2 tablespoons water in small bowl. Lightly brush tops and sides of each loaf with egg mixture. Sprinkle tops of loaves with coarse salt, if desired.

5. Preheat oven to 375°F. Bake 30 minutes or until golden brown. Immediately remove loaves from baking sheets and allow to cool on wire rack.   *Makes 2 loaves*

BASIC YEAST BREAD

 2 **cups milk**
 $\frac{1}{4}$ **cup unsalted butter, softened**
 $6\frac{1}{2}$ **to $7\frac{1}{2}$ cups all-purpose flour, divided**
 2 **packages active dry yeast**
 $\frac{1}{4}$ **cup sugar**
 2 **teaspoons salt**
 2 **eggs**

1. Heat milk and butter in small saucepan over medium heat just until butter is melted. Remove from heat; cool to about 120° to 130°F.

2. Combine 4 cups flour, yeast, sugar and salt in large bowl. Add milk mixture and eggs. Beat vigorously 2 minutes. Add remaining flour, $\frac{1}{4}$ cup at a time, until dough begins to pull away from sides of bowl.

3. Turn out dough onto lightly floured work surface; flatten slightly. Knead 10 minutes or until smooth and elastic, adding flour if necessary to prevent sticking.

4. Shape dough into a ball. Place in large lightly oiled bowl; turn dough over once to oil surface. Cover with towel; let rise in warm place about 1 hour or until doubled in bulk.

5. Turn out dough onto lightly oiled work surface; divide in half. Shape each half of dough into loaf; place in prepared pans. Cover with towel; let rise in warm place 45 minutes.

6. Preheat oven to 375°F. Bake 25 minutes or until loaves are golden and sound hollow when tapped. Immediately remove bread from pans and cool on wire rack.

Makes 2 loaves

Cheddar Pepper Bread

Bayou Yam Muffins

    1 cup all-purpose flour
    1 cup yellow cornmeal
    ¼ cup sugar
    1 tablespoon baking powder
 1¼ teaspoons ground cinnamon
    ½ teaspoon salt
    2 eggs
    1 cup mashed yams or sweet potatoes
    ½ cup very strong cold coffee
    ¼ cup butter or margarine, melted
    ½ teaspoon TABASCO® brand Pepper Sauce

Preheat oven to 425°F. Grease 12 (3×1½-inch) muffin cups. Combine flour, cornmeal, sugar, baking powder, cinnamon and salt in large bowl. Beat eggs in medium bowl; stir in yams, coffee, butter and TABASCO® Sauce. Make a well in center of dry ingredients; add yam mixture and stir just to combine. Spoon batter into prepared muffin cups. Bake 20 to 25 minutes or until cake tester inserted in center of muffin comes out clean. Cool 5 minutes on wire rack. Remove from pans. Serve warm or at room temperature.   *Makes 12 muffins*

Microwave Directions: Prepare muffin batter as directed above. Spoon approximately ⅓ cup batter into each of 6 paper baking cup-lined 6-ounce custard cups or microwave-safe muffin pan cups. Cook uncovered on High (100% power) 4 to 5½ minutes or until cake tester inserted in center of muffin comes out clean; turn and rearrange cups or turn muffin pan ½ turn once during cooking. Remove muffins with small spatula. Cool 5 minutes on wire rack. Remove from pans. Repeat procedure with remaining batter. Serve warm or at room temperature.

This Tabasco bottle is a replica of the original 1868 bottle, reproduced for the 125th anniversary of TABASCO® brand Pepper Sauce in 1993. When Edmund McIlhenny first created his sauce, he poured it into cologne bottles with cork stoppers which were sealed with green wax. He included with each bottle a sprinkler fitment which consumers attached after purchase to dispense the sauce a drop at a time.

APRICOT-ALMOND COFFEE RING

1 cup dried apricots, sliced
1 cup water
3½ teaspoons EQUAL® FOR RECIPES or
  12 packets EQUAL® sweetener or
  ½ cup EQUAL® SPOONFUL™
⅛ teaspoon ground mace
1 loaf (16 ounces) frozen Italian bread
  dough, thawed
⅓ cup sliced or slivered almonds
  Skim milk
1 teaspoon EQUAL® FOR RECIPES or
  3 packets EQUAL® sweetener or
  2 tablespoons EQUAL® SPOONFUL™

• Heat apricots, water, 3½ teaspoons Equal® for Recipes or 12 packets Equal® sweetener or ½ cup Equal® Spoonful™ and mace to boiling in small saucepan; reduce heat and simmer, covered, until apricots are tender and water is absorbed, about 10 minutes. Simmer, uncovered, until no water remains, 2 to 3 minutes. Cool.

• Roll dough on floured surface into 14×8-inch rectangle. Spread apricot mixture on dough to within 1 inch of edges; sprinkle with ¼ cup almonds. Roll dough up jelly-roll style, beginning with long edge; pinch edge of dough to seal. Place dough seam side down on greased cookie sheet, forming circle; pinch ends to seal.

• Using scissors, cut dough from outside edge almost to center, making cuts 1 inch apart. Turn each section cut side up so filling shows. Let rise, covered, in warm place until dough is double in size, about 1 hour.

• Brush top of dough lightly with milk; sprinkle with remaining almonds and 1 teaspoon Equal® for Recipes or 3 packets Equal® sweetener or 2 tablespoons Equal® Spoonful™. Bake coffee cake in preheated 375°F oven until golden, 25 to 30 minutes. Cool on wire rack.

Makes about 12 servings

CRISPY ONION CRESCENT ROLLS

1 can (8 ounces) refrigerated crescent
  dinner rolls
1⅓ cups FRENCH'S® French Fried Onions,
  slightly crushed
1 egg, beaten

Preheat oven to 375°F. Line large baking sheet with foil. Separate refrigerated rolls into 8 triangles. Sprinkle center of each triangle with about 1½ tablespoons French Fried Onions. Roll-up triangles from short side, jelly-roll fashion. Sprinkle any excess onions over top of crescents.

Arrange crescents on prepared baking sheet. Brush with beaten egg. Bake 15 minutes or until golden brown and crispy. Transfer to wire rack; cool slightly. *Makes 8 servings*

Prep Time: 15 minutes
Cook Time: 15 minutes

PEACH GINGERBREAD MUFFINS

2 cups all-purpose flour
2 teaspoons baking powder
1 teaspoon ground ginger
½ teaspoon salt
½ teaspoon ground cinnamon
¼ teaspoon ground cloves
½ cup sugar
½ cup MOTT'S® Chunky Apple Sauce
¼ cup MOTT'S® Apple Juice
¼ cup GRANDMA'S® Molasses
1 egg
2 tablespoons vegetable oil
1 (16-ounce) can peaches in juice, drained and chopped

1. Preheat oven to 400°F. Line 12 (2½-inch) muffin cups with paper liners or spray with nonstick cooking spray.

2. In large bowl, combine flour, baking powder, ginger, salt and spices.

3. In small bowl, combine sugar, apple sauce, apple juice, molasses, egg and oil.

4. Stir apple sauce mixture into flour mixture just until moistened. Fold in peaches.

5. Spoon evenly into prepared muffin cups.

6. Bake 20 minutes or until toothpick inserted in centers comes out clean. Immediately remove from pan; cool on wire rack 10 minutes. Serve warm or cool completely.

Makes 12 servings

Mott's was founded in 1842 when Sam R. Mott began making cider and vinegar in a small mill in Bouckville, New York. These products caught the fancy of his neighbors and as demand grew so did the size of his mill. In 1900, Mott merged with the W.B. Duffy Cider Company. Sam Mott quickly incorporated Duffy's method for preserving apple cider in wood which further increased the size of the market. In 1930, apple sauce was added to the Mott's line. Today, Mott's produces over 13 million cases of apple juice and apple sauce every year.

Peach Gingerbread Muffins

ONION-ZUCCHINI BREAD

1 large zucchini (¾ pound), shredded
2½ cups all-purpose flour*
1⅓ cups FRENCH'S® French Fried Onions
⅓ cup grated Parmesan cheese
1 tablespoon baking powder
1 tablespoon chopped fresh basil or
    1 teaspoon dried basil leaves
½ teaspoon salt
¾ cup milk
½ cup (1 stick) butter or margarine, melted
¼ cup packed light brown sugar
2 eggs

*You may substitute 1¼ cups whole wheat flour for 1¼ cups of all-purpose flour.

Preheat oven to 350°F. Grease 9×5×3-inch loaf pan. Drain zucchini in colander. Combine flour, French Fried Onions, cheese, baking powder, basil and salt in large bowl.

Combine milk, butter, brown sugar and eggs in medium bowl; whisk until well blended. Place zucchini in kitchen towel; squeeze out excess liquid. Stir zucchini into milk mixture.

Stir milk mixture into flour mixture, stirring just until moistened. Do not overmix. (Batter will be very stiff and dry.) Pour batter into prepared pan. Run knife down center of batter.

Bake 50 to 65 minutes or until toothpick inserted in center comes out clean. Cool in pan on wire rack 10 minutes. Remove bread from pan to wire rack; cool completely. Cut into slices to serve.**

Makes 10 to 12 servings

**For optimum flavor, wrap bread overnight and serve the next day. Great when toasted!

CRANBERRY ORANGE BREAD

2 cups all-purpose flour
1 cup QUAKER® Oats (quick or old
    fashioned, uncooked)
¼ cup granulated sugar *or* 2 tablespoons
    fructose
1 teaspoon baking powder
½ teaspoon baking soda
¼ teaspoon salt (optional)
¾ cup skim milk
¾ cup egg substitute *or* 3 whole eggs
⅓ cup unsweetened orange juice
¼ cup vegetable oil
1 tablespoon grated orange peel
½ cup chopped cranberries, fresh or frozen
¼ cup chopped nuts* (optional)

*To toast nuts for extra flavor, spread evenly in small baking pan. Bake in 350°F oven 7 to 10 minutes or until light golden brown.

Heat oven to 350°F. Grease and flour 9×5-inch loaf pan. Combine flour, oats, granulated sugar, baking powder, baking soda and salt; mix well. Set aside. Beat milk, egg substitute, orange juice, vegetable oil and orange peel until thoroughly mixed. Add to dry ingredients, mixing just until moistened. Stir in cranberries and nuts. Pour into prepared pan. Bake 60 to 70 minutes or until wooden pick inserted in center comes out clean. Cool 10 minutes; remove from pan. Cool completely.

Makes 16 servings

Onion-Zucchini Bread

CRISPY RANCH BREADSTICKS

2 tablespoons dry ranch party dip mix
2 tablespoons sour cream
1 package (10 ounces) refrigerated pizza
   dough
   Butter, melted

1. Preheat oven to 400°F. Combine dip mix and sour cream in small bowl; set aside.

2. Unroll pizza dough on lightly floured work surface. Shape dough into 16×10-inch rectangle. Brush with melted butter. Spread dip mixture evenly over top of dough; cut into 24 (10-inch) strips. Shape into desired shapes.

3. Place breadsticks, ¹/₂ inch apart, on parchment-lined or well-greased baking sheets. Bake 10 minutes or until golden brown. Serve immediately or place on wire rack to cool. *Makes 24 breadsticks*

Crispy Spiced Nut Breadsticks: Place 1 cup chopped pecans and 1 tablespoon vegetable oil in plastic bag; toss to coat. Combine ¹/₄ teaspoon chili powder, ¹/₄ teaspoon ground cumin, ¹/₄ teaspoon curry powder, ¹/₈ teaspoon ground cinnamon and a dash of ground red pepper in small bowl. Add to nuts; toss to coat. Place nuts in small pan over medium heat and stir constantly until nuts are lightly toasted. Sprinkle nut mixture with 1 teaspoon garlic salt; cool to room temperature. Instead of spreading dough with sour cream mixture, sprinkle ¹/₂ cup very finely chopped spiced nuts over dough (store remaining nuts in tightly covered container). Cut into 24 (10-inch) strips. Shape into desired shapes. Bake as directed.

PINEAPPLE ZUCCHINI BREAD

1 cup vegetable oil
3 eggs
3¹/₂ teaspoons EQUAL® FOR RECIPES *or*
   12 packets EQUAL® sweetener *or*
   ¹/₂ cup EQUAL® SPOONFUL™
1 teaspoon vanilla
2 cups shredded zucchini
1 can (8¹/₂ ounces) unsweetened crushed
   pineapple in juice, drained
3 cups all-purpose flour
1¹/₂ teaspoons ground cinnamon
1 teaspoon baking soda
³/₄ teaspoon ground nutmeg
³/₄ teaspoon salt
1 cup raisins
¹/₂ cup chopped walnuts, optional

• Mix oil, eggs, Equal® and vanilla in large bowl; stir in zucchini and pineapple. Combine flour, cinnamon, baking soda, nutmeg and salt in medium bowl; stir into oil mixture. Stir in raisins and walnuts, if desired. Spread batter evenly in 2 greased and floured 8¹/₂×4¹/₂×2¹/₂-inch loaf pans.

• Bake in preheated 350°F oven until breads are golden and toothpick inserted in centers comes out clean, 50 to 60 minutes. Cool in pans on wire rack 10 minutes; remove from pans and cool completely on wire rack.
Makes 2 loaves (about 16 slices each)

*Top to bottom: Crispy Spiced Nut Breadsticks
and Crispy Ranch Breadsticks*

GREEK FLAT BREADS

Basic Yeast Bread (page 60)
1 cup chopped kalamata olives
6 cloves garlic, minced
8 ounces crumbled feta cheese
2 tablespoons olive oil
2 eggs
2 tablespoons water
Coarse salt (optional)

1. Prepare Basic Yeast Bread through Step 4. Grease 2 baking sheets; set aside. Turn out dough onto lightly oiled work surface; divide in half. Keep remaining half of dough covered. Divide dough into 16 equal pieces. Form each piece into ball. Cover with towel; let rest 5 minutes.

2. Combine olives, garlic, cheese and oil in medium bowl; set aside. Beat eggs with water in small bowl.

3. Flatten each ball of dough to $\frac{1}{2}$-inch thickness. Place 2 inches apart on prepared baking sheet. Brush dough with beaten egg. Sprinkle each round of dough with olive mixture; press topping into dough slightly. Cover with towel; let rise 45 minutes. Repeat with remaining half of dough.

4. Place heavy baking or roasting pan on lower rack of oven. Preheat oven to 400°F.

5. Sprinkle tops of dough with coarse salt, if desired. Place bread in oven. Carefully place 4 to 5 ice cubes in heavy pan; close door. Bake 15 minutes or until lightly browned. Immediately remove bread from baking sheets and place on wire rack to cool.

Makes 32 flat breads

APPLE BUTTER SPICE MUFFINS

$\frac{1}{2}$ cup sugar
1 teaspoon ground cinnamon
$\frac{1}{4}$ teaspoon ground nutmeg
$\frac{1}{8}$ teaspoon ground allspice
$\frac{1}{2}$ cup pecans or walnuts, chopped
2 cups all-purpose flour
2 teaspoons baking powder
$\frac{1}{4}$ teaspoon salt
1 cup milk
$\frac{1}{4}$ cup vegetable oil
1 egg
$\frac{1}{4}$ cup apple butter

Preheat oven to 400°F. Grease or paper-line 12 (2$\frac{1}{2}$-inch) muffin cups.

Combine sugar, cinnamon, nutmeg and allspice in large bowl. Toss 2 tablespoons sugar mixture with pecans in small bowl; set aside.

Add flour, baking powder and salt to remaining sugar mixture.

Combine milk, oil and egg in medium bowl. Stir into flour mixture just until moistened.

Spoon 1 tablespoon batter into each prepared muffin cup. Spoon 1 teaspoon apple butter into each cup. Spoon remaining batter evenly over apple butter. Sprinkle reserved pecan mixture over each muffin. Bake 20 to 25 minutes or until golden brown and wooden toothpick inserted in center comes out clean. Immediately remove from pan; cool on wire rack 10 minutes. Serve warm or cold.

Makes 12 muffins

Greek Flat Breads

LEMON POPPY SEED TEA LOAF

TEA LOAF

2½ cups all-purpose flour
¼ cup poppy seeds
1 tablespoon grated lemon peel
2 teaspoons baking powder
½ teaspoon baking soda
½ teaspoon salt
1 cup sugar
⅔ cup MOTT'S® Natural Apple Sauce
1 whole egg
2 egg whites, lightly beaten
2 tablespoons vegetable oil
1 teaspoon vanilla extract
⅓ cup skim milk

LEMON SYRUP

¼ cup lemon juice
¼ cup sugar

1. Preheat oven to 350°F. Spray 9×5-inch loaf pan with nonstick cooking spray.

2. To prepare Tea Loaf, in large bowl, combine flour, poppy seeds, lemon peel, baking powder, baking soda and salt.

3. In medium bowl, combine 1 cup sugar, apple sauce, whole egg, egg whites, oil and vanilla.

4. Stir apple sauce mixture into flour mixture alternately with milk. Mix until thoroughly moistened. Spread batter into prepared pan.

5. Bake 40 to 45 minutes or until toothpick inserted in center comes out clean. Cool in pan 10 minutes. Invert onto wire rack; turn right side up.

6. To prepare Lemon Syrup, in small saucepan, combine lemon juice and ¼ cup sugar. Cook, stirring frequently, until sugar dissolves. Cool slightly.

7. Pierce top of loaf with metal skewer. Brush lemon syrup over loaf. Let stand until cool. Cut into 16 slices. *Makes 16 servings*

BANANA-NANA PECAN BREAD

1 cup QUAKER® Oats (quick or old fashioned, uncooked)
½ cup chopped pecans
3 tablespoons margarine or butter, melted
2 tablespoons firmly packed brown sugar
1 (14-ounce) package banana bread quick bread mix
1 cup water
½ cup mashed ripe banana (about 1 large)
2 eggs, lightly beaten
3 tablespoons vegetable oil

Heat oven to 375°F. Lightly grease and flour bottom only of 9×5-inch loaf pan. Combine oats, pecans, margarine and sugar; mix well. Reserve ½ cup oat mixture for topping; set aside. In large bowl, combine remaining oat mixture, quick bread mix, water, banana, eggs and oil. Mix just until dry ingredients are moistened. Pour into prepared pan. Sprinkle top of loaf with reserved oat mixture. Bake 50 to 55 minutes or until wooden pick inserted in center comes out clean. Cool 10 minutes in pan; remove to wire rack. Cool completely.
Makes 12 servings

The man on the package of Quaker Oats—the company logo—is the personification of a man who stands for purity and integrity. The founder of the Quaker Oats Company chose this name and symbol over one hundred years ago, and they are still used today.

SAVORY CHEESE BREAD

6 to 7 cups flour, divided
2 tablespoons sugar
4 teaspoons instant minced onion
2 teaspoons salt
2 packages active dry yeast
$\frac{1}{2}$ teaspoon caraway seeds
1$\frac{3}{4}$ cups milk
$\frac{1}{2}$ cup water
3 tablespoons butter or margarine
1 teaspoon TABASCO® brand Pepper Sauce
2 cups (8 ounces) shredded sharp Cheddar
    cheese, divided
1 egg, lightly beaten

Combine 2$\frac{1}{2}$ cups flour, sugar, onion, salt, yeast and caraway seeds in large bowl of electric mixer. Combine milk, water and butter in small saucepan. Heat milk mixture until very warm (120° to 130°F); stir in TABASCO® Sauce.

With mixer at medium speed, gradually add milk mixture to dry ingredients; beat 2 minutes. Add 1 cup flour. Beat at high speed 2 minutes. With wooden spoon stir in 1$\frac{1}{2}$ cups cheese and enough flour to make a stiff dough. Turn dough out onto lightly floured surface. Knead 8 to 10 minutes or until dough is smooth and elastic, adding as much remaining flour as needed to prevent sticking. Place dough in large greased bowl and turn once to grease surface. Cover with towel; let rise in warm place (90° to 100°F) 1 hour or until doubled in bulk.

Punch dough down. Divide dough into 16 equal pieces; shape each piece into a ball. Place half the balls in well-greased 10-inch tube pan. Sprinkle with remaining $\frac{1}{2}$ cup cheese. Arrange remaining balls on top. Cover with towel; let rise in warm place 45 minutes or until doubled in bulk. Preheat oven to 375°F. Brush dough with egg. Bake 40 to 50 minutes or until golden brown. Remove from pan. Cool completely on wire rack.

Makes 1 (10-inch) round loaf

WALNUT-CHOCOLATE QUICK BREAD

1½ cups milk
1 cup sugar
⅓ cup vegetable oil
1 egg, beaten
1 tablespoon molasses
1 teaspoon vanilla
3 cups all-purpose flour
3 tablespoons unsweetened cocoa powder
2 teaspoons baking soda
2 teaspoons baking powder
1 teaspoon salt
1 cup chocolate chips
½ cup walnuts, coarsely chopped

1. Preheat oven to 350°F. Grease four 5×3-inch loaf pans; set aside.

2. Combine milk, sugar, oil, egg, molasses and vanilla in medium bowl. Stir until sugar is dissolved; set aside.

3. Whisk together flour, cocoa, baking soda, baking powder and salt in large bowl. Add chocolate chips, nuts and sugar mixture; stir just until combined. Pour into prepared pans.

4. Bake 30 minutes or until toothpick inserted near center of loaf comes out clean. Cool in pan 15 minutes. Remove from pan and cool on wire rack. *Makes 4 loaves*

Muffin Variation: Preheat oven to 375°F. Spoon batter into 12 greased muffin cups. Bake 20 minutes or until toothpick inserted near center of muffin comes out clean.

FESTIVE CORNMEAL BISCUITS

1¾ cups all-purpose flour
½ cup yellow cornmeal
1 tablespoon baking powder
1 tablespoon sugar
1 teaspoon salt
¼ teaspoon baking soda
3 tablespoons margarine
¾ cup buttermilk
1 egg white, beaten
Peach or strawberry preserves (optional)

1. Preheat oven to 425°F. Combine flour, cornmeal, baking powder, sugar, salt and baking soda in large bowl; mix well. Cut in margarine with pastry blender or two knives until mixture forms coarse crumbs. Add buttermilk; mix just until dough holds together.

2. Turn dough out onto lightly floured surface; knead 8 to 10 times. Pat dough to ½-inch thickness; cut with decorative 2-inch cookie or biscuit cutter. Spray baking sheet with nonstick cooking spray and place biscuits on sheet. Brush tops lightly with beaten egg white.

3. Bake 12 to 13 minutes or until light golden brown. Serve with preserves, if desired.
Makes 1 dozen biscuits

Festive Cornmeal Biscuits

SPICY PUMPKIN SOUP WITH GREEN CHILI SWIRL

 1 can (4 ounces) diced green chilies
 ¼ cup reduced-fat sour cream
 ¼ cup fresh cilantro leaves
 1 can (15 ounces) solid-pack pumpkin
 1 can (about 14 ounces) fat-free reduced-sodium chicken broth
 ½ cup water
 1 teaspoon ground cumin
 ½ teaspoon chili powder
 ¼ teaspoon garlic powder
 ⅛ teaspoon ground red pepper (optional)

1. Combine green chilies, sour cream and cilantro in food processor or blender; process until smooth.

2. Combine pumpkin, chicken broth, water, cumin, chili powder, garlic powder and pepper, if desired, in medium saucepan; stir in ¼ cup green chili mixture. Bring to a boil; reduce heat to medium. Simmer, uncovered 5 minutes, stirring occasionally.

3. Pour into serving bowls. Top each serving with a small dollop of remaining green chili mixture. Run tip of spoon through dollop to swirl. *Makes 4 servings*

Spicy Pumpkin Soup with Green Chili Swirl

MINESTRONE

1 tablespoon extra virgin olive oil
1 cup chopped red onion
2 teaspoons minced garlic
5 cups low sodium chicken broth
1 cup water
1 can (16 ounces) low sodium whole
    tomatoes, chopped and juices reserved
1 bay leaf
½ teaspoon salt or to taste
¼ teaspoon freshly ground black pepper
¾ cup uncooked ditalini pasta (mini
    macaroni)
2 packages (10 ounces each) frozen Italian
    vegetables
1 can (16 ounces) cannellini beans, rinsed
    and drained
⅓ cup slivered fresh basil leaves
1 cup (4 ounces) shredded ALPINE LACE®
    Fat Free Pasteurized Process Skim Milk
    Cheese Product—For Parmesan Lovers

1. In an 8-quart Dutch oven, heat the oil over medium-high heat. Add the onion and garlic and sauté for 5 minutes or until the onion is soft.

2. Stir in the broth, water, tomatoes and their juices, the bay leaf, salt and pepper. Bring to a rolling boil, add the pasta and return to a rolling boil. Cook, uncovered, for 10 minutes or until the pasta is almost tender.

3. Stir in the vegetables and beans. Return to a boil. Reduce the heat to low and simmer 5 minutes longer or until the vegetables are tender. Remove the bay leaf and discard. Stir in the basil, sprinkle with the cheese and serve immediately.
*Makes 10 first-course servings (1 cup each)
or 5 main-dish servings (2 cups each)*

CAMPBELL'S® TURKEY CORN CHOWDER

1 can (10¾ ounces) CAMPBELL'S®
    Condensed Cream of Celery Soup *or*
    98% Fat Free Cream of Celery Soup
1 soup can milk
½ cup PACE® Picante Sauce *or* Thick &
    Chunky Salsa
1 can (about 8 ounces) whole kernel corn,
    drained
1 cup cubed cooked turkey *or* chicken
4 slices bacon, cooked and crumbled
    Shredded Cheddar cheese
    Sliced green onions

In medium saucepan mix soup, milk, picante sauce, corn, turkey and bacon. Over medium heat, heat through, stirring occasionally. Top with cheese, onions and additional picante sauce. *Makes 4 servings*

Tip: Give this rich and creamy chowder an extra flavor accent with PEPPERIDGE FARM® Flavor Blasted™ Goldfish® snacks in Extra Cheddar or Extra Nacho varieties.

Prep Time: 10 minutes
Cook Time: 10 minutes

Minestrone

ZUCCHINI-TOMATO-NOODLE SOUP

10 cups cubed zucchini
¾ cup water
4 cups chopped onion
½ cup butter
8 cups quartered tomatoes
4 chicken bouillon cubes
3 cloves garlic, chopped
1 teaspoon Beau Monde seasoning
1 teaspoon salt
1 teaspoon black pepper
4 cups uncooked 100% durum noodles, hot cooked and drained
Garlic bread (optional)

Combine zucchini and water in Dutch oven. Cook over medium heat until crisp-tender. Cook and stir onion in hot butter in small skillet over medium heat until tender. Add onion mixture, tomatoes, bouillon cubes, garlic, seasoning, salt and pepper to zucchini mixture. Simmer until tender. Add noodles; heat through. Serve with garlic bread, if desired.   *Makes 8 servings*

Favorite recipe from **North Dakota Wheat Commission**

CHUNKY POTATO SOUP

6 slices OSCAR MAYER® Bacon, chopped
1 large leek, chopped *or* ½ cup chopped green onions
1 can (13¾ ounces) chicken broth
1 cup milk
1 package (8 ounces) PHILADELPHIA® Cream Cheese, cubed
4 cups diced peeled potatoes

COOK bacon in 5-quart Dutch oven or saucepot on medium heat until crisp, turning frequently. Drain bacon, reserving 2 tablespoons drippings in Dutch oven. Set bacon aside.

ADD leek to reserved 2 tablespoons drippings in Dutch oven; cook and stir 5 minutes or until tender. Stir in broth, milk and cream cheese; stir on low heat until cream cheese is melted.

ADD potatoes; cook on low heat 20 to 25 minutes or until potatoes are tender, stirring occasionally.   *Makes 6 (1-cup) servings*

Prep Time: 15 minutes
Cooking Time: 25 minutes

Zucchini-Tomato-Noodle Soup

TURKEY VEGETABLE SOUP

4 cups fat-free turkey or chicken broth
1 (14-ounce) can Italian tomatoes, undrained
1 medium zucchini, cut into ½-inch slices
1 medium carrot, cut into ½-inch slices
1 stalk celery, cut into ½-inch slices
1 leek, thinly sliced
1 cup green beans, cut into 2-inch pieces
½ cup lima beans
3 tablespoons pearl barley
1 tablespoon parsley flakes (if using fresh, triple amount)
1 teaspoon garlic
¾ teaspoon pepper
½ teaspoon dried oregano (if using fresh, triple amount)
¼ teaspoon salt
2 cups cooked turkey, cut into 1-inch chunks
1 cup broccoli florets
½ cup peas
1 ear corn, cut into ½-inch slices or removed from cob

1. In 5-quart saucepan, combine broth, tomatoes, zucchini, carrot, celery, leek, green beans, lima beans, barley, parsley, garlic, pepper, oregano and salt. Bring to boil; cover and reduce heat to simmer and cook 20 minutes.

2. Add turkey, broccoli, peas and corn; cook an additional 5 minutes.   *Makes 6 servings*

Favorite recipe from **National Turkey Federation**

According to the National Turkey Federation (NTF), about 270 million turkeys were raised in 1997. 45 million of those turkeys were eaten at Thanksgiving, 22 million at Christmas and 19 million at Easter. 91% of Americans surveyed by NTF eat turkey at Thanksgiving.

HEARTY FETTUCCINE, HAM AND BEAN SOUP

2 tablespoons olive oil
1 cup canned chunky Italian tomato sauce
1 cup diced, cooked ham
2 cloves garlic, chopped
4 cups canned no-fat, low-salt chicken broth, divided
1 (15-ounce) can garbanzo beans, drained, divided
4 ounces fettuccine (broken in thirds), elbows or rotini
Parmesan cheese

Heat oil in saucepan over medium heat. Add tomato sauce, ham and garlic. Simmer 5 minutes. Add 3 cups broth; stir to blend. Purée remaining broth and 1 cup beans in blender. Add to saucepan; add remaining beans. Bring to a boil, reduce heat and simmer 10 minutes. Add pasta; cook until tender, about 10 minutes. Serve, passing Parmesan cheese separately.   *Makes 4 to 6 servings*

Favorite recipe from **North Dakota Wheat Commission**

Pappa al Pomodoro alla Papa Newman (Bread and Tomato Soup)

¾ cup olive oil plus extra for drizzling on soup, divided
3 large cloves garlic, smashed
1 teaspoon dried sage
12 ounces stale Italian or French bread, thinly sliced, crusts removed (about 30 slices), divided
1 jar NEWMAN'S OWN® Bombolina Sauce (about 3 cups)
4 cups chicken broth
½ teaspoon hot red pepper flakes
½ teaspoon freshly ground black pepper
   Freshly grated Parmesan cheese

1. In large skillet, heat ¼ cup oil over medium heat. Add garlic and sage and cook, stirring frequently, 1 to 2 minutes. Remove garlic from oil. Add ⅓ of bread slices and cook, turning once, until golden brown on both sides, 2 to 3 minutes per side. Remove from heat; repeat with remaining oil and bread.

2. In large heavy saucepan, heat Newman's Own® Bombolina Sauce and chicken broth over medium-high heat to boiling. Reduce heat to low. Add red pepper flakes, black pepper and bread; simmer, covered, 30 minutes. Remove from heat and let stand 30 minutes to 1 hour. Ladle into soup bowls. Drizzle lightly with olive oil and sprinkle with Parmesan cheese.   *Makes 6 to 8 servings*

Spicy Senegalese Soup

1 tablespoon unsalted butter
1 large white onion, chopped
4 cloves garlic, chopped
2 tablespoons all-purpose flour
4 teaspoons curry powder
2 cans (14½ ounces each) chicken broth
½ cup water
1 tart cooking apple, peeled, cored and sliced
1 cup thinly sliced carrots
¼ cup golden raisins
¼ cup FRANK'S® REDHOT® Hot Sauce
1 cup half 'n' half

1. Melt butter in large saucepan over medium heat. Add onion and garlic; cook 5 minutes or until tender, stirring occasionally. Add flour and curry powder; cook and stir 1 minute.

2. Gradually blend in broth and water. Add apple, carrots, raisins and REDHOT sauce. Bring to a boil. Reduce heat to low. Cook, covered, 25 minutes or until carrots are tender.

3. Place one-third of the soup in blender or food processor. Cover securely; process on low speed until mixture is puréed. Transfer to large bowl. Repeat with remaining soup. Return puréed mixture to saucepan. Stir in half 'n' half. Cook until heated through.

4. Serve hot or cold. Garnish with chopped apple and dollop of sour cream, if desired.
        Makes 6 servings (about 6 cups)

Prep Time: 25 minutes
Cook Time: 30 minutes

CHEDDAR BROCCOLI SOUP

1 tablespoon olive or vegetable oil
1 rib celery, chopped (about ½ cup)
1 carrot, chopped (about ½ cup)
1 small onion, chopped (about ½ cup)
½ teaspoon dried thyme leaves, crushed
    (optional)
2 cans (13¾ ounces each) chicken broth
1 jar (17 ounces) RAGÚ® Cheese
    Creations!™ Double Cheddar Pasta
    Sauce
1 box (10 ounces) frozen chopped
    broccoli, thawed and drained

In 3-quart saucepan, heat oil over medium
heat and cook celery, carrot, onion and thyme
3 minutes or until vegetables are almost
tender. Add chicken broth and bring to a boil
over high heat. Reduce heat to medium and
simmer uncovered 10 minutes.

In food processor or blender, purée vegetable
mixture until smooth; return to saucepan. Stir
in Ragú® Cheese Creations!™ Pasta Sauce and
broccoli. Cook 10 minutes or until heated
through.   *Makes 6 (1-cup) servings*

---

*Make simple soup into a super
supper by serving it in individual
bread bowls. Purchase small, round
loaves of a hearty bread, such as
Italian or sourdough. Cut a small
slice from the top and then remove
the inside of the loaf, leaving a 1½-
inch shell. Pour in soup and serve.*

TURKEY SAUSAGE JAMBALAYA

2 packages BUTTERBALL® Lean Fresh
    Turkey Hot Italian Sausage
2 tablespoons vegetable oil
2 cups chopped onion
⅔ cup chopped green bell pepper
⅔ cup chopped red bell pepper
⅔ cup chopped celery
4 to 6 cloves garlic, minced
4 cups chopped tomato
¼ to ½ teaspoon cayenne pepper
¼ teaspoon ground thyme
2 cans (14½ ounces each) chicken broth
2 cups uncooked long grain rice
⅓ cup chopped fresh parsley
    Salt and black pepper

Heat oil in large skillet over medium heat until
hot. Brown turkey sausage in skillet 8 minutes,
turning occasionally. Add onion, bell peppers,
celery and garlic. Cook and stir 3 to 5
minutes. Stir in tomato, cayenne pepper and
thyme. Add chicken broth; bring to a boil. Stir
in rice; cover. Reduce heat to low; simmer 20
minutes. Remove from heat. Stir in parsley.
Add salt and pepper to taste. Cover; let stand
5 minutes before serving.

Makes 10 servings

Preparation Time: 30 to 40 minutes

Cheddar Broccoli Soup

Oniony Mushroom Soup

2 cans (10¾ ounces each) condensed
   golden mushroom soup
1 can (13¾ ounces) reduced-sodium beef
   broth
1⅓ cups FRENCH'S® French Fried Onions,
   divided
½ cup water
⅓ cup dry sherry wine
4 slices French bread, cut ½ inch thick
1 tablespoon olive oil
1 clove garlic, finely minced
1 cup (4 ounces) shredded Swiss cheese

Combine mushroom soup, beef broth, *1 cup*
French Fried Onions, water and sherry in large
saucepan. Bring to a boil over medium-high
heat, stirring often. Reduce heat to low.
Simmer 15 minutes, stirring occasionally.

Preheat broiler. Place bread on baking sheet.
Combine oil and garlic in small bowl. Brush
oil over both sides of bread slices. Broil bread
until toasted and crisp, turning once.

Ladle soup into 4 broiler-safe bowls. Place
1 slice of bread in each bowl. Sprinkle evenly
with cheese and remaining *⅓ cup* onions.
Place bowls on baking sheet. Place under
broiler about 1 minute or until cheese is
melted and onions are golden.

Makes 4 servings

Tip: Make all your soups special by topping
with French Fried Onions. They'll give your
soups a wonderful oniony flavor.

Prep Time: 20 minutes
Cook Time: 18 minutes

Swanson® Skinny Potato Soup

1 can (14½ ounces) SWANSON® Chicken
   Broth (1¾ cups)
⅛ teaspoon pepper
4 green onions, sliced (about ½ cup)
1 stalk celery, sliced (about ½ cup)
3 medium potatoes (about 1 pound),
   peeled and sliced ¼ inch thick
1½ cups milk

1. In medium saucepan mix broth, pepper,
onions, celery and potatoes. Over high heat,
heat to a boil. Reduce heat to low. Cover and
cook 15 minutes or until vegetables are tender.
Remove from heat.

2. In blender or food processor, place **half** the
broth mixture and ¾ **cup** milk. Cover and
blend until smooth. Repeat with remaining
broth mixture and remaining milk. Return to
pan. Over medium heat, heat through.

Makes 5 servings

Tip: In warm weather, serve Chilled Swanson®
Skinny Potato Soup. After blending, pour soup
into a serving bowl. Refrigerate at least 2
hours.

Note: 2g fat per serving (traditional vichyssoise
recipe: 15g fat per serving)

Prep Time: 15 minutes
Cook Time: 30 minutes

Oniony Mushroom Soup

CREAMY CORN BISQUE WITH SPICY RED PEPPER CREAM

RED PEPPER CREAM

  1 jar (7 ounces) roasted red peppers, drained and patted dry
  3 tablespoons sour cream
  2 tablespoons FRANK'S® REDHOT® Hot Sauce

CORN BISQUE

  1 tablespoon olive oil
  1 large leek (white portion only), well rinsed and chopped* (1½ cups)
  2 carrots, diced
  ¾ teaspoon dried thyme leaves
  ½ teaspoon dried basil leaves
  1 can (14½ ounces) reduced-sodium chicken broth
  ¾ pound potatoes, peeled and cut into ½-inch pieces (2 cups)
  1 can (10¾ ounces) condensed cream of corn soup
  1 cup half 'n' half
  1 cup frozen corn
  ¼ teaspoon salt
  1 tablespoon FRANK'S® REDHOT® Hot Sauce

*You may substitute 6 small green onions (white portion only), chopped.

1. Combine roasted peppers, sour cream and 2 tablespoons REDHOT sauce in blender or food processor. Cover; process until puréed. Set aside.

2. Heat oil in large saucepan. Add leek and carrots; cook over medium heat 4 minutes until just tender. Add thyme and basil; cook 1 minute. Stir in chicken broth and potatoes.

Bring to a boil. Reduce heat to low; cook, covered, 5 minutes or until potatoes are just tender. Stir in corn soup, 1 cup water, half 'n' half, corn and salt. Bring just to a boil. Reduce heat to low; cook 3 minutes, stirring. Stir in 1 tablespoon REDHOT sauce.

3. Ladle soup into bowls. Top with dollop of reserved red pepper cream; swirl into soup. Garnish with chives, if desired.

Makes 6 servings (7 cups soup, 1 cup pepper cream)

Prep Time: 30 minutes
Cook Time: about 15 minutes

ITALIAN TOMATO SOUP

  ½ pound lean ground beef
  ½ cup chopped onion
  1 clove garlic, minced
  1 can (28 ounces) tomatoes, undrained, cut into pieces
  1 can (15 ounces) white kidney beans, drained, rinsed
  ½ cup thinly sliced carrots
  ¾ cup HEINZ® Tomato Ketchup
  1 teaspoon dried basil leaves
  ¼ teaspoon salt

In medium saucepan, brown beef, onion and garlic; drain excess fat. Add tomatoes and remaining ingredients. Cover; simmer 15 minutes.

Makes 4 to 6 servings (about 6 cups)

Creamy Corn Bisque with Spicy Red Pepper Cream

BUTTERNUT SQUASH SOUP

1 cup finely chopped onions
1 (3-pound) butternut squash, peeled and
     cubed
4 cups defatted* chicken broth
1½ cups MOTT'S® Natural Apple Sauce
½ teaspoon salt
¼ teaspoon ground white pepper
¼ teaspoon ground nutmeg
¼ teaspoon ground cloves
¼ teaspoon curry powder
¼ teaspoon ground coriander

*To defat chicken broth, chill canned broth thoroughly. Use can opener to punch two holes in top of can. Quickly pour out the contents of the can into bowl. Most of the fat will remain in the can and the remaining broth is "defatted."

1. Spray large saucepan or Dutch oven with nonstick cooking spray; heat over medium heat until hot. Add onions; cook and stir about 5 minutes or until transparent.

2. Add squash, chicken broth, apple sauce, salt, pepper, nutmeg, cloves, curry powder and coriander. Increase heat to high; bring mixture to a boil. Cover; reduce heat to low. Simmer 10 to 15 minutes or until squash is fork-tender, stirring occasionally.

3. In food processor or blender, process soup in small batches until smooth. Return soup to saucepan. Cook over low heat 5 minutes or until hot, stirring occasionally. Refrigerate leftovers.   *Makes 8 servings*

Microwave Directions: In large microwave-safe bowl, combine onions, squash, chicken broth, apple sauce, salt, pepper, nutmeg, cloves, curry powder and coriander. Cover; cook at HIGH (100% power) 15 minutes or until squash is fork-tender, stirring once. In food processor or blender, process soup in small batches until smooth. Return soup to bowl. Cover; cook at HIGH 3 minutes or until hot. Refrigerate leftovers.

BUTCH'S BLACK BEAN SOUP

¼ cup olive oil
4 cloves garlic, minced
1 medium onion, diced
4 cups water
2 chicken-flavored bouillon cubes
3 celery stalks, diced
1 medium potato, peeled and diced
2 carrots, diced
1 large can (2 pounds, 8 ounces) black
     beans, rinsed and drained
2 cups canned corn (15 ounces),
     undrained
1 cup uncooked rice or orzo
¼ cup fresh cilantro, minced
2 (11-ounce) jars NEWMAN'S OWN®
     Bandito Salsa (medium or hot) *or*
     1 (26-ounce) jar NEWMAN'S OWN®
     Diavolo Spicy Simmer Sauce

Heat oil; cook and stir garlic and onion over high heat until onion is translucent. Add water and bouillon cubes; bring to a boil. Reduce heat to medium; add celery, potato, carrots, beans, corn, rice and cilantro. Stir in Newman's Own® Bandito Salsa and simmer until rice and vegetables are cooked, about 30 minutes.   *Makes 8 servings*

QUICK CORN, POTATO AND FRANK SOUP

2 cans (about 15 ounces each) cream-style corn
2 cans (10½ ounces each) condensed chicken broth
2 cups frozen ready-to-cook hash browned potatoes with onions and peppers
½ teaspoon hot pepper sauce
1 package (12 ounces) HEBREW NATIONAL® Beef Franks or Reduced Fat Beef Franks
½ cup sliced green onions, including tops

Combine corn, broth, potatoes with onions and peppers and hot sauce in large saucepan. Bring to a boil over high heat. Slice franks crosswise into ½-inch pieces; stir into broth mixture. Simmer, uncovered, 10 to 12 minutes. Stir in onions; simmer 3 minutes.

Makes 6 servings

WILD RICE SOUP

½ cup uncooked wild rice
1 pound lean ground beef
1 can (14½ ounces) chicken broth
1 can (10¾ ounces) condensed cream of mushroom soup
2 cups milk
1 cup (4 ounces) shredded Cheddar cheese
⅓ cup shredded carrot
1 package (.4 ounce) HIDDEN VALLEY® Buttermilk Recipe Original Ranch® salad dressing mix
Chopped green onions with tops

Cook rice according to package directions to make about 1½ cups cooked rice. In Dutch oven or large saucepan, brown beef; drain off excess fat. Stir in rice, chicken broth, cream of mushroom soup, milk, cheese, carrot and dry salad dressing mix. Heat to a simmer over low heat, stirring occasionally, about 15 minutes. Serve in warmed soup bowls; top with green onions. Garnish with additional green onions, if desired.

Makes 6 to 8 servings

HEARTY CHICKEN AND RICE SOUP

10 cups chicken broth
1 medium onion, chopped
1 cup sliced celery
1 cup sliced carrots
¼ cup snipped parsley
½ teaspoon cracked black pepper
½ teaspoon dried thyme leaves
1 bay leaf
1½ cups chicken cubes (about ¾ pound)
2 cups cooked rice
2 tablespoons lime juice
Lime slices for garnish

Combine broth, onion, celery, carrots, parsley, pepper, thyme and bay leaf in Dutch oven. Bring to a boil; stir once or twice. Reduce heat; simmer, uncovered, 10 to 15 minutes. Add chicken; simmer, uncovered, 5 to 10 minutes or until chicken is no longer pink in center. Remove and discard bay leaf. Stir in rice and lime juice just before serving. Garnish with lime slices.

Makes 8 servings

Favorite recipe from **USA Rice Federation**

HAM AND CAULIFLOWER CHOWDER

1 bag (16 ounces) BIRDS EYE® frozen Cauliflower
2 cans (10¾ ounces each) cream of mushroom or cream of celery soup
2½ cups milk or water
½ pound ham, cubed
⅓ cup shredded colby cheese (optional)

• Cook cauliflower according to package directions.

• Combine cauliflower, soup, milk and ham in saucepan; mix well.

• Cook over medium heat 4 to 6 minutes, stirring occasionally. Top individual servings with cheese.   *Makes 4 to 6 servings*

Prep Time: 2 minutes
Cook Time: 10 to 12 minutes

CREAMY VEGETABLE BISQUE

1 bag (16 ounces) BIRDS EYE® frozen Broccoli Cuts
2 teaspoons butter or margarine
⅓ cup chopped celery or onion (or a combination)
1 can (10¾ ounces) cream of celery soup
1¼ cups milk or water
1 tablespoon chopped parsley

• Cook broccoli according to package directions.

• Melt butter in saucepan. Add celery; cook and stir 3 to 5 minutes or until hot.

• Blend in broccoli, soup, milk and parsley; cook over medium heat 4 to 5 minutes.
                    Makes 4 to 6 servings

Prep Time: 2 to 3 minutes
Cook Time: 8 to 10 minutes

In the early 1900's, Clarence Birdseye worked as a field naturalist near the Arctic, where he made a chilling discovery that changed the history of the food industry. He noticed that freshly caught fish placed on Arctic ice froze solid almost immediately, and when thawed and eaten still retained all their fresh characteristics. He later turned this knowledge into a successful business and the beginning of the frozen foods industry.

Ham and Cauliflower Chowder

SOUTH-OF-THE-BORDER CORN AND ONION SOUP

2 cans (13¾ ounces each) chicken broth
1 package (16 ounces) frozen whole kernel corn
1 cup mild taco sauce
1⅓ cups FRENCH'S® French Fried Onions, divided
1 tablespoon FRANK'S® REDHOT® Hot Sauce
½ teaspoon ground cumin
1 cup (4 ounces) shredded Cheddar or Monterey Jack cheese with jalapeño pepper
1 can (4 ounces) chopped green chilies, drained
1 cup low-fat sour cream

Combine chicken broth, corn, taco sauce, ⅔ cup French Fried Onions, REDHOT sauce and cumin in large saucepan. Bring to a boil over high heat, stirring often. Reduce heat to low. Simmer, uncovered, 10 minutes, stirring occasionally.

Pour one third of the soup into blender or food processor. Cover tightly; process until puréed. Transfer to large bowl. Repeat with remaining soup, processing in batches. Return all puréed mixture to saucepan.

Add cheese; whisk until cheese melts and mixture is well blended. Stir in green chilies and sour cream. Cook over low heat until heated through. Do not boil. Ladle soup into individual bowls. Garnish with additional sour cream, if desired. Sprinkle with remaining ⅔ cup onions.   *Makes 6 to 8 servings*

Prep Time: 30 minutes
Cook Time: 15 minutes

DIJON ROASTED VEGETABLE SOUP

2 plum tomatoes, halved
1 medium zucchini, split lengthwise and halved
1 large onion, quartered
1 red bell pepper, sliced
1 cup sliced carrots
2 to 3 cloves garlic
5 cups chicken broth
¼ teaspoon ground cumin
¼ teaspoon crushed red pepper flakes
2 cups diced cooked chicken (about 10 ounces)
½ cup GREY POUPON® Dijon Mustard
¼ cup chopped parsley

On large baking sheet, arrange tomatoes, zucchini, onion, bell pepper, carrots and garlic. Bake at 325°F for 30 to 45 minutes or until golden and tender. Remove from oven and cool. Chop vegetables.

In 3-quart pot, over high heat, heat chicken broth, chopped vegetables, cumin and red pepper flakes to a boil; reduce heat. Simmer for 5 minutes. Stir in chicken and mustard; cook for 5 minutes more. Stir in parsley and serve warm.   *Makes 8 servings*

South-of-the-Border Corn and Onion Soup

CHRISTMAS RIBBON

2 packages (4-serving size each) or
    1 package (8-serving size) JELL-O®
    Brand Strawberry Flavor Gelatin
    Dessert
5 cups boiling water, divided
⅔ cup sour cream or plain or vanilla lowfat
    yogurt, divided
2 packages (4-serving size each) or
    1 package (8-serving size) JELL-O®
    Brand Lime Flavor Gelatin Dessert

Dissolve strawberry flavor gelatin in 2½ cups of the boiling water. Pour 1½ cups gelatin into 6-cup ring mold. Chill until set but not firm, about 30 minutes. Chill remaining gelatin in bowl until slightly thickened; gradually blend in ⅓ cup of the sour cream. Spoon over gelatin in mold. Chill until set but not firm, about 15 minutes.

Repeat with lime flavor gelatin, using remaining 2½ cups boiling water and ⅓ cup sour cream. Chill dissolved gelatin before measuring and pouring into mold. Chill at least 2 hours. Unmold.   *Makes 12 servings*

Chill Time: 3 hours
Prep Time: 30 minutes

GREEN BEAN SALAD

1 pound fresh green beans, trimmed
3 tablespoons lemon juice
1 tablespoon FILIPPO BERIO® Extra Virgin
    Olive Oil
½ teaspoon dried oregano leaves
    Salt

In medium saucepan, cook beans in boiling salted water 10 to 15 minutes or until tender. Drain well; cool slightly. In small bowl, whisk together lemon juice, olive oil and oregano. Pour over green beans; toss until lightly coated. Cover; refrigerate several hours or overnight before serving. Season to taste with salt.   *Makes 6 servings*

Note: May also be served as an appetizer.

SASSY SWEET AND SOUR DRESSING

1 cup plain low-fat yogurt
⅓ cup cider vinegar
2 tablespoons finely chopped onion
1¾ teaspoons EQUAL® FOR RECIPES *or*
    6 packets EQUAL® sweetener *or* ¼ cup
    EQUAL® SPOONFUL™
1 teaspoon dry mustard
1 teaspoon celery seed
½ teaspoon salt

• Process all ingredients in food processor or blender until smooth and well mixed. Refrigerate until ready to serve.
    Makes 12 servings

Variation: Substitute 1 tablespoon poppy seed for celery seed.

Christmas Ribbon

ITALIAN ANTIPASTO SALAD

1 box (9 ounces) BIRDS EYE® frozen
    Deluxe Artichoke Heart Halves
1 box (9 ounces) BIRDS EYE® frozen
    Deluxe Whole Green Beans
12 lettuce leaves
1 pound salami, cut into ¾-inch cubes
¾ pound provolone cheese, cut into ¾-inch
    cubes
1 jar (7 ounces) roasted red peppers*
⅓ cup Italian salad dressing

*Or, substitute pimientos, drained and cut into thin strips.

• In large saucepan, cook artichokes and green beans according to package directions; drain. Rinse under cold water to cool; drain again.

• Place lettuce on serving platter. Arrange cooked vegetables, salami, cheese and peppers in separate piles.

• Drizzle with dressing just before serving.

Makes 6 servings

Serving Suggestion: Add pitted ripe olives and jarred pepperoncini, if desired.

Prep Time: 10 minutes
Cook Time: 5 minutes

CLASSIC VINAIGRETTE

¼ cup FILIPPO BERIO® Olive Oil
¼ cup white wine vinegar
1 teaspoon Dijon mustard
¼ teaspoon sugar
    Salt and freshly ground black pepper

In small screw-topped jar, combine olive oil, vinegar, mustard and sugar. Shake vigorously until well blended. Season to taste with salt and pepper. Store dressing in refrigerator up to 1 week. Shake well before using.

Makes about ½ cup

Garlic Vinaigrette: Add 1 small, halved garlic clove to oil mixture; let stand 1 hour. Discard garlic. Store and serve as directed above.

Lemon Vinaigrette: Use 2 tablespoons lemon juice in place of vinegar; add finely grated peel of 1 small lemon to oil mixture. Store and serve as directed above.

Herb Vinaigrette: Whisk 1 to 2 tablespoons finely chopped fresh herbs (basil, oregano or chives) into dressing just before serving. Store and serve as directed above.

Shallot Vinaigrette: Add 1 to 2 finely chopped shallots to oil mixture; let stand at least 1 hour before serving. Store and serve as directed above.

Italian Antipasto Salad

CREAMY GARLIC DRESSING

12 ounces (2 cartons) ALPINE LACE®
    Reduced Fat Cream Cheese with
    Garlic & Herbs
1/2 cup 2% reduced fat milk
1/4 cup fat free sour cream
2 tablespoons fresh lemon juice
1 tablespoon prepared horseradish
1/2 teaspoon freshly ground black pepper
    Radish slices (optional)

1. In a food processor or blender, process all of the ingredients for 30 seconds or until well blended. Refrigerate until ready to serve. Garnish with the radish slices, if you wish.

2. Serve this dressing over vegetable or meat salads. It's also a great sauce for grilled meat, chicken and fish. *Makes 2 cups*

CRANBERRY WALDORF FLUFF

1 1/2 cups cranberries, finely chopped
1 cup miniature marshmallows
1/4 cup sugar
1 1/2 cups finely chopped apple
1/2 cup MIRACLE WHIP® Salad Dressing
1/4 cup chopped walnuts
1/8 teaspoon ground cinnamon

Combine cranberries, miniature marshmallows and sugar; mix lightly. Cover; chill. Add remaining ingredients; mix lightly.
Makes 6 servings

Prep Time: 20 minutes plus chilling

CREAMY PESTO SALAD DRESSING

1/2 cup packed fresh basil leaves, washed
2 tablespoons olive oil
1 tablespoon grated Parmesan cheese
1 teaspoon pine nuts (optional)
1 1/2 teaspoons LAWRY'S® Garlic Powder with
    Parsley
1/2 teaspoon LAWRY'S® Seasoned Salt
1 cup mayonnaise
1/2 cup dairy sour cream
1/2 cup buttermilk
2 tablespoons red wine vinegar

Using food processor or blender, combine basil and oil until well blended. Add Parmesan cheese, pine nuts, Garlic Powder with Parsley and Seasoned Salt; process until smooth. Set aside. In small bowl, combine mayonnaise, sour cream and buttermilk with wire whisk. Add basil mixture and vinegar; blend until smooth. Refrigerate before serving.
Makes 2 cups

Serving Suggestion: Delicious over a salad of mixed romaine and iceberg lettuce, pitted ripe olives and slivered red bell peppers. Or, serve over a mixture of hot cooked rotini pasta, sliced green Spanish olives and slivered red bell peppers.

Creamy Garlic Dressing

ROASTED PEPPER AND PARMESAN SALAD WITH BASIL VINAIGRETTE

1 red bell pepper
1 green bell pepper
8 small or 4 large Belgian endive
4 arugula leaves or watercress sprigs
½ cup shaved or grated Parmesan cheese
¼ cup FILIPPO BERIO® Olive Oil
2 tablespoons balsamic vinegar
1 tablespoon chopped fresh basil *or*
    ½ teaspoon dried basil leaves
Salt and freshly ground black pepper

Place bell peppers on baking sheet. Broil, 4 to 5 inches from heat, 5 minutes on each side or until entire surface of each bell pepper is blistered and blackened slightly. Place bell peppers in paper bag. Close bag; cool 15 to 20 minutes. Cut around cores of bell peppers; twist and remove. Cut bell peppers lengthwise in half. Peel off skins with paring knife; rinse under cold water to remove seeds. Slice bell peppers into strips. Peel leaves from endive; rinse under cold water and pat dry. Arrange endive in spoke-like fashion on 4 plates. Top with bell peppers and arugula.

Sprinkle with cheese. In small bowl, whisk together olive oil, vinegar and basil. Drizzle over endive mixture. Season to taste with salt and black pepper.   *Makes 4 servings*

CRANBERRY HOLIDAY RING

2¼ cups water, divided
1 (3-ounce) package strawberry flavored gelatin
1 (10½-ounce) can frozen cranberry-orange relish, thawed
1 (8-ounce) can crushed pineapple
1 (3-ounce) package lemon flavored gelatin
2 cups miniature marshmallows
½ cup MIRACLE WHIP® Salad Dressing
1 cup whipping cream, whipped

Bring 1 cup water to boil. Gradually add to strawberry gelatin, stirring until dissolved. Add cranberry-orange relish; mix well. Pour into lightly oiled 6½-cup ring mold; cover. Chill until almost set. Drain pineapple, reserving liquid. Bring remaining 1¼ cups water to boil. Gradually add to lemon gelatin, stirring until dissolved. Add marshmallows; stir until melted. Add reserved pineapple liquid; cover. Chill until partially set. Add salad dressing and pineapple to marshmallow mixture. Fold in whipped cream; pour over strawberry layer. Cover; chill until firm. Unmold. Garnish as desired.   *Makes 12 servings*

Variation: Substitute 12×8-inch baking dish for ring mold. Do not unmold.

Prep Time: 1½ hours plus final chilling

CRUNCHY FENNEL AND RED ONION SALAD

1½ ounces JARLSBERG LITE™ Cheese, cut into small cubes (about ½ cup)
2 fennel bulbs, cleaned and shredded *or* 1½ cups chopped celery
1 medium red onion, coarsely chopped
1 cup canned garbanzo beans, drained
2 tomatoes, seeded and cut into medium dice (1½ cups)
1 cucumber, peeled and cut into medium dice (⅔ cup)
⅓ cup walnuts, finely chopped
4 tablespoons vinegar
2 tablespoons chopped parsley
2 cloves garlic, minced

In large mixing bowl, combine all ingredients. Let marinate in refrigerator ½ hour. Divide among four salad plates.   *Makes 4 servings*

VEGETABLE BEAN SALAD

4 medium zucchini, thinly sliced
1 can (7 ounces) whole kernel corn, drained
1 can (8¾ ounces) kidney beans, drained
½ red onion, julienne-cut into ½-inch pieces
2½ tablespoons rice or red wine vinegar
3½ teaspoons sesame or vegetable oil
¾ teaspoon LAWRY'S® Seasoned Salt
¾ teaspoon LAWRY'S® Seasoned Pepper
½ teaspoon LAWRY'S® Garlic Powder with Parsley

In medium bowl, combine zucchini, corn, beans and onion; set aside. In small bowl, combine remaining ingredients; mix well. Pour over zucchini mixture; cover and refrigerate 30 minutes.   *Makes 4 servings*

Serving Suggestion: Serve with any grilled entrée.

Tip: Can be made a day or two ahead of time. Refrigerate in covered container.

Hint: Use Lawry's® Red Wine Viniagrette with Cabernet Sauvignon in place of the last 5 ingredients.

CARROT SALAD

2 pounds carrots
2 cups plain yogurt
¼ cup FILIPPO BERIO® Olive Oil
2 cloves garlic, chopped
Salt
1 tomato, sliced
1 cucumber, peeled and sliced
1 onion, thinly sliced
½ cup oil-cured black olives

Wash carrots; do not peel. In large saucepan, cook carrots in boiling salted water 10 to 15 minutes or until tender when pierced with fork. Drain; cool slightly. Grate carrots using largest holes on metal hand grater. In medium bowl, combine yogurt and olive oil. Stir in garlic. Season to taste with salt. In large bowl, combine carrots, tomato, cucumber and onion. Pour yogurt mixture over carrot mixture; toss until lightly coated. Top with olives.   *Makes 4 servings*

MOZZARELLA & TOMATO WITH LEMON DIJON DRESSING

⅓ cup olive oil
¼ cup GREY POUPON® COUNTRY DIJON® Mustard*
2 tablespoons lemon juice
2 teaspoons finely chopped fresh basil leaves
½ teaspoon sugar
3 medium tomatoes, sliced
6 ounces mozzarella cheese, sliced
2 cups mixed salad greens
¼ cup coarsely chopped pitted ripe olives
Chopped fresh basil leaves

*GREY POUPON® Peppercorn Mustard may be substituted for Country Dijon® Mustard.

In small bowl, whisk oil, mustard, lemon juice, basil and sugar; set aside.

Arrange tomato and cheese slices over salad greens on serving platter. Top with chopped olives and basil leaves; garnish as desired. Drizzle with prepared dressing before serving.

Makes 6 appetizer servings

IMPERIAL SALAD

1 can (8 ounces) crushed or chunk pineapple in juice, undrained
1 package (4-serving size) JELL-O® Brand Gelatin Dessert, Lemon or Lime Flavor
1 cup boiling water
1 to 2 tablespoons vinegar
1 cup diced cucumber
¼ cup finely chopped red pepper
Salad greens, for garnish
Cucumber slices, for garnish

DRAIN pineapple, reserving juice. Add water to juice to make ¾ cup.

DISSOLVE gelatin in boiling water. Add measured pineapple juice and vinegar. Chill until slightly thickened. Fold in pineapple, cucumber and red pepper.

POUR gelatin mixture into 3-cup mold or individual molds. Chill until firm, about 3 hours. Unmold. Garnish with crisp salad greens and cucumber slices, if desired.

Makes 6 servings

Prep Time: 20 minutes
Chill Time: 3½ hours

Mozzarella & Tomato with Lemon Dijon Dressing

MEDITERRANEAN GREEK SALAD

½ cup olive oil
⅓ cup red wine vinegar
2 teaspoons chopped fresh oregano *or*
   ¾ teaspoon dried oregano
1 teaspoon LAWRY'S® Seasoned Salt
1 teaspoon LAWRY'S® Garlic Powder with
   Parsley
3 medium cucumbers, peeled and chopped
3 to 4 medium tomatoes, seeded and
   coarsely chopped
1 medium onion, thinly sliced and
   separated into rings
1 can (6 ounces) Greek or ripe olives,
   drained, pitted
1 cup (4 ounces) crumbled feta cheese

In container with stopper or lid, combine oil,
vinegar, oregano and seasonings. Cover; shake
well. Set dressing aside. In medium bowl,
combine cucumbers, tomatoes, onion, olives
and cheese; mix lightly. Shake dressing. Add
to salad; toss lightly to coat. Refrigerate 30
minutes.   *Makes 8 servings*

Serving Suggestion: Heat pita bread and
spread with herb-flavored butter.

Tip: Substitute a Lawry's® classic dressing such
as Caesar or Red Wine Vinaigrette for first 5
ingredients.

FRESH SPINACH SALAD WITH RED WINE VINAIGRETTE DRESSING

½ pound spinach leaves, torn into pieces
2 hard-cooked eggs, peeled and chopped
6 bacon slices, cooked and crumbled
2 cups sliced fresh mushrooms
¾ cup LAWRY'S® Classic Red Wine
   Vinaigrette with Cabernet Sauvignon
   Dressing

In large salad bowl, gently toss together all
ingredients, except dressing; chill. Toss with
dressing just before serving.
                        Makes 6 servings

Serving Suggestion: Chill salad plates and
forks, too, if desired.

CUCUMBER AND ONION SALAD

½ cup MIRACLE WHIP® FREE® Nonfat
   Dressing
4 cucumbers, peeled, halved lengthwise,
   seeded, sliced
2 onions, sliced, halved
½ cup thin red bell pepper strips

Mix together dressing, cucumbers and onions
in large bowl. Top with peppers; refrigerate.
                Makes 12 servings (6 cups)

Prep Time: 10 minutes plus refrigerating

Mediterranean Greek Salad

Roasted Pepper and Avocado Salad

2 red bell peppers
2 orange bell peppers
2 yellow bell peppers
2 ripe avocados, halved, pitted and peeled
3 shallots, thinly sliced
$\frac{1}{4}$ cup FILIPPO BERIO® Extra Virgin Olive Oil
1 clove garlic, crushed
   Finely grated peel and juice of 1 lemon
   Salt and freshly ground black pepper

Place bell peppers on baking sheet. Broil, 4 to 5 inches from heat, 5 minutes on each side or until entire surface of each bell pepper is blistered and blackened slightly. Place bell peppers in paper bag. Close bag; cool 15 to 20 minutes. Cut around cores of bell peppers; twist and remove. Cut bell peppers lengthwise in half. Peel off skin with paring knife; rinse under cold water to remove seeds. Slice bell peppers into $\frac{1}{2}$-inch-thick strips; place in shallow dish. Cut avocados into $\frac{1}{4}$-inch-thick slices; add to bell peppers. Sprinkle with shallots.

In small bowl, whisk together olive oil, garlic, lemon peel and juice. Pour over bell pepper mixture. Cover; refrigerate at least 1 hour before serving. Season to taste with salt and black pepper. *Makes 6 servings*

Oriental Toss

   Boiling water
$\frac{1}{4}$ pound fresh snow peas, trimmed
$\frac{1}{4}$ pound fresh bean sprouts
1 head curly leaf lettuce, washed and drained
$\frac{1}{4}$ pound fresh mushrooms, sliced
$\frac{1}{4}$ cup distilled white vinegar
2 tablespoons sugar
2 tablespoons KIKKOMAN® Soy Sauce
2 tablespoons water
$\frac{1}{2}$ teaspoon ground ginger

Pour enough boiling water over snow peas in small bowl to cover; let stand 10 minutes. Drain; cool under cold water and drain thoroughly. Pour boiling water over bean sprouts in colander; cool immediately under cold water and drain thoroughly. Tear lettuce into bite-size pieces; combine with snow peas, bean sprouts and mushrooms in large serving bowl. Cover and refrigerate until chilled. Meanwhile, combine vinegar, sugar, soy sauce, water and ginger until sugar dissolves. Pour desired amount of dressing over salad mixture; toss well to coat all ingredients.
Makes 6 servings

Roasted Pepper and Avocado Salad

CONFETTI BARLEY SALAD

4 cups water
1 cup dry pearl barley
1/3 cup GREY POUPON® Dijon Mustard
1/3 cup olive oil
1/4 cup red wine vinegar
2 tablespoons chopped parsley
2 teaspoons chopped fresh rosemary leaves
    or 1/2 teaspoon dried rosemary leaves
2 teaspoons grated orange peel
1 teaspoon sugar
1 1/2 cups diced red, green or yellow bell
    peppers
1/2 cup sliced green onions
1/2 cup sliced pitted ripe olives
    Fresh rosemary and orange and tomato
    slices, for garnish

In 3-quart saucepan, over medium-high heat, heat water and barley to a boil; reduce heat. Cover; simmer for 45 to 55 minutes or until tender. Drain and cool.

In small bowl, whisk mustard, oil, vinegar, parsley, rosemary, orange peel and sugar until blended; set aside.

In large bowl, combine barley, bell peppers, green onions and olives. Stir in mustard dressing, tossing to coat well. Chill several hours to blend flavors. To serve, spoon barley mixture onto serving platter; garnish with rosemary and orange and tomato slices.

Makes 6 to 8 servings

OLIVE AND BROCCOLI SALAD WITH ITALIAN TOMATO DRESSING

1 can (6 ounces) CONTADINA® Tomato
    Paste
1 cup Italian dressing
1/2 teaspoon hot pepper sauce
5 cups (10 ounces) dry rotini or bow tie
    pasta, cooked, drained, chilled
3 cups broccoli flowerets, cooked
1 cup halved pitted ripe olives, drained
1 medium red onion, cut into thin strips
1/2 cup diced cucumber
1 to 2 tablespoons pine nuts, toasted

1. Combine tomato paste, dressing and hot pepper sauce in small bowl.

2. Combine pasta, broccoli, olives, onion and cucumber in large bowl; toss well. Add tomato paste mixture; mix lightly. Transfer salad to platter; sprinkle with pine nuts.

Makes 8 servings

Prep Time: 10 minutes
Cook Time: 12 minutes

FOUR-SEASON FRUIT SLAW

4 cups (10 ounces) DOLE® Classic Cole
    Slaw
1/2 cup DOLE® Chopped Dates or Pitted
    Prunes, chopped
1/3 cup DOLE® Golden or Seedless Raisins
1/4 cup sliced green onions
1/2 cup fat free or reduced fat mayonnaise
2 tablespoons apricot or peach fruit spread
1/3 cup DOLE® Slivered Almonds, toasted

• Toss together cole slaw, dates, raisins and green onions in large serving bowl.

• Stir together mayonnaise and fruit spread until blended in small bowl. Add to cole slaw; toss well to evenly coat.

• Chill 30 minutes. Stir in almonds before serving. *Makes 6 servings*

Prep Time: 15 minutes
Cook Time: 5 minutes
Chill Time: 30 minutes

COOL & CREAMY CUCUMBER DRESSING

1 large cucumber, peeled, seeded and
    coarsely chopped
$\frac{1}{2}$ cup reduced-fat sour cream
2 tablespoons chopped fresh dill *or*
    2 teaspoons dried dill weed
2 tablespoons FRENCH'S® Dijon Mustard
1 tablespoon olive oil
1 tablespoon cider vinegar
1 clove garlic, pressed
$\frac{1}{8}$ teaspoon salt
$\frac{1}{8}$ teaspoon black pepper

1. Combine cucumber, sour cream, dill, mustard, oil, vinegar, garlic, salt and pepper in blender or food processor. Cover and process until well blended. Cover and chill in refrigerator until ready to serve.

2. Serve over mixed salad greens, if desired.
Makes 1⅓ cups dressing

Prep Time: 15 minutes

COUSCOUS SALAD

1 bag (16 ounces) BIRDS EYE® frozen Farm
    Fresh Mixtures Broccoli, Corn & Red
    Peppers, thawed
1 can (15 ounces) black beans, drained
    and rinsed
$\frac{1}{2}$ cup chopped red onion
1 cup LAWRY'S® Classic Red Wine
    Vinaigrette
1 package (10 ounces) instant couscous
1 tablespoon olive oil

• In large saucepan, cook vegetables according to package directions; drain and refrigerate until chilled.

• In medium bowl, combine vegetables, beans, onion and vinaigrette.

• Prepare couscous according to package directions, substituting olive oil for margarine.

• Fluff couscous with fork; cool 10 minutes.

• Add couscous to vegetable mixture; toss to blend. *Makes 4 servings*

Serving Suggestion: Serve with pita bread rounds and fruit. Stir in chopped leftover turkey and $\frac{1}{2}$ teaspoon hot pepper sauce for an added treat.

Prep Time: 15 minutes
Cook Time: 10 minutes

ORANGE-BERRY SALAD

½ cup prepared HIDDEN VALLEY® Original
   Ranch® salad dressing
2 tablespoons orange juice
1 teaspoon grated orange peel
½ cup heavy cream, whipped
1 can (11 ounces) mandarin orange
   segments
2 packages (3 ounces each) strawberry- or
   raspberry-flavored gelatin
1 can (16 ounces) whole-berry cranberry
   sauce
½ cup walnut pieces
   Mint sprigs
   Whole fresh strawberries and raspberries

In large bowl, whisk together salad dressing, orange juice and peel. Fold in whipped cream; cover and refrigerate. Drain oranges, reserving juice. Add water to juice to measure 3 cups; pour into large saucepan and bring to a boil. Stir in gelatin until dissolved. Cover and refrigerate until partially set. Fold orange segments, cranberry sauce and walnuts into gelatin. Pour into lightly oiled 6-cup ring mold. Cover and refrigerate until firm; unmold. Garnish with mint, fresh strawberries and raspberries. Serve with chilled dressing.

Makes 8 servings

OVEN-BROILED ITALIAN STYLE SALAD

¼ cup FILIPPO BERIO® Olive Oil
1 clove garlic, crushed
2 medium red onions, thinly sliced into
   rounds
3 large beefsteak tomatoes, thinly sliced
   into rounds
1 (8-ounce) package thinly sliced part-skim
   mozzarella cheese
1 tablespoon balsamic vinegar
3 tablespoons shredded fresh basil *or*
   1 tablespoon dried basil leaves
   Salt and freshly ground black pepper

In small bowl, combine olive oil and garlic. Brush 2 tablespoons olive oil mixture over onion slices. In large nonstick skillet, cook onions over medium heat 5 minutes or until beginning to brown, turning halfway through cooking time. In large, shallow, heatproof serving dish, arrange slightly overlapping slices of onion, tomato and mozzarella. Whisk vinegar into remaining 2 tablespoons olive oil mixture; drizzle over onion mixture. Broil, 4 to 5 inches from heat, 4 to 5 minutes or until cheese just begins to melt. Sprinkle with basil. Season to taste with salt and pepper.

Makes 4 servings

Orange-Berry Salad

SPINACH-TOMATO SALAD

1 package (8 ounces) DOLE® Complete
    Spinach Salad
2 medium tomatoes, halved and cut into
    thin wedges
½ medium cucumber, thinly sliced
½ small onion, thinly sliced
1 can (14 to 16 ounces) low-sodium kidney
    or garbanzo beans, drained

• Toss spinach, croutons and bacon from salad
bag with tomatoes, cucumber, onion and
beans in medium serving bowl.

• Pour dressing from packet over salad; toss to
coat evenly.   *Makes 4 servings*

Prep Time: 10 minutes

TOMATO BASIL DRESSING

½ cup tomato juice
3 tablespoons red wine vinegar*
2 tablespoons scallions, chopped
1 tablespoon lemon juice
1 tablespoon sugar
1 teaspoon dried oregano
½ teaspoon dried basil leaves

*For more tomato taste use only 2 tablespoons
vinegar.

Combine all ingredients in jar with tight-fitting
lid. Cover and shake vigorously. Chill or serve
immediately over green salad or pasta salad.
        Makes 4 servings

Favorite recipe from **The Sugar Association, Inc.**

HOLIDAY FRUIT SALAD

3 packages (3 ounces each) strawberry
    flavor gelatin
3 cups boiling water
2 ripe DOLE® Bananas
1 package (16 ounces) frozen strawberries
1 can (20 ounces) DOLE® Crushed
    Pineapple
1 package (8 ounces) cream cheese,
    softened
1 cup dairy sour cream or plain yogurt
¼ cup sugar
    Crisp DOLE® Lettuce leaves

• In large bowl, dissolve gelatin in boiling
water. Slice bananas into gelatin mixture. Add
frozen strawberries and undrained pineapple.
Reserve half of the mixture at room
temperature. Pour remaining mixture into
13×9-inch pan. Refrigerate 1 hour or until
firm.

• In mixer bowl, beat cream cheese with sour
cream and sugar; spread over chilled layer.
Gently spoon reserved gelatin mixture on top.
Refrigerate until firm, about 2 hours.

• Cut into squares; serve on lettuce-lined salad
plates. Garnish with additional pineapple and
mint leaves, if desired.   *Makes 12 servings*

Spinach-Tomato Salad

Tangy Garlic Tortellini Salad

¼ cup mayonnaise
¼ cup plain yogurt
1 tablespoon plus 1½ teaspoons lemon juice
1 tablespoon olive oil
2 teaspoons chopped fresh chives or ¼ cup chopped green onion
1 teaspoon LAWRY'S® Seasoned Pepper
1 to 1¼ teaspoons LAWRY'S® Garlic Salt
9 ounces fresh cheese-filled tortellini or 8 ounces spiral pasta, cooked and drained
1 medium-sized red bell pepper, cut into thin strips
1 medium zucchini, cut into julienne strips
2 medium carrots, cut into julienne strips

In small bowl, combine all ingredients except pasta and vegetables. In medium bowl, combine pasta and vegetables; mix lightly. Add dressing; toss lightly to coat. Refrigerate at least 30 minutes. Garnish as desired.

Makes 4 to 6 servings

Serving Suggestion: Serve with crusty French or sourdough bread.

Two-in-One Salad

3 tablespoons vegetable oil
2 tablespoons KIKKOMAN® Soy Sauce
2 tablespoons distilled white vinegar
2 tablespoons minced fresh parsley
¾ teaspoon sugar
¼ teaspoon garlic powder
1 small cucumber, peeled, halved and seeded
1 medium tomato
½ small red onion, thinly sliced
1 medium head romaine, green leaf *or* butter lettuce, washed, drained and chilled

Combine oil, soy sauce, vinegar, parsley, sugar and garlic powder in small bowl. Cut cucumber halves crosswise into ⅛-inch-thick slices; cut tomato into 1-inch pieces. Add cucumbers and tomatoes to soy sauce mixture with red onions, tossing gently to coat all pieces well. Let stand 1 hour, stirring occasionally. Meanwhile, tear lettuce into bite-size pieces into large salad bowl. Just before serving, pour cucumber mixture over lettuce; toss to combine. Serve immediately.

Makes 4 to 6 servings

Tangy Garlic Tortellini Salad

Merry Meats
MERRY MEATS

HERBED ROAST

    1 beef top round roast (about 3 pounds)
 ⅓ cup Dijon-style mustard
1½ teaspoons dried thyme, crushed
    1 teaspoon dried rosemary, crushed
    1 teaspoon LAWRY'S® Seasoned Pepper
    1 teaspoon LAWRY'S® Garlic Powder with Parsley
 ½ teaspoon LAWRY'S® Seasoned Salt

Brush all sides of roast with mustard. In small bowl, combine remaining ingredients; sprinkle on top and sides of roast, pressing into meat. Place roast, fat side up, on rack in roasting pan. Roast in 325°F oven, 50 minutes to 1 hour or until internal temperature reaches 160°F. Remove roast from oven. Let stand, covered, 15 minutes. *Makes 6 to 8 servings*

Serving Suggestion: Slice thinly and serve with roasted potato wedges and steamed vegetables.

Herbed Roast

VEAL CHOPS WITH BRANDIED APRICOTS AND PECANS

8 dried apricot halves
¼ cup water
¼ cup honey
4 (¾-inch-thick) boneless veal chops
   (about 5 ounces each)*
¼ teaspoon salt
¼ teaspoon ground black pepper
3 tablespoons all-purpose flour
2 tablespoons butter or margarine
16 pecan halves
2 tablespoons brandy
   Celery or mint leaves for garnish

*If boneless chops are unavailable, chops with bones may be substituted.

1. Cut apricot halves into ¼-inch slivers.

2. Combine water and honey in 2-cup glass measuring cup; microwave on HIGH (100% power) 2 minutes or until mixture begins to boil. Stir in slivered apricots; cover with plastic wrap, turning back 1 corner to vent. Microwave 30 seconds more; let stand, covered, 1 hour.

3. Meanwhile, sprinkle veal chops with salt and pepper. Place flour in shallow bowl; dredge veal chops, 1 at a time, in flour, shaking off excess.

4. Melt butter in large skillet over medium heat; arrange veal chops and pecan halves in single layer in skillet. Cook veal chops and pecans 5 minutes per side or until browned.

5. Add apricot mixture and brandy; bring to a boil. Reduce heat to low; cover and simmer 10 minutes or until veal chops are tender.

6. Transfer veal chops and pecans to 4 warm serving plates with slotted spatula. Bring apricot mixture in skillet to a boil over high heat; cook 1 minute or until slightly thickened. To serve, spoon apricot mixture over veal chops. Garnish, if desired.

Makes 4 servings

HEARTY BEEF BOURGUIGNONNE

4 slices bacon, chopped
1 medium onion, chopped
1 large carrot, chopped
2 pounds boneless sirloin steak, cut into
   ¾-inch cubes
½ cup dry red wine or beef broth
1 jar (28 ounces) RAGÚ® Hearty Robust
   Blend Pasta Sauce

In 6-quart saucepan or Dutch oven, cook bacon over medium heat, stirring occasionally, 4 minutes or until crisp. Stir in onion and carrot and cook, stirring occasionally, 5 minutes. Stir in steak and cook over medium-high heat, stirring occasionally, 5 minutes or until steak is no longer pink. Add wine and Ragú® Hearty Robust Blend Pasta Sauce; bring to a boil over high heat. Reduce heat to low and simmer covered, stirring occasionally, 30 minutes. Serve, if desired, with hot cooked rice or noodles. *Makes 4 servings*

Recipe Tip: If cooking with wine, use the quality of wine which you would also enjoy drinking. For this classic dinner—your best Burgundy!

Veal Chop with Brandied Apricots and Pecans

BEEF TENDERLOINS IN WILD MUSHROOM SAUCE

2 boxes UNCLE BEN'S® Butter & Herb Long Grain & Wild Rice
4 bacon slices, cut into 1-inch pieces
4 beef tenderloin steaks (4 ounces each) *or* 1 pound beef top sirloin steak, cut into 4 pieces
1 package (4 ounces) sliced mixed exotic mushrooms (crimini, shiitake and oyster) or button mushrooms
1 cup chopped onion
²⁄₃ cup half-and-half
2 tablespoons Dijon mustard
2 tablespoons Worcestershire sauce

1. Prepare rice according to package directions.

2. Meanwhile, cook bacon over medium-high heat in large skillet until crisp; remove bacon from skillet, reserving 1 tablespoon drippings. Drain bacon on paper towels; set aside.

3. Add steaks to drippings in skillet; cook 2 minutes on each side or until browned. Reduce heat to medium; continue to cook steaks 3 to 4 minutes on each side for medium-rare or to desired doneness. Remove steaks from skillet, reserving drippings in skillet; cover steaks to keep warm.

4. Add mushrooms and onion to drippings in skillet; cook and stir over medium heat until tender, about 5 minutes, stirring occasionally.

5. In small bowl, combine half-and-half, mustard and Worcestershire sauce; mix well. Add to skillet with bacon; cook 3 minutes or until sauce thickens, stirring occasionally.

6. Return steaks to skillet. Continue to cook 3 minutes or until hot, turning steaks over once.

7. Season with salt and pepper to taste, if desired. Transfer steaks to serving plates; top with sauce. Serve with rice.

Makes 4 servings

VEAL PARMESAN

¼ cup egg substitute or 1 large egg
1 large egg white
1 tablespoon water
¾ cup seasoned dry bread crumbs
¼ cup (1 ounce) shredded ALPINE LACE® Fat Free Pasteurized Process Skim Milk Cheese Product—For Parmesan Lovers
6 veal cutlets (3 ounces each), pounded thin
2 tablespoons unsalted butter substitute, divided
½ cup chopped yellow onion
2 teaspoons minced garlic
1 can (28 ounces) crushed tomatoes, undrained
½ cup slivered fresh basil leaves
½ teaspoon freshly ground black pepper
2 cups (8 ounces) shredded ALPINE LACE® Reduced Fat Mozzarella Cheese
¼ cup finely chopped fresh parsley

1. Preheat the oven to 425°F. Spray a 13×9-inch baking dish and a large nonstick skillet with nonstick cooking spray.

2. In a pie plate, whisk the egg substitute (or the whole egg) with the egg white and water until foamy. On a separate plate, toss the bread crumbs with the Parmesan. Dip the veal into the egg mixture, letting the excess drip off, then coat with the bread crumb mixture.

3. In the skillet, melt 1 tablespoon of the butter over medium-high heat. Sauté the veal for 2 minutes on each side or until golden brown, turning once. Using a slotted spatula, transfer to a plate.

4. In the same skillet, melt the remaining tablespoon of butter; add the onion and garlic and sauté 5 minutes. Stir in the tomatoes and their juices, the basil and pepper. Lower the heat; simmer, uncovered, for 5 minutes.

5. Spread half of the sauce in the baking dish. Top with the veal, then the remaining sauce and the mozzarella. Bake, uncovered, 10 minutes or until bubbly. Sprinkle with the parsley and serve hot.　　*Makes 6 servings*

HOLIDAY BEEF STEAKS WITH VEGETABLE SAUTÉ AND HOT MUSTARD SAUCE

　2 pounds boneless beef top loin steaks,
　　　cut 1 inch thick
　½ cup plain yogurt
　1 teaspoon cornstarch
　¼ cup condensed beef broth
　2 teaspoons coarse-grained mustard
　1 teaspoon *each:* prepared grated
　　　horseradish and Dijon-style mustard
　¼ teaspoon sugar
　½ teaspoon lemon-pepper
　1 package (16 ounces) frozen whole green
　　　beans
　1 cup quartered large mushrooms
　1 tablespoon butter
　¼ cup water

Place yogurt and cornstarch in medium saucepan and stir until blended. Stir in beef broth, coarse-grained mustard, horseradish, Dijon-style mustard and sugar; reserve. Press an equal amount of lemon-pepper into surface of boneless beef top loin steaks. Place steaks on rack in broiler pan so surface of steaks is 3 to 4 inches from heat. Broil steaks 13 to 17 minutes for medium rare to medium doneness, turning once. Meanwhile, cook beans and mushrooms in butter in large frying pan over medium heat 6 minutes, stirring occasionally. Add water; cover and continue cooking 6 to 8 minutes, stirring occasionally until beans are tender. Cook reserved sauce over medium-low heat 5 minutes, stirring until sauce is slightly thickened. Serve steaks and vegetables with sauce.　　*Makes 6 servings*

Note: A boneless beef top loin steak will yield three to four 3-ounce cooked servings per pound.

Prep Time: 15 minutes
Cook Time: 15 minutes

Favorite recipe from **National Cattlemen's Beef Association**

PREGO® BAKED ZITI SUPREME

1 pound ground beef
1 medium onion, chopped (about ½ cup)
1 jar (28 ounces) PREGO® Pasta Sauce
    with Fresh Mushrooms
1½ cups shredded mozzarella cheese
    (6 ounces)
5 cups hot cooked medium tube-shaped
    macaroni (about 3 cups uncooked)
¼ cup grated Parmesan cheese

1. In large saucepan over medium-high heat, cook beef and onion until beef is browned, stirring to separate meat. Pour off fat.

2. Stir in pasta sauce, *1 cup* mozzarella cheese and macaroni. Spoon into 3-quart shallow baking dish. Sprinkle with remaining mozzarella cheese and Parmesan cheese. Bake at 350°F. for 30 minutes.

Makes 6 servings

Tip: A salad of mixed greens and hot toasted garlic bread team perfectly with this quick and easy casserole.

Prep Time: 25 minutes
Cook Time: 30 minutes

VEAL IN GINGERED SWEET BELL PEPPER SAUCE

1 teaspoon olive oil
¾ pound veal cutlets, thinly sliced
½ cup skim milk
1 tablespoon finely chopped fresh tarragon
2 teaspoons crushed capers
1 jar (7 ounces) roasted red peppers,
    drained
1 tablespoon lemon juice
½ teaspoon freshly grated ginger
½ teaspoon ground black pepper

1. Heat oil in medium saucepan over high heat. Add veal; lightly brown both sides. Reduce heat to medium. Add milk, chopped tarragon and capers. Cook, uncovered, 5 minutes or until veal is fork-tender and milk evaporates.

2. Place roasted peppers, lemon juice, ginger and black pepper in food processor or blender; process until smooth. Set aside.

3. Remove veal from pan with slotted spoon; place in serving dish. Spoon roasted pepper sauce over veal. Sprinkle with cooked capers and fresh tarragon, if desired.

Makes 4 servings

Prego® Baked Ziti Supreme

LONDON BROIL WITH MARINATED VEGETABLES

¾ **cup olive oil**
¾ **cup red wine**
2 **tablespoons red wine vinegar**
2 **tablespoons finely chopped shallots**
2 **teaspoons bottled minced garlic**
½ **teaspoon dried marjoram leaves**
½ **teaspoon dried oregano leaves**
½ **teaspoon dried basil leaves**
½ **teaspoon black pepper**
2 **pounds top round London broil
   (1½ inches thick)**
1 **medium red onion, cut into ¼-inch-thick
   slices**
1 **package (8 ounces) sliced mushrooms**
1 **medium red bell pepper, cut into strips**
1 **medium zucchini, cut into ¼-inch-thick
   slices**

1. Combine olive oil, wine, vinegar, shallots, garlic, marjoram, oregano, basil and pepper in medium bowl; whisk to combine.

2. Combine London broil and ¾ cup marinade in large resealable food storage bag. Seal bag and turn to coat. Marinate up to 24 hours in refrigerator, turning once or twice.

3. Combine onion, mushrooms, bell pepper, zucchini and remaining marinade in separate large food storage bag. Seal bag and turn to coat. Refrigerate up to 24 hours, turning once or twice.

4. Preheat broiler. Remove meat from marinade and place on broiler pan; discard marinade. Broil 4 to 5 inches from heat about 9 minutes per side or until desired doneness. Let stand 10 minutes before slicing. Cut meat into thin slices.

5. While meat is standing, drain marinade from vegetables and arrange on broiler pan. Broil 4 to 5 inches from heat about 9 minutes or until edges of vegetables just begin to brown. Serve meat and vegetables immediately on platter.

Makes 6 servings

A roast or any large cut of meat can be part of a beautiful holiday platter. The meat can be left whole and surrounded by colorful vegetables, then sliced at the table. Or, slice the meat ahead of time, arrange the slices overlapping around the outer portion of the platter and fill the center with vegetables. Garnish either presentation with plenty of fresh herbs on the platter, or evergreens or other decorative greens around the platter.

London Broil with Marinated Vegetables

MUSHROOM-STUFFED VEAL BREAST

    4 teaspoons olive oil, divided
1½ cups chopped mushrooms
    ½ cup finely chopped red bell pepper
    2 cloves garlic, minced
    ½ teaspoon dried rosemary, crushed
    1 (2½- to 3-pound) boneless veal breast
    ½ teaspoon salt
    ⅓ cup *each* marsala and water

Heat 2 teaspoons oil in 10-inch nonstick skillet over medium heat until hot. Add mushrooms, bell pepper and garlic; cook and stir about 5 minutes or just until mushrooms are tender. Stir in rosemary. Remove from heat; cool. Unroll boneless veal breast; trim excess surface fat. Sprinkle evenly with salt. Spread cooled mushroom mixture evenly over surface. Roll up veal; tie securely with string. Heat remaining 2 teaspoons oil in Dutch oven over medium heat until hot. Add veal; cook until browned on all sides. Add marsala and water. Cover and simmer over low heat 1 hour and 30 minutes to 1 hour and 45 minutes until veal is tender. Transfer veal to platter; keep warm. Skim fat from pan juices, if necessary. Cook over high heat until reduced by one third. Slice veal; discard strings. Spoon pan juices over each serving.

Makes 8 to 10 servings

Note: A boneless veal breast will yield 3½ (3-ounce) cooked, trimmed servings per pound.

Prep Time: 20 minutes
Cook Time: 1 hour and 45 minutes to 2 hours

Favorite recipe from **National Cattlemen's Beef Association**

TOURNEDOS WITH MUSHROOM WINE SAUCE

    ¼ cup finely chopped shallots
    2 tablespoons margarine or butter
    ¼ pound small mushrooms, halved
    ½ cup A.1.® Steak Sauce
    ¼ cup Burgundy or other dry red wine
    ¼ cup chopped parsley
    4 (4-ounce) beef tenderloin steaks
        (tournedos), about 1 inch thick

In medium saucepan, over medium heat, sauté shallots in margarine until tender. Stir in mushrooms; sauté 1 minute. Stir in steak sauce and wine; heat to a boil. Reduce heat; simmer for 10 minutes. Stir in parsley; keep warm.

Grill steaks over medium heat for 10 to 12 minutes or until done, turning occasionally. Serve steaks topped with warm sauce.

Makes 4 servings

Mushroom-Stuffed Veal Breast

BEEF TENDERLOIN WITH ROASTED VEGETABLES

1 beef tenderloin (3 pounds), well trimmed
½ cup chardonnay or other dry white wine
½ cup reduced-sodium soy sauce
2 cloves garlic, sliced
1 tablespoon fresh rosemary
1 tablespoon Dijon mustard
1 teaspoon dry mustard
1 pound small red or white potatoes, cut into 1-inch pieces
1 pound brussels sprouts
12 ounces baby carrots

1. Place tenderloin in resealable plastic food storage bag. Combine chardonnay, soy sauce, garlic, rosemary, Dijon mustard and dry mustard in small bowl. Pour over tenderloin, turning to coat. Seal bag. Marinate in refrigerator 4 to 12 hours, turning several times.

2. Preheat oven to 425°F. Spray 13×9-inch baking pan with nonstick cooking spray. Place potatoes, brussels sprouts and carrots in pan. Remove tenderloin from marinade. Pour marinade over vegetables; toss to coat well. Cover vegetables with foil. Bake 30 minutes; stir. Place tenderloin on vegetables. Bake 40 minutes or until meat thermometer registers 135°F for rare, 155°F for medium or 165°F for well done. Remove tenderloin from pan and place on serving platter; tent with foil. Temperature of meat will increase about 5 degrees during 15-minute standing time.

3. Stir vegetables; test for doneness and continue to bake if not tender. Slice tenderloin; arrange on serving platter with roasted vegetables. Garnish with fresh rosemary, if desired. *Makes 10 servings*

HOLIDAY PORK ROAST

1 tablespoon minced fresh ginger
2 cloves garlic, minced
1 teaspoon dried sage leaves, crushed
¼ teaspoon salt
1 (5- to 7-pound) pork loin roast
⅓ cup apple jelly
½ teaspoon TABASCO® brand Pepper Sauce
2 medium carrots, sliced
2 medium onions, sliced
1¾ cups water, divided
1 teaspoon browning and seasoning sauce

Preheat oven to 325°F. Combine ginger, garlic, sage and salt; rub over pork. Place in shallow roasting pan. Roast pork 1½ hours. Remove from oven; score meat in diamond pattern.

Combine jelly and TABASCO® Sauce; spread generously over roast. Arrange carrots and onions around meat; add 1 cup water. Roast 1 hour until meat thermometer registers 170°F. Remove roast to serving platter; keep warm.

Skim fat from drippings in pan; discard fat. Place vegetables and drippings in food processor or blender; process until puréed. Return purée to roasting pan. Stir in remaining ¾ cup water and browning sauce; heat. Serve sauce with roast. *Makes 6 to 8 servings*

Beef Tenderloin with Roasted Vegetables

STUFFED PORK TENDERLOIN

2 teaspoons minced garlic
2 teaspoons snipped fresh rosemary leaves
    or ½ teaspoon dried rosemary
2 teaspoons snipped fresh thyme leaves
    or ½ teaspoon dried thyme
1 teaspoon salt
½ teaspoon freshly ground black pepper
1 boneless end-cut rolled pork loin with
    tenderloin attached (4 pounds), tied
1 tablespoon unsalted butter substitute
1 cup thin strips yellow onion
2 large tart apples, peeled, cored and
    thinly sliced (2 cups)
10 thin slices (½ ounce each) ALPINE LACE®
    Reduced Fat Swiss Cheese
1 cup apple cider or apple juice

1. Preheat the oven to 325°F. Fit a 13×9×3-inch baking pan with a rack. In a small bowl, combine the garlic, rosemary, thyme, salt and pepper. Untie and unroll the pork loin, laying it flat. Rub half of the spice mixture onto the pork.

2. In a medium-size skillet, melt the butter over medium-high heat. Add the onion and apples and sauté for 5 minutes or until soft. Spread this mixture evenly on the pork and cover with the cheese slices.

3. Starting from one of the widest ends, re-roll the pork, jelly-roll style. Tie the roast with cotton string at 1-inch intervals and rub the outside with the remaining spice mixture. Place the roast on the rack in the pan and pour the apple cider over it.

4. Roast, uncovered, basting frequently with the pan drippings, for 2 to 2½ hours or until a thermometer inserted in the thickest part registers 160°F. Let stand 15 minutes before slicing.   *Makes 16 servings*

HERBED TOMATO PORK CHOPS AND STUFFING

1 tablespoon oil
4 pork chops, ½ inch thick
1 can (8 ounces) stewed tomatoes
1 can (8 ounces) tomato sauce
1 medium green bell pepper, chopped
½ teaspoon dried oregano leaves
¼ teaspoon ground pepper
2 cups STOVE TOP® Stuffing Mix for
    Chicken in the Canister
1 cup (4 ounces) shredded mozzarella
    cheese, divided

HEAT oil in large skillet on medium-high heat. Add chops; brown on both sides.

STIR in tomatoes, tomato sauce, green pepper, oregano and ground pepper. Bring to boil. Reduce heat to low; cover and simmer 15 minutes or until chops are cooked through. Remove chops from skillet.

STIR stuffing mix and ½ cup of the cheese into skillet. Return chops to skillet. Sprinkle with remaining ½ cup cheese; cover. Remove from heat. Let stand 5 minutes.

Makes 4 servings

Prep Time: 5 minutes
Cook Time: 25 minutes

Stuffed Pork Tenderloin

APRICOT GLAZED HAM

2 tablespoons butter
½ cup dry sherry
½ cup apricot jam
12 dried apricots
8 slices HILLSHIRE FARM® Smoked Spiral
Sliced Ham

Preheat oven to 325°F.

Melt butter over low heat in small casserole or ovenproof skillet. Add sherry, jam and apricots. Stir until sauce is smooth.

Add Smoked Ham to casserole; spoon sauce over ham. Cover and bake 30 minutes. Baste ham; bake until ham is glazed, 5 to 10 minutes. Do not overcook. Serve immediately.

Makes 4 servings

BRONZED PORK CHOPS

2 ounces (½ stick) unsalted butter
6 (6-ounce) pork chops, about ¾ inch
thick, at room temperature (see Note)
1 tablespoon CHEF PAUL PRUDHOMME'S
Pork & Veal Magic® or CHEF PAUL
PRUDHOMME'S Meat Magic®

Melt the butter in pan or skillet large enough to hold pork chops; set aside.

Heat 10-inch skillet, preferably nonstick, over high heat to 350°F, about 4 minutes.

Be sure meat is at room temperature (so butter will adhere but not congeal). Dip chops in melted butter to coat both sides lightly and evenly. Place meat on plate and sprinkle (don't pour) ¼ teaspoon Pork and Veal (or Meat) Magic on one side of each chop. Carefully place chops, two at a time, seasoned side down, in skillet and reduce heat to medium. Sprinkle ¼ teaspoon Pork and Veal (or Meat) Magic on top of each chop. Cook, turning several times, to desired doneness. Serve piping hot. Wipe out skillet, reheat to 350°F and repeat process with remaining chops. Serve immediately.

Makes 6 servings

Note: If you must use cold meat, you will have to adjust the cooking time and turn the chops almost continuously to avoid burning.

Chef Paul Prudhomme is well known not only for his celebrated New Orleans restaurant, K-Paul's Louisiana Kitchen, but also for his warmth, knowledge and personality. Due to the popularity of his famous eatery, Chef Paul's Magic Seasoning Blends® became available nationally and internationally.

Roasted Pork in Pineapple-Chile Adobo

1 DOLE® Fresh Pineapple
3 tablespoons packed brown sugar, divided
1 to 2 tablespoons chopped canned
    chipotle peppers
2 tablespoons lime juice
1 tablespoon yellow mustard
2 teaspoons dried oregano leaves, crushed
¼ teaspoon ground black pepper
1½ pounds pork tenderloin
    Lime wedges

• Twist off crown from pineapple. Cut pineapple in half lengthwise. Cut one half crosswise into about 1-inch thick slices. Cut remaining half in half. Refrigerate one quarter for later use. Core, skin and finely chop remaining quarter. Set aside.

• Arrange pineapple slices in single layer on large baking sheet. Sprinkle with half of sugar. Set aside.

• Combine chopped pineapple, peppers, lime juice, mustard, oregano and black pepper in shallow roasting pan. Add pork; spoon mixture over pork to cover all sides.

• Bake pork and pineapple at 400°F, 40 to 50 minutes until pork is no longer pink in center and pineapple is golden, turning pineapple halfway through cooking and sprinkling with remaining sugar. Let pork stand 5 minutes. Slice pork into ½-inch-thick slices. Serve with pineapple and lime wedges.

Makes 6 servings

Prep Time: 15 minutes
Bake Time: 50 minutes

Pork Tenderloin with Peach Mango Chutney

⅔ cup GREY POUPON® COUNTRY
    DIJON® Mustard
½ cup peach preserves
1 tablespoon cider vinegar
2 teaspoons chopped chives
½ cup chopped celery
1 clove garlic, minced
1 tablespoon vegetable oil
½ cup chopped mango
¼ cup dark seedless raisins
1 tablespoon chopped parsley
2 pork tenderloins (¾ pound each)

In small bowl, blend mustard, preserves, vinegar and chives. Set aside ⅓ cup mixture for glazing pork tenderloins.

In small saucepan, over medium-high heat, sauté celery and garlic in oil until tender. Stir in remaining mustard mixture; cook 2 minutes. Remove from heat; cool slightly. Stir in mango, raisins and parsley; set aside.

Place tenderloins on rack in roasting pan. Roast pork at 450°F for 10 minutes. Reduce to 350°F and bake 30 to 35 minutes or until done. Brush pork with reserved mustard mixture during last 15 minutes of roasting. Slice pork and serve with mango chutney.

Makes 6 servings

Baked Holiday Ham with Cranberry-Wine Compote

2 teaspoons peanut oil
⅔ cup chopped onion
½ cup chopped celery
1 cup red wine
1 cup honey
½ cup sugar
1 package (12 ounces) fresh cranberries
1 fully-cooked smoked ham (10 pounds)
Whole cloves
Kumquats and currant leaves for garnish

1. For Cranberry-Wine Compote, heat oil in large saucepan over medium-high heat until hot; add onion and celery. Cook until tender, stirring frequently. Stir in wine, honey and sugar; bring to a boil. Add cranberries; return to a boil. Reduce heat to low; cover and simmer 10 minutes. Cool completely.

2. Carefully ladle enough clear syrup from cranberry mixture into glass measuring cup to equal 1 cup; set aside. Transfer remaining cranberry mixture to small serving bowl; cover and refrigerate.

3. Slice away skin from ham with sharp utility knife.

4. Preheat oven to 325°F. Score fat on ham in diamond design with sharp utility knife; stud with whole cloves. Place ham, fat side up, on rack in shallow roasting pan.

5. Bake, uncovered, 1½ hours. Baste ham with reserved cranberry-wine syrup. Insert meat thermometer into thickest part of ham, not touching bone. Bake 1 to 2 hours more until meat thermometer registers 140°F, basting with cranberry-wine syrup twice.*

6. Let ham stand 10 minutes before transferring to warm serving platter. Slice ham with large carving knife. Serve warm with chilled Cranberry-Wine Compote. Garnish, if desired.

Makes 16 to 20 servings

*Total cooking time for ham should be 18 to 24 minutes per pound.

Peachy Pork Roast

1 (3- to 4-pound) rolled boneless pork loin roast
1 cup (12-ounce jar) SMUCKER'S® Currant Jelly
½ cup SMUCKER'S® Peach Preserves
Fresh peach slices and currants for garnish, if desired

Place pork in roasting pan; insert meat thermometer into one end of roast. Bake at 325°F for 30 to 40 minutes or until browned. Turn roast and bake an additional 30 minutes to brown the bottom. Turn roast again and drain off drippings.

In saucepan over medium heat, melt currant jelly and peach preserves. Brush roast generously with sauce. Continue baking until meat thermometer reads 160°F, about 15 minutes, basting occasionally with sauce.

Remove roast from oven. Garnish with peach slices and currants. Serve with remaining sauce.

Makes 8 to 10 servings

Note: Canned, sliced peaches can be substituted for fresh peaches.

Baked Holiday Ham with Cranberry-Wine Compote

Maple-Cranberry Pork Chops

4 well-trimmed center cut pork chops
  (½ inch thick)
1 cup dry red wine or apple juice
½ cup maple syrup*
½ cup dried cranberries
1 tablespoon water
2 teaspoons cornstarch

*Pure maple or maple-flavored syrup may be used.

1. Spray large nonstick skillet with nonstick cooking spray. Heat skillet over medium-high heat until hot. Add pork chops; cook 3 to 5 minutes per side or just until browned and pork is no longer pink in center. Remove from skillet; keep warm.

2. Add wine, syrup and cranberries to skillet; cook and stir over medium-high heat 2 to 3 minutes.

3. Combine water and cornstarch in small bowl; stir until smooth. Add cornstarch mixture to skillet; cook and stir about 1 minute or until thickened and clear. Reduce heat to medium. Return pork chops to skillet; spoon sauce over and simmer 1 minute.

Makes 4 servings

Prep and Cook Time: 20 minutes

Stuffed Pork Loin Genoa Style

1 (4- to 5-pound) boneless pork loin roast
1¼ cups fresh parsley, chopped and divided
½ cup fresh basil leaves, chopped
½ cup pine nuts
½ cup grated Parmesan cheese
6 cloves garlic, peeled and chopped
½ pound ground pork
½ pound Italian sausage
1 cup dry bread crumbs
¼ cup milk
1 egg
1 teaspoon ground black pepper

In food processor or blender, blend 1 cup parsley, basil, pine nuts, Parmesan cheese and garlic. Set aside.

Mix together ground pork, Italian sausage, bread crumbs, milk, egg, remaining ¼ cup parsley and pepper.

Place roast fat-side down on cutting board. Spread with the herb-cheese mixture; place ground pork mixture along center of loin. Fold in half; tie with kitchen string. Roast on rack in shallow baking pan at 350°F for 1½ hours or until internal temperature reaches 155°F. Slice to serve. *Makes 10 servings*

Prep Time: 15 minutes
Cook Time: 90 minutes

Favorite recipe from **National Pork Producers Council**

Maple-Cranberry Pork Chop

Pork Roast with Dried Cranberries and Apricots

1 center cut pork loin roast (3½ pounds)
1½ cups cranberry apple juice, divided
1 cup chardonnay or other dry white wine
1½ teaspoons ground ginger
1 teaspoon ground cardamom
2 tablespoons apricot preserves
¼ cup water
1 tablespoon plus 1 teaspoon cornstarch
½ cup dried cranberries
½ cup chopped dried apricots
2 tablespoons golden raisins

1. Place pork roast in resealable plastic food storage bag. Combine 1 cup cranberry apple juice, chardonnay, ginger and cardamom in medium bowl. Pour over roast, turning to coat. Seal bag. Marinate in refrigerator 4 hours or overnight, turning several times.

2. Preheat oven to 350°F. Remove roast from marinade; reserve marinade. Place roast in roasting pan. Pour marinade over roast. Bake, loosely covered with foil, 1 hour. Remove foil and continue baking 30 minutes or until meat thermometer inserted in center of roast registers 155°F. Remove from oven. Loosely cover roast with foil; set aside.

3. Measure juices from pan. Add enough remaining cranberry apple juice to equal 1½ cups. Combine juices and apricot preserves in small saucepan. Stir water into cornstarch in cup until smooth; stir into juice mixture. Bring to a boil over medium heat.

Cook until thickened, stirring frequently. Add dried cranberries, apricots and raisins. Cook 2 minutes; remove from heat. Cut roast into thin slices. Drizzle some sauce over roast; serve with remaining sauce. Garnish, if desired.

Makes 10 servings

Baked Ham with Apple-Raspberry Sauce

1 (3-pound) canned ham
1 cup chopped apples
½ cup SMUCKER'S® Red Raspberry Preserves
½ cup SMUCKER'S® Apple Jelly
¾ cup apple cider
1 tablespoon cider vinegar
2 tablespoons cornstarch
Endive or parsley sprigs
Whole crabapples

Bake ham according to package directions.

Mix chopped apples, preserves and jelly in medium saucepan. Combine cider, vinegar and cornstarch; stir into saucepan. Heat to boiling; boil, stirring constantly, until thickened, about 1 minute.

Slice ham and arrange on platter; garnish with endive and crabapples. Serve with sauce.

Makes 8 to 10 servings

Pork Roast with Dried Cranberries and Apricots

PORK TENDERLOIN MOLE

1½ pounds pork tenderloin (about 2 whole)
1 teaspoon vegetable oil
½ cup chopped onion
1 clove garlic, minced
1 cup Mexican-style chili beans, undrained
¼ cup chili sauce
¼ cup raisins
2 tablespoons water
1 tablespoon peanut butter
1 teaspoon unsweetened cocoa
   Dash each salt, ground cinnamon and
      ground cloves

Place tenderloin in shallow baking pan. Roast at 350°F for 30 minutes or until juicy and slightly pink in center.

Heat oil in medium saucepan. Cook onion and garlic over low heat for 5 minutes. Combine onion and garlic with remaining ingredients in food processor; process until almost smooth. Heat mixture in saucepan thoroughly over low temperature, stirring frequently. Serve over tenderloin slices.

Makes 6 servings

Favorite recipe from **National Pork Producers Council**

FIESTA PORK ROAST

1 (6- to 7-pound) pork loin roast
1 tablespoon salt
2 teaspoons onion powder
2 teaspoons garlic powder
½ teaspoon pepper
1½ cups water
8 small whole onions, peeled
¾ cup currant jelly
½ teaspoon hot pepper sauce
8 small seedless oranges, peeled
¼ cup water
3 tablespoons all-purpose flour

Combine salt, onion powder, garlic powder and pepper. Sprinkle on pork roast; rub into roast. Place roast in shallow roasting pan; insert meat thermometer. Roast at 325°F for 1 hour. Add 1½ cups water to pan. Place onions around roast. Combine currant jelly and hot pepper sauce; brush on roast and onions. Continue to roast for 1 hour or until meat thermometer registers 155°F to 160°F. Remove roast; let stand 5 to 10 minutes before slicing. Meanwhile, add oranges to hot liquid in pan; heat thoroughly. Remove onions and oranges; keep warm. To make gravy, combine ¼ cup water and flour; mix until smooth. Bring pan liquid to a boil; gradually stir in flour mixture. Cook and stir until thickened. Serve with onions and oranges.

Makes 16 servings

Favorite recipe from **National Pork Producers Council**

Sun-Dried Tomato and Pepper Stuffed Leg of Lamb with Garlic Chèvre Sauce

1 (6- to 7-pound) leg of lamb, boned and butterflied
Salt and black pepper
4½ ounces sun-dried tomatoes in oil, drained (about ¾ cup)
2 red or green bell peppers, roasted, peeled and seeded
1½ cups olive oil
2 tablespoons minced fresh rosemary
2 tablespoons minced fresh thyme
3 cloves garlic, minced
1 teaspoon TABASCO® brand Pepper Sauce
Garlic Chèvre Sauce (recipe follows)

Set lamb, skin side down, on work surface. Pat dry. Sprinkle with salt and black pepper. Arrange tomatoes and bell peppers down center of lamb. Roll up lamb; secure with kitchen string. Set in roasting pan. Whisk oil, herbs, garlic and TABASCO® Sauce in small bowl. Pour over lamb, turning to coat. Cover and refrigerate 24 hours. Preheat oven to 450°F. Place lamb, uncovered, in oven and reduce temperature to 325°F. Cook about 2 hours or 20 minutes per pound. Let stand 15 minutes before slicing. Serve with Garlic Chèvre Sauce.   *Makes 8 servings*

Garlic Chèvre Sauce

1 (4-ounce) package goat cheese
½ cup light cream
3 cloves garlic, minced
¼ teaspoon TABASCO® brand Pepper Sauce
1 sprig fresh rosemary

Combine goat cheese, cream, garlic and TABASCO® Sauce in microwavable dish; stir to combine. Microwave, uncovered, at MEDIUM (50% power) 45 seconds. Let stand 5 minutes and refrigerate. Garnish with rosemary sprig.

Avery Island, located just above the Louisiana Gulf Coast, is the birthplace of Tabasco® brand Pepper Sauce. It isn't an island in the classic sense, but a salt dome—a 2,500-acre hill surrounded by marshes, swamps and bayous. Today, Tabasco® Sauce remains a high-quality product made from only three ingredients—peppers grown from Avery Island seed, Avery Island salt, and pure, strong vinegar.

ROAST LEG OF LAMB

3 tablespoons coarse-grained mustard
2 cloves garlic, minced*
1½ teaspoons dried rosemary leaves,
**   crushed**
½ teaspoon ground black pepper
1 leg of lamb, well trimmed, boned, rolled
**   and tied (about 4 pounds)**
Mint jelly (optional)

*For more intense garlic flavor inside the meat, cut garlic into slivers. Cut small pockets at random intervals throughout roast with tip of sharp knife; insert garlic slivers.

Preheat oven to 400°F. Combine mustard, garlic, rosemary and pepper. Rub mustard mixture over lamb.** Place roast on meat rack in shallow, foil-lined roasting pan. Insert meat thermometer in thickest part of roast. Roast 15 minutes. *Reduce oven temperature to 325°F;* roast 20 minutes per pound until thermometer registers 150°F for medium.

Transfer roast to carving board; tent with foil. Let stand 10 minutes before carving. Temperature will continue to rise 5° to 10°F during stand time.

Cut strings; discard. Carve roast into thin slices; serve with mint jelly, if desired.

Makes 6 to 8 servings

**At this point lamb may be covered and refrigerated up to 24 hours before roasting.

Although the food is the main attraction, spectacular table settings can make the holiday meal complete—and they don't have to cost a fortune or take hours or days to prepare!

• Tie each napkin with sheer, shimmery ribbon. Tuck in sprigs of fresh herbs, greenery or a candy cane for added color.

• Make fun and festive place card holders for the table: bake extra gingerbread people and write guests' names in icing (prop the cookies up against a glass); purchase inexpensive small picture frames to hold guests' names and/or photos; cut slits in the sides of apples and insert place cards (alternate green and red apples and tie ribbon around each one).

• Arrange an instant centerpiece by filling a large glass bowl with Christmas balls or red and green apples, then surround the bowl with small votives. Or, float flowers and star candles in a glass bowl.

Roast Leg of Lamb

LEG OF LAMB WITH APRICOT STUFFING

1 (6-ounce) package dried apricots, snipped
¼ cup apple juice
¼ cup wild rice, rinsed and drained
1½ cups chicken broth
½ cup long-grain rice
¼ cup chutney
¼ cup sliced green onions
2 teaspoons dried basil leaves
½ teaspoon lemon pepper
3 to 3½ pounds American leg of lamb, shank half, boned and butterflied
¼ teaspoon salt
¼ teaspoon ground black pepper

In bowl, combine apricots and apple juice; let stand 20 minutes, stirring occasionally. In saucepan, combine wild rice and broth. Bring to a boil; reduce heat. Cover and simmer 40 minutes. Add long-grain rice. Cover and simmer 15 minutes more. Remove from heat. Let stand, covered, 5 minutes. Stir in apricot mixture, chutney, green onions, basil and lemon pepper.

Trim any fat from lamb. With boned side up, pound meat with meat mallet to even thickness, about 4 inches by 20 inches. Sprinkle lightly with salt and pepper. Spread rice mixture over meat. Roll up, starting with narrow end; tie securely. Place roast on end, spiral side up, on rack in shallow roasting pan. Cover exposed rice mixture with small piece of foil. Roast at 325°F for 1¾ hours, or to medium doneness (150° to 160°F). Remove from oven. Let stand about 10 minutes before serving. *Makes 12 servings*

Favorite recipe from **American Lamb Council**

LAMB CHOPS WITH FRESH HERBS

⅓ cup red wine vinegar
⅓ cup vegetable oil
2 tablespoons soy sauce
2 tablespoons sherry
1 tablespoon lemon juice
1 tablespoon LAWRY'S® Seasoned Salt
1 teaspoon LAWRY'S® Garlic Powder with Parsley
1 teaspoon chopped fresh oregano
1 teaspoon chopped fresh rosemary
1 teaspoon chopped fresh thyme
1 teaspoon chopped fresh marjoram
1 teaspoon dry mustard
½ teaspoon white pepper
8 lamb loin chops (about 2 pounds), cut 1 inch thick

In large resealable plastic food storage bag, combine all ingredients except chops; mix well. Remove ½ cup marinade for basting. Add chops; seal bag. Marinate in refrigerator at least 1 hour. Remove chops; discard used marinade. Grill or broil chops 8 minutes or until desired doneness, turning once and basting often with additional ½ cup marinade. *Do not baste during last 5 minutes of cooking.* Discard any remaining marinade.
Makes 4 to 6 servings

Serving Suggestion: Serve with mashed potatoes and fresh green beans.

Hint: Substitute ¼ to ½ teaspoon dried herbs for each teaspoon of fresh herbs.

Lamb Chops with Fresh Herbs

PERFECT POULTRY

MEDITERRANEAN CORNISH HENS

1 cup UNCLE BEN'S® Instant Rice
¾ cup chopped fresh spinach
¼ cup chopped sun-dried tomatoes in oil, drained
2 Cornish hens, thawed (about 1 pound each)
1 tablespoon butter or margarine, melted
1 clove garlic, minced

1. Heat oven to 425°F. Cook rice according to package directions. Stir in spinach and sun-dried tomatoes; cool.

2. Spoon ½ rice mixture into cavity of each hen. Tie drumsticks together with cotton string. Place hens on rack in roasting pan. Combine butter and garlic; brush each hen with garlic butter.

3. Roast 45 to 50 minutes* or until juices run clear, basting occasionally with drippings.   *Makes 2 servings*

*If hens weigh over 18 ounces, roast 60 to 70 minutes.

Cook's Tip: Do not store garlic in the refrigerator. Garlic heads will keep up to two months if stored in an open container in a dark, cool place. Unpeeled cloves will keep for up to two weeks.

Mediterranean Cornish Hen

TRADITIONAL CHICKEN AND RICE

1 tablespoon olive oil
4 boneless, skinless chicken breasts (about 1 pound)
2¼ cups water
1 box COUNTRY INN® Brand Chicken Rice Dishes
½ cup chopped red bell pepper
½ cup frozen peas, thawed
¼ cup Parmesan cheese

1. Heat oil in large skillet. Add chicken, cook over medium-high heat 10 to 15 minutes or until lightly browned on both sides.

2. Add water, rice, contents of seasoning packet, bell pepper and peas; mix well. Bring to a boil. Cover; reduce heat and simmer 10 minutes or until chicken is no longer pink in center. Remove from heat. Sprinkle with cheese; let stand covered 5 minutes or until liquid is absorbed.   *Makes 4 servings*

BUFFET CHICKEN MEDLEY

4 boneless, skinless chicken breasts, quartered (about 2½ pounds)
2 tablespoons butter or margarine
1 large onion, cut into ¼-inch pieces
1 jar (6 ounces) marinated artichoke hearts, drained and sliced (reserve marinade)
4 tomatoes, cut into wedges
1 teaspoon salt, divided
½ teaspoon pepper, divided
1 avocado, halved, peeled, pitted and cut into ½-inch wedges
1 cup (4 ounces) crumbled feta cheese

In 10-inch skillet, melt butter over medium-high heat. Add chicken pieces; cook, turning, about 5 minutes or until lightly browned. Remove chicken to warm dish.

Add onion to pan juices; cook over medium heat 3 minutes, stirring frequently. Add artichokes, reserved marinade and tomatoes; cook about 2 minutes. Remove from heat. In 2-quart baking dish, place half of chicken; sprinkle with ½ teaspoon salt and ¼ teaspoon pepper. Spoon half of artichoke mixture over chicken; add half of avocado and half of cheese. Top with remaining chicken; repeat layers. Bake at 350°F about 25 minutes or until chicken is no longer pink in center.
          Makes 8 servings

Favorite recipe from **National Broiler Council**

Traditional Chicken and Rice

CHICKEN DIANE

6 ounces uncooked pasta
¾ cup unsalted butter, divided
1 tablespoon plus 2 teaspoons CHEF PAUL
   PRUDHOMME'S Poultry Magic®
¾ pound boneless, skinless chicken breasts,
   cut into strips
3 cups sliced mushrooms (about 8 ounces)
¼ cup minced green onion tops
3 tablespoons minced fresh parsley
1 teaspoon minced garlic
1 cup defatted chicken stock or water

Cook pasta according to package directions. Drain immediately; rinse with hot water, then with cold water. Drain again.

Combine ¼ cup butter, Poultry Magic® and chicken in medium bowl. Heat large skillet over high heat until hot, about 4 minutes. Add chicken; brown both sides. Add mushrooms; cook 2 minutes. Add green onion tops, parsley, garlic and stock. Cook 2 minutes or until sauce boils rapidly. Add remaining butter (cut into pats), stirring constantly. Cook 3 minutes. Add cooked pasta; mix well. Serve immediately. Garnish as desired.

Makes 2 servings

FESTIVE CHICKEN ROLLS

1 can (8 ounces) crushed pineapple, well
   drained, divided
2 slices cinnamon raisin bread, toasted,
   cubed
⅓ cup chopped toasted walnuts
4 large skinless boneless chicken breast
   halves
1 tablespoon vegetable oil
½ cup HEINZ® Tomato Ketchup
½ cup whole berry cranberry sauce
¼ cup orange juice
3 tablespoons orange marmalade
⅛ teaspoon ground cloves

Measure ½ cup pineapple; reserve remainder. For stuffing, combine ½ cup pineapple, toast and walnuts. Flatten chicken breasts to uniform thickness. Place about ⅓ cup stuffing across center of each breast; fold edges to center and secure with toothpicks. In skillet, brown chicken in oil on all sides. Combine ketchup with reserved pineapple and remaining ingredients; pour over chicken. Simmer, uncovered, 13 to 15 minutes, turning and basting frequently. Remove toothpicks before serving.

Makes 4 servings

Chicken Diane

CHICKEN PUTTANESCA-STYLE

2 tablespoons olive or vegetable oil
1 (2½- to 3-pound) chicken, cut into
    pieces
1 medium onion, sliced
¼ cup balsamic vinegar
1 jar (27.7 ounces) RAGÚ® Old World
    Style® Pasta Sauce
1 cup pitted ripe olives
1 tablespoon drained capers

In 12-inch skillet, heat oil over medium-high
heat and brown chicken. Remove chicken and
set aside; drain.

In same skillet, add onion and vinegar and
cook over medium heat, stirring occasionally,
3 minutes. Stir in Ragú® Old World Style Pasta
Sauce. Return chicken to skillet and simmer
covered 25 minutes or until chicken is no
longer pink. Stir in olives and capers; heat
through. Serve, if desired, over hot cooked rice
and garnish with chopped fresh parsley.

Makes 4 servings

Recipe Tip: Be sure to use the best quality
balsamic vinegar you can afford. In general,
the longer it's been aged, the deeper and
tastier the flavor.

CHICKEN DIJON WITH WHITE WINE

2 tablespoons olive oil
6 boneless, skinless chicken breast halves
    Salt and pepper to taste
1 medium onion, chopped
1 cup sliced mushrooms
2 cloves garlic, minced
1 container (6.5 ounces) ALOUETTE®
    Garlic et Herbes
½ cup chicken broth
¼ cup white wine
1 tablespoon GREY POUPON® Dijon
    Mustard
    Fresh parsley, chopped

• Heat olive oil in large skillet over medium
heat.

• Season chicken breasts with salt and pepper.
Add to skillet; brown 10 minutes on each side,
adding onion, mushrooms and garlic to skillet
while chicken is browning on second side.

• In small bowl, mix Alouette® with broth,
wine and mustard.

• Pour Alouette® mixture over chicken and
simmer for 10 to 15 minutes.

• Sprinkle with parsley.   *Makes 6 servings*

Note: Any extra sauce may be served over
potatoes, rice or pasta.

Chicken Puttanesca-Style

STUFFED CHICKEN BREASTS À LA FRANÇAISE

6 boneless, skinless chicken breast halves, with pockets (6 ounces each)
6 ounces (1 carton) ALPINE LACE® Reduced Fat Cream Cheese with Garlic & Herbs
½ cup finely chopped green onions (tops only)
2 teaspoons snipped fresh rosemary leaves or ¾ teaspoon dried rosemary
½ cup all-purpose flour
1 teaspoon freshly ground black pepper
⅓ cup low sodium chicken broth
⅓ cup dry white wine or low sodium chicken broth
8 sprigs fresh rosemary, about 3 inches long (optional)

1. Preheat the oven to 350°F. Spray a 13×9×2-inch baking dish with nonstick cooking spray. Rinse the chicken and pat dry with paper towels. In a medium-size bowl, mix the cream cheese with the green onions and rosemary until well blended. Stuff the pockets of the chicken breasts with this mixture.

2. On a piece of wax paper, blend the flour and pepper. Roll each chicken breast in the seasoned flour, then arrange in the baking dish. Pour over the broth and the wine.

3. Cover the dish tightly with foil and bake for 30 minutes. Uncover and bake 10 minutes more or until the juices run clear when the thickest piece of chicken is pierced with fork.

4. Transfer the chicken to a serving platter and garnish each with a sprig of rosemary, if you wish. *Makes 6 servings*

CHICKEN ROSEMARY

2 boneless skinless chicken breast halves
1 teaspoon margarine
1 teaspoon olive oil
Salt and pepper
½ small onion, sliced
1 large clove garlic, minced
½ teaspoon dried rosemary
⅛ teaspoon ground cinnamon
½ cup DOLE® Pineapple Juice
1 tablespoon orange marmalade
2 cups sliced DOLE® Carrots

Place chicken between 2 pieces of waxed paper or plastic wrap. Pound with flat side of meat mallet or rolling pin to ½-inch thickness. In medium skillet, brown chicken on both sides in margarine and oil. Sprinkle with salt and pepper. Stir in onion, garlic, rosemary and cinnamon. Cook and stir until onion is soft. Blend in juice and marmalade. Spoon over chicken. Cover; simmer 10 minutes. Stir in carrots. Cover; simmer 5 minutes or until carrots are tender-crisp and chicken is no longer pink in center. Garnish as desired.
Makes 2 servings

Prep Time: 10 minutes
Cook Time: 20 minutes

Stuffed Chicken Breast à la Française

CHICKEN WITH BRANDIED FRUIT SAUCE

4 broiler-fryer chicken breast halves,
    boned, skinned
½ teaspoon salt
¼ teaspoon ground nutmeg
2 tablespoons butter or margarine
1 tablespoon cornstarch
¼ teaspoon ground red pepper
    Juice of 1 orange
    Juice of 1 lemon
    Juice of 1 lime
⅓ cup orange marmalade
2 tablespoons brandy
1 cup red seedless grapes

Pound chicken to ½-inch thickness on hard surface with meat mallet or rolling pin. Sprinkle salt and nutmeg over chicken. Heat butter in large skillet over medium-high heat. Add chicken and cook, turning, about 8 minutes or until chicken is brown and fork-tender. Mix cornstarch and red pepper in small bowl. Stir in orange juice, lemon juice and lime juice; set aside. Remove chicken to serving platter. Add marmalade to same skillet; heat until melted. Stir in juice mixture; cook and stir until mixture boils and thickens. Add brandy and grapes. Return chicken to pan; spoon sauce over chicken. Cook over low heat 5 minutes. *Makes 4 servings*

Favorite recipe from **Delmarva Poultry Industry, Inc.**

LEMON-HERB ROAST CHICKEN

1 (2½-to 3-pound) whole roasting chicken

BASTING SAUCE

⅓ cup lemon juice
¼ cup HOLLAND HOUSE® Vermouth
    Cooking Wine
¼ cup oil
½ teaspoon dried rosemary leaves
½ teaspoon dried thyme leaves
1 garlic clove, minced

Remove giblets from chicken. Rinse chicken; pat dry. In large nonmetal bowl, combine all ingredients for Basting Sauce; mix well. Add chicken, turning to coat all sides. Cover; refrigerate 1 to 2 hours, turning several times.

Heat oven to 375°F. Remove chicken from Basting Sauce; reserve Basting Sauce. Using string, tie legs and tail together. Twist wing tips under back. Place chicken, breast side up, on rack in shallow roasting pan. Brush with Basting Sauce. Roast at 375°F for 55 to 65 minutes, or until chicken is tender and juices run clear, brushing with Basting Sauce halfway through roasting. Let stand 5 to 10 minutes before carving. *Makes 4 servings*

Chicken with Brandied Fruit Sauce

Mahogany Glazed Chicken with Wild Rice Stuffing

2 disposable aluminum foil pans (9 inches each)
1 package (6 ounces) white & wild rice mix
¼ pound thick sliced bacon or pancetta (Italian bacon), chopped
1 package (6 ounces) mushrooms, wiped clean and chopped
3 carrots, chopped
1 medium onion, finely chopped
½ cup chopped fresh parsley
2 tablespoons FRENCH'S® Worcestershire Sauce
½ cup red currant jelly or seedless raspberry jam
2 tablespoons FRENCH'S® Dijon Mustard
1 whole chicken (about 4 pounds)
  Olive oil vegetable cooking spray
  Seasoned salt

To prepare grill, place doubled foil pans in center of grill under grilling rack. Arrange hot coals or lava rocks around foil pan. Fill pan with cold water.

To prepare stuffing, cook rice mix according to package directions, omitting butter. Cook bacon in large skillet over high heat 2 minutes or until wilted. Add mushrooms, carrots and onion. Cook 5 minutes or until vegetables are tender, stirring often. Stir in parsley, Worcestershire and cooked rice; mix well. Cool slightly.

To prepare glaze, microwave jelly in small microwave-safe bowl on HIGH 1 to 2 minutes until jelly is melted, whisking once. Whisk in mustard; set aside.

With fingertips, carefully loosen breast skin of chicken. Spoon cooled stuffing under skin and into body cavity. Shape stuffing under skin. (Keep extra stuffing warm and serve on the side.) Secure skin and openings with metal poultry skewers. Twist wing tips under back and tie legs together with kitchen string. Coat chicken with vegetable cooking spray; sprinkle with seasoned salt. Place chicken on greased grid. Grill, on covered grill, over medium-low to medium coals 1½ hours or until meat thermometer inserted into thigh, but not touching bone, reaches 180°F, basting frequently with glaze during last hour of cooking. Carve and serve with stuffing.

Makes 4 to 6 servings

Prep Time: 30 minutes
Cook Time: 1 hour 30 minutes

Chili Cranberry Chicken

½ cup HEINZ® Chili Sauce
½ cup whole berry cranberry sauce
2 tablespoons orange marmalade
⅛ teaspoon ground allspice
4 to 6 skinless boneless chicken breast halves (about 1½ pounds)
2 teaspoons vegetable oil

Combine first 4 ingredients; set aside. In large skillet, slowly brown chicken on both sides in oil. Pour reserved chili sauce mixture over chicken. Simmer, uncovered, 8 to 10 minutes or until chicken is cooked and sauce is of desired consistency, turning and basting occasionally.

Makes 4 to 6 servings and about 1 cup sauce

APRICOT-GLAZED HENS WITH WILD RICE STUFFING

1/4 cup butter or margarine
1/2 cup chopped onion
3/4 cup diced celery
1 (6-ounce) package long grain and wild rice mix
2 1/2 cups water
1 cup (12-ounce jar) SMUCKER'S® Apricot Preserves, divided
2 tablespoons chopped parsley
1/3 cup chopped toasted pecans
4 Cornish game hens (about 22 ounces each)
Salt and pepper
Lemon slices and celery leaves

Melt butter in large saucepan; remove 2 tablespoons melted butter and set aside. Add onion and celery to saucepan. Sauté over medium heat, stirring frequently, until onion begins to turn golden. Add rice mix and water; cover and cook according to package directions. Add 1/4 cup apricot preserves, parsley and pecans. Use mixture to stuff hens, or serve as a side dish in 3- to 4-cup casserole dish.

Fill hens with stuffing; secure cavities with poultry pins or toothpicks. Brush hens with reserved butter; sprinkle lightly with salt and pepper.

Roast at 350°F for 70 to 75 minutes or until legs of hens can be moved easily. Baste hens with remaining apricot preserves during last 15 minutes of roasting.

To serve, remove poultry pins from hens; place hens on large serving platter. Garnish with lemon slices and celery leaves. Serve apricot drippings from hens as sauce in small dish; thin with water and heat, if necessary.

Makes 4 servings

OVEN CHICKEN & RICE

1 package (4.3 ounces) RICE-A-RONI® Long Grain & Wild Rice Pilaf
4 bone-in chicken breast halves
1/2 teaspoon dried thyme leaves or dried basil leaves
1/4 teaspoon garlic powder
1 tablespoon margarine or butter, melted
1/2 teaspoon paprika
1 cup chopped tomato or red bell pepper

1. Heat oven to 375°F. In 11×7-inch glass baking dish or 1 1/2-quart casserole, combine 1 1/4 cups water, rice and contents of seasoning packet; mix well.

2. Place chicken over rice. Sprinkle evenly with thyme and garlic powder. Brush with margarine; sprinkle with paprika.

3. Cover with foil; bake 45 minutes. Stir in tomato. Bake, uncovered, 15 minutes or until liquid is absorbed and chicken is no longer pink inside. *Makes 4 servings*

STUFFED CHICKEN BREASTS WITH HERBED BUTTER SAUCE

8 boneless skinless chicken breast halves (about 3 pounds)
½ teaspoon salt
¼ teaspoon black pepper
½ cup butter or margarine, softened
2 tablespoons chopped fresh parsley
½ teaspoon dried oregano leaves
½ teaspoon dried rosemary leaves, crushed
½ teaspoon dried basil leaves
4 ounces Swiss cheese, cut into 8 strips
¼ cup all-purpose flour
1 egg, beaten
⅔ cup dry bread crumbs
½ cup dry white wine
1 teaspoon vegetable oil
½ cup red bell pepper strips
½ cup green bell pepper strips
4 cups cooked rice
1 tablespoon cornstarch
1 tablespoon cold water
Fresh oregano and rosemary sprigs for garnish

Place chicken between plastic wrap; pound with meat mallet or rolling pin to ¼-inch thickness. Sprinkle chicken with salt and black pepper. Combine butter, parsley, oregano, rosemary and basil in small bowl. Place 1½ teaspoons herb butter on centers of chicken breast halves, reserving remaining herb butter. Place 1 cheese strip in center of each chicken breast half. Roll up chicken with cheese inside; tuck in ends. Roll in flour, then dip in egg. Coat with bread crumbs. Place in ungreased 13×9-inch baking dish; bake at 375°F 15 minutes. Stir wine into remaining herb butter in small saucepan; heat over low heat until butter melts. Pour over chicken; bake 20 minutes more. Heat oil in large skillet over medium heat until hot. Add red and green bell peppers; cook and stir until crisp-tender. Add rice; toss lightly. Heat thoroughly. Serve chicken over rice. Pour pan drippings into small saucepan. Dissolve cornstarch in water. Add to drippings; heat until mixture boils and thickens, stirring constantly. Serve with chicken and rice. Garnish, if desired.

Makes 8 servings

Favorite recipe from **National Broiler Council**

NBC
National Broiler Council

The National Broiler Council is the nonprofit trade organization for the broiler chicken industry. Membership includes broiler producers and processors, firms that supply goods and services to the broiler industry and other companies involved in the industry. Members produce, process and market over 90% of all U.S. broilers.

Stuffed Chicken Breast with Herbed Butter Sauce

CORNISH HENS WITH CITRUS CHUTNEY GLAZE

Grated peel and juice of 1 SUNKIST®
    orange
Grated peel and juice of 1 SUNKIST®
    lemon
¼ cup bottled mango chutney
1 tablespoon margarine or butter
4 Rock Cornish game hens (1¼ to 1½
    pounds each), thawed if frozen (giblets
    and necks removed)

For glaze, in small saucepan combine citrus peel and juices, chutney and margarine. Simmer 5 minutes to blend flavors, breaking up any mango pieces with back of spoon. Tie legs of each hen together with string and turn wing tips under back of each hen. Brush hens lightly with glaze and arrange, breast side up, in shallow baking pan lined with aluminum foil. Bake at 350°F for 1 hour to 1 hour and 15 minutes or until hens are tender, brushing occasionally with remaining glaze. (Cover legs and wings with small pieces of foil if they start to become too brown.) Remove string before serving. *Makes 4 servings*

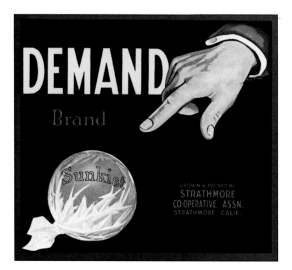

Sunkist Growers is the oldest, best-known agricultural marketing cooperative in the world, owned by 6,500 grower-members in California and Arizona, most of whom are small family farmers. Sunkist is responsible for starting the orange juice industry, being first to promote the benefits of Vitamin C and convincing consumers to add lemon to their tea, fish and even their water.

Cornish Hen with Citrus Chutney Glaze

Tomato Chutney Chicken

4 broiler-fryer chicken breast halves,
    boned, skinned
1 can (16 ounces) tomatoes with juice,
    cut up
1 cup peeled and chopped cooking apple
1/4 cup chopped onion
1/4 cup chopped green pepper
1/4 cup golden raisins
2 tablespoons brown sugar
2 tablespoons lemon juice
1 teaspoon grated lemon peel
1 clove garlic, minced
1/2 teaspoon ground cinnamon
1/4 teaspoon red pepper flakes
1/4 teaspoon salt

In large skillet, place tomatoes, apple, onion, green pepper, raisins, brown sugar, lemon juice, lemon peel, garlic, cinnamon and red pepper flakes; stir to mix. Cook, stirring, over medium-high heat until mixture boils. Sprinkle salt over chicken breasts. Place chicken over tomato mixture. Reduce heat to medium-low; cover and cook, stirring and turning frequently, about 15 minutes or until chicken is fork-tender. Arrange chicken on serving platter; spoon sauce over chicken.

Makes 4 servings

Favorite recipe from **Delmarva Poultry Industry, Inc.**

Rosemary Roasted Chicken and Potatoes

1 BUTTERBALL® Fresh Young Roaster,
    giblets removed
3 cloves garlic, minced
    Grated peel and juice of 1 lemon
2 tablespoons vegetable oil
1 tablespoon fresh rosemary leaves
1 teaspoon cracked black pepper
1/4 teaspoon salt
6 medium potatoes, cut into pieces

Preheat oven to 425°F. Mix garlic, lemon peel, lemon juice, oil, rosemary, pepper and salt in medium bowl. Place chicken, breast side up, in lightly oiled large roasting pan. Place potatoes around chicken. Drizzle garlic mixture over chicken and onto potatoes. Bake 20 to 25 minutes per pound or until internal temperature reaches 180°F in thigh. Stir potatoes occasionally to brown evenly. Let chicken stand 10 minutes before carving.

Makes 8 servings

Preparation Time: 15 minutes plus roasting time

Tomato Chutney Chicken

SPICY MARINATED CHICKEN KABABS OVER RICE

½ cup white wine
¼ cup lime juice
¼ cup vegetable oil
2 cloves garlic, minced
1 jalapeño, seeded and finely chopped
2 tablespoons chopped fresh cilantro
½ teaspoon salt
½ teaspoon ground black pepper
1½ pounds boneless, skinless chicken breast, cut into 1-inch cubes
1 medium-size red onion, cut into 1-inch pieces
2 medium-size red or green bell peppers, cut into 1-inch pieces
2 medium-size yellow squash, cut into 1-inch pieces
12 wooden or metal skewers*
3 cups hot cooked rice

*Soak wooden skewers in water 20 minutes before using to prevent burning.

Combine wine, lime juice, oil, garlic, jalapeño, cilantro, salt and black pepper in gallon size resealable plastic food storage bag. Add chicken, onion, bell peppers and squash. Seal; turn to coat. Marinate in refrigerator 30 to 45 minutes. Remove chicken and vegetables. Place marinade in small saucepan. Bring to a boil over medium-high heat; keep warm. Alternate chicken and vegetables on skewers. Place on broiler rack coated with cooking spray; brush with marinade. Broil 4 to 6 inches from heat 8 to 10 minutes, turning and basting frequently with marinade. Serve over hot rice.

Makes 6 servings

Favorite recipe from **USA Rice Federation**

APPLE RAISIN-STUFFED CHICKEN

1 package (6 ounces) STOVE TOP® Savory Herbs Stuffing Mix or STOVE TOP® Stuffing Mix for Chicken
1½ cups hot water
¼ cup (½ stick) butter or margarine, cut into pieces
1 apple, cored, chopped
¼ cup raisins
¼ cup toasted chopped walnuts
6 boneless skinless chicken breast halves
Vegetable oil
Paprika

HEAT oven to 375°F.

MIX contents of vegetable/seasoning packet, hot water and butter in large bowl until butter is melted. Stir in stuffing crumbs, apple, raisins and walnuts just to moisten. Let stand 5 minutes.

POUND chicken to ¼-inch thickness. Spoon ¼ cup of the stuffing over each chicken breast half; roll up. Reserve remaining stuffing. Place chicken, seam side down, in 13×9-inch baking pan. Brush with oil; sprinkle with paprika.

BAKE 20 minutes. Spoon reserved stuffing into center of pan. Bake 20 minutes or until chicken is no longer pink in center.

Makes 6 servings

Spicy Marinated Chicken Kababs Over Rice

LEMON-GARLIC CHICKEN & RICE

4 skinless, boneless chicken breast halves
1 teaspoon paprika
   Salt and pepper (optional)
2 tablespoons margarine or butter
2 cloves garlic, minced
1 package (6.9 ounces) RICE-A-RONI®
   Chicken Flavor
2 tablespoons lemon juice
1 cup chopped red or green bell pepper
½ teaspoon grated lemon peel

1. Sprinkle chicken with paprika, salt and pepper.

2. In large skillet, melt margarine over medium-high heat. Add chicken and garlic; cook 2 minutes on each side or until browned. Remove from skillet; set aside, reserving drippings. Keep warm.

3. In same skillet, sauté rice-vermicelli mix in reserved drippings over medium heat until vermicelli is golden brown. Stir in 2¼ cups water, lemon juice and contents of seasoning packet. Top rice with chicken; bring to a boil over high heat.

4. Cover; reduce heat. Simmer 10 minutes. Stir in red pepper and lemon peel.

5. Cover; continue to simmer 10 minutes or until liquid is absorbed, rice is tender and chicken is no longer pink inside.

Makes 4 servings

BUTTERFLIED CORNISH GAME HENS

2 Cornish game hens (about 3 pounds)*
   Olive oil vegetable cooking spray
   Seasoned salt
   Ground black pepper
½ cup FRENCH'S® Dijon Mustard
   Grilled vegetables (optional)

*You may substitute 3 pounds chicken parts (skinned, if desired) for the game hens.

Remove neck and giblets from hens; discard. Wash hens and pat dry. Place 1 hen, breast side down, on cutting board. With kitchen shears or sharp knife, cut along one side of backbone, cutting as close to bone as possible. Cut down other side of backbone; remove backbone. Spread bird open and turn breast side up, pressing to flatten. Repeat with remaining hen.

To keep drumsticks flat, make small slit through skin with point of knife between thigh and breast. Push end of leg through slit. Repeat on other side of bird and with remaining hen. Coat both sides of hens with vegetable cooking spray. Sprinkle with seasoned salt and pepper. Generously brush mustard onto both sides of hens.

Place hens, skin sides up, on oiled grid. Grill over medium-high coals 35 to 45 minutes until meat is no longer pink near bone and juices run clear, turning and basting often with remaining mustard. (Do not baste during last 10 minutes of cooking.) Serve with grilled vegetables, if desired. *Makes 4 servings*

Lemon-Garlic Chicken & Rice

CHICKEN BREASTS DIAVOLO

6 chicken breast halves, boned, skinned
    and slightly flattened
½ cup finely minced fresh parsley
1 teaspoon lemon pepper seasoning
    Dash salt
    Dash garlic powder
3 tablespoons olive oil
3 (6-ounce) jars marinated artichoke
    hearts
1 tablespoon fresh lemon juice
1 (26-ounce) jar NEWMAN'S OWN®
    Diavolo Sauce
½ cup red wine (preferably Chianti)
1½ cups shredded mozzarella cheese
1½ cups onion-garlic flavor croutons (tossed
    with 1 tablespoon olive oil)
6 cups hot cooked pasta or rice

Preheat oven to 350°F. Sprinkle chicken breasts with parsley, lemon pepper seasoning, salt and garlic powder. Roll each breast, seasoned side in; secure with wooden toothpicks. Cook chicken in olive oil in large skillet until golden brown on all sides. Remove from pan with tongs and place in 13×9-inch baking dish. Carefully remove toothpicks.

Drain artichoke hearts; sprinkle with lemon juice and distribute among rolled chicken breasts.

Combine Newman's Own® Diavolo Sauce with wine; pour over chicken and artichokes. Sprinkle cheese evenly over top. Sprinkle with crouton mixture. Bake 30 to 40 minutes until golden brown and bubbly.

Spoon chicken over pasta or rice. Serve with crusty Italian bread or rolls, a green salad and remaining red wine. *Makes 6 servings*

For years, Paul Newman packaged homemade salad dressing in old wine bottles for Christmas gifts. One day, he and longtime friend A. E. Hotchner decided to market it. The overnight success of Newman's Own Salad Dressing led to the expansion of the company's line of all-natural food products to include popcorn, spaghetti sauce, salsa, lemonade, ice cream and steak sauce. Newman's Own has grown into a multimillion dollar business from which Paul Newman donates 100% of his after-tax profits to charitable and educational causes, including The Hole in the Wall Gang Camp, which he founded in 1988, for children with cancer and other serious blood-related illnesses.

BRAISED DUCKLING AND PEARS

1 (4- to 5-pound) frozen duckling, thawed and quartered
1 can (16 ounces) pear halves in heavy syrup
⅓ cup KIKKOMAN® Stir-Fry Sauce
1 cinnamon stick, about 3 inches long

Wash duckling quarters; dry thoroughly with paper towels. Heat large skillet or Dutch oven over medium heat. Add duckling; brown slowly on both sides, about 15 minutes, or until golden. Meanwhile, drain pears; reserve all syrup. Remove ¼ cup pear syrup and combine with stir-fry sauce; set aside. Drain off fat from pan. Pour syrup mixture over duckling; add cinnamon stick. Cover and simmer 40 minutes or until tender, turning quarters over once. Remove duckling to serving platter; keep warm. Remove and discard cinnamon stick. Pour drippings into measuring cup; skim off fat. Combine ½ cup drippings with 2 tablespoons reserved pear syrup; return to pan with pears. Gently bring to boil and cook until pears are heated through, stirring occasionally. Serve duckling with pears and sauce.

Makes 3 to 4 servings

ROAST TURKEY WITH FRESH HERB STUFFING

4 cups cubed fresh herb- or garlic-flavored breadsticks
1 turkey (8 to 10 pounds)
1 tablespoon margarine
1½ cups sliced mushrooms
1 cup chopped onion
⅔ cup chopped celery
¼ cup chopped fresh parsley
2 tablespoons chopped fresh tarragon
1 tablespoon chopped fresh thyme
¼ teaspoon black pepper
¼ cup reduced-sodium chicken broth

1. Preheat oven to 350°F. Place cubed breadsticks on nonstick baking sheet. Bake 20 minutes to dry.

2. Remove giblets from turkey. Rinse turkey and cavities; pat dry with paper towels. Melt margarine in large nonstick skillet. Add mushrooms, onion and celery. Cook and stir 5 minutes or until onion is soft and golden; remove from heat. Add parsley, tarragon, thyme, pepper and bread cubes; stir until blended. Gently mix chicken broth into bread cube mixture. Fill turkey cavities with stuffing.

3. Spray roasting pan with nonstick cooking spray. Place turkey, breast side up, in roasting pan. Bake in 350°F oven 3 hours or until meat thermometer inserted in thigh registers 180°F and juices run clear.

4. Transfer turkey to serving platter. Cover loosely with foil; let stand 20 minutes. Remove and discard skin. Slice turkey and serve with herb stuffing. Garnish, if desired.

Makes 10 servings

ROASTED TURKEY BREAST WITH CHERRY & APPLE RICE STUFFING

3¾ cups water
  3 boxes UNCLE BEN'S® Butter & Herb Long Grain & Wild Rice
  ½ cup butter or margarine, divided
  ½ cup dried red tart cherries
  1 large apple, peeled and chopped (about 1 cup)
  ½ cup sliced almonds, toasted*
  1 bone-in turkey breast (5 to 6 pounds)

*To toast almonds, place them on a baking sheet. Bake 10 to 12 minutes in preheated 325°F oven or until golden brown, stirring occasionally.

1. In large saucepan, combine water, rice, contents of seasoning packets, 3 tablespoons butter and cherries. Bring to a boil. Cover; reduce heat to low and simmer 25 minutes or until all water is absorbed. Stir in apple and almonds; set aside.

2. Preheat oven to 325°F. Place turkey breast, skin side down, on rack in roasting pan. Loosely fill breast cavity with rice stuffing. (Place any remaining stuffing in greased baking dish; cover and refrigerate. Bake alongside turkey for 35 to 40 minutes or until heated through.)

3. Place sheet of heavy-duty foil over stuffing, molding it slightly over sides of turkey. Carefully invert turkey, skin side up, on rack. Melt remaining 5 tablespoons butter; brush some of butter over surface of turkey.

4. Roast turkey, uncovered, 1 hour; baste with melted butter. Continue roasting 1¼ to 1¾ hours, basting occasionally with melted butter, until meat thermometer inserted into center of thickest part of turkey breast, not touching bone, registers 170°F. Let turkey stand, covered, 15 minutes before carving.

Makes 6 to 8 servings

ROASTED TURKEY PAN GRAVY

  1 can (14½ ounces) SWANSON® Chicken Broth (1¾ cups)
  3 tablespoons all-purpose flour

Remove turkey from roasting pan. Pour off fat. In roasting pan gradually mix broth into flour. Over medium heat, cook until mixture boils and thickens, stirring constantly.

Makes about 4 servings

Note: ½g fat per serving (traditional turkey gravy recipe: 8g fat per serving)

Prep Time: 5 minutes
Cook Time: 10 minutes

Roasted Turkey Breast with Cherry & Apple Rice Stuffing

CAMPBELL'S® EASY TURKEY & BISCUITS

1 can (10¾ ounces) CAMPBELL'S®
  Condensed Cream of Celery Soup or
  98% Fat Free Cream of Celery Soup
1 can (10¾ ounces) CAMPBELL'S®
  Condensed Cream of Potato Soup
1 cup milk
¼ teaspoon dried thyme leaves, crushed
¼ teaspoon pepper
4 cups cooked cut-up vegetables*
2 cups cubed cooked turkey, chicken or
  ham
1 package (7½ or 10 ounces) refrigerated
  buttermilk biscuits (10 biscuits)

*Use a combination of broccoli flowerets, cauliflower flowerets and sliced carrots or broccoli flowerets and sliced carrots or broccoli flowerets, sliced carrots and peas.

1. In 3-quart shallow baking dish mix soups, milk, thyme, pepper, vegetables and turkey.

2. Bake at 400°F. for 15 minutes or until hot.

3. Stir. Arrange biscuits over turkey mixture. Bake 15 minutes more or until biscuits are golden.   *Makes 5 servings*

Tip: To microwave vegetables, in 2-quart shallow microwave-safe baking dish arrange vegetables and ¼ cup water. Cover. Microwave on HIGH 10 minutes.

Prep Time: 15 minutes
Cook Time: 30 minutes

VEGETABLE-STUFFED TURKEY BREAST

¾ cup chopped onion
2 tablespoons FLEISCHMANN'S® Original
  Margarine, divided
1 cup cooked regular long-grain rice
1 cup shredded carrots
1 cup sliced mushrooms
½ cup chopped fresh parsley
¼ cup EGG BEATERS® Healthy Real Egg
  Substitute
½ teaspoon poultry seasoning
1 whole turkey breast (about 5 pounds)

In small skillet, over medium heat, sauté onion in 1 tablespoon margarine until tender; set aside.

In large bowl, combine rice, carrots, mushrooms, parsley, Egg Beaters® and poultry seasoning; stir in onion. Remove skin from turkey breast. Place rice mixture into cavity of turkey breast; cover cavity with foil.

Place turkey, breast-side up, on rack in roasting pan. Melt remaining margarine; brush over turkey. Roast at 350°F according to package directions or until meat thermometer registers 170°F. If necessary, tent breast with foil after 30 minutes to prevent overbrowning. Let turkey stand 15 minutes before carving. Portion 3 ounces sliced turkey and ½ cup stuffing per serving. (Freeze remaining turkey for another use.)   *Makes 8 servings*

Prep Time: 30 minutes
Cook Time: 2 hours

Campbell's® Easy Turkey & Biscuits

PEPPERIDGE FARM® TURKEY & STUFFING BAKE

1 can (14½ ounces) SWANSON® Chicken
    Broth (1¾ cups)
  Generous dash pepper
1 stalk celery, chopped (about ½ cup)
1 small onion, coarsely chopped (about
    ¼ cup)
4 cups PEPPERIDGE FARM® Herb Seasoned
    Stuffing
4 servings sliced roasted *or* deli turkey
    (about 12 ounces)
1 jar (12 ounces) FRANCO-AMERICAN®
    Slow Roast™ Turkey Gravy

1. In medium saucepan mix broth, pepper,
celery and onion. Over high heat, heat to a
boil. Reduce heat to low. Cover and cook 5
minutes or until vegetables are tender. Add
stuffing. Mix lightly.

2. Spoon into 2-quart shallow baking dish.
Arrange turkey over stuffing. Pour gravy over
turkey.

3. Bake at 350°F. for 30 minutes or until hot.
Makes 4 servings

Prep Time: 15 minutes
Cook Time: 30 minutes

RASPBERRY-GLAZED TURKEY

½ cup SMUCKER'S® Seedless Red
    Raspberry Jam
6 tablespoons raspberry vinegar
¼ cup Dijon mustard
4 small turkey breast tenderloins

In large saucepan, stir together jam, vinegar
and mustard. Bring to a boil over high heat;
cook and stir 3 minutes. Reserve about ½ cup
of glaze; coat turkey with some of remaining
glaze.

Set turkey on rack in broiler pan. Broil about 4
inches from heat for 15 to 20 minutes or until
no longer pink in center, turning and basting
once with remaining glaze.

Slice turkey crosswise. Serve with reserved
glaze. *Makes 4 to 6 servings*

MUSTARD HERB CRUSTED TURKEY TENDERLOINS

1 package BUTTERBALL® Fresh Boneless
    Turkey Breast Tenderloins
1 cup fresh bread crumbs
2 tablespoons olive oil
2 tablespoons minced fresh parsley
1 clove garlic, minced
2 teaspoons Dijon mustard
½ teaspoon dried savory leaves
½ teaspoon salt

Preheat oven to 400°F. Mix bread crumbs, oil,
parsley, garlic, mustard, savory and salt in
small bowl to form a coarse paste. Spread
crumb mixture over tenderloins. Place in small
roasting pan sprayed with nonstick cooking
spray. Roast 30 minutes or until no longer pink
in center. *Makes 4 servings*

Preparation Time: 10 minutes plus roasting
time

Pepperidge Farm® Turkey & Stuffing Bake

ORANGE-CRANBERRY TURKEY SLICES

1 pound turkey breast slices or cutlets
  Salt and pepper
2 tablespoons margarine
2 tablespoons packed brown sugar
1/3 cup orange juice
1 cup fresh cranberries*
1/4 cup raisins
2 tablespoons chopped green onion
2 tablespoons orange-flavored liqueur
  (optional)

*If fresh cranberries are not available, delete brown sugar, reduce orange juice to 2 tablespoons and substitute 1/4 cup canned whole cranberry sauce for 1 cup fresh cranberries.

1. Season turkey slices with salt and pepper. Brown turkey slices in margarine in skillet 2 to 3 minutes per side. Remove to platter; keep warm.

2. Add brown sugar, orange juice and cranberries to skillet; cook 5 minutes or until cranberries pop.

3. Stir in raisins, green onion and liqueur, if desired; heat through.

4. Serve sauce over warm turkey slices.

Makes 6 servings

Favorite recipe from **National Turkey Federation**

Terrific turkey facts from the National Turkey Federation:

- *Only tom turkeys gobble.*

- *Hen turkeys make a clicking noise.*

- *Domesticated turkeys cannot fly.*

- *Wild turkeys can fly for short distances up to 55 miles an hour and can run.*

GRILLED TURKEY

Sage-Garlic Baste (recipe follows) or
  Chinese 5-Spice Butter Baste (recipe
  follows)
1 whole turkey (9 to 13 pounds), thawed if
  frozen
  Salt and black pepper
3 lemons, halved (optional)

Prepare Sage-Garlic Baste. Remove neck and giblets from turkey. Rinse turkey under cold running water; pat dry with paper towels. Season turkey cavity with salt and pepper; place lemons in cavity, if desired. Lightly brush outer surface of turkey with part of Sage-Garlic Baste. Pull skin over neck and secure with skewer. Tuck wing tips under back and tie legs together with cotton string. Insert meat thermometer into thickest part of thigh, not touching bone. Arrange medium-hot KINGSFORD® Briquets on each side of large rectangular metal or foil drip pan. Pour hot tap water into drip pan until half full. Place turkey, breast side up, on grid directly above drip pan. Grill turkey on covered grill 9 to 13 minutes per pound or until thermometer registers 180°F, basting every 20 minutes with remaining Sage-Garlic Baste. Add a few briquets to both sides of fire every hour or as necessary to maintain constant temperature.* Let turkey stand 15 minutes before carving. Refrigerate leftovers promptly.

Makes 8 to 10 servings

*For larger turkey, add 15 briquets every 50 to 60 minutes.

SAGE-GARLIC BASTE

**Grated peel and juice of 1 lemon
3 tablespoons olive oil
2 tablespoons minced fresh sage *or*
    1½ teaspoons rubbed sage
2 cloves garlic, minced
½ teaspoon salt
¼ teaspoon black pepper**

Combine all ingredients in small saucepan; cook and stir over medium heat 4 minutes. Use as baste for turkey or chicken.

Makes about ½ cup

CHINESE 5-SPICE BUTTER BASTE

**⅓ cup melted butter
1 tablespoon soy sauce
2 teaspoons Chinese 5-spice powder**

Combine all ingredients in small bowl. Use as baste for turkey or chicken.

Makes about 6 tablespoons

SIDE BY SIDE SOUTHERN STUFFING AND TURKEY

**1 (3-pound) BUTTERBALL® Boneless Breast
    of Young Turkey with Gravy Packet,
    thawed
Vegetable oil
1 can (14½ ounces) chicken broth
½ cup chopped onion
½ cup chopped celery
4 tablespoons butter or margarine
4 cups packaged cornbread stuffing
1 can (16 ounces) sliced peaches, drained
    and coarsely chopped
½ cup chopped pecans**

Spray small roasting pan with nonstick cooking spray. Place boneless breast on one side of roasting pan. Brush with vegetable oil. Combine chicken broth, onion, celery and butter in large saucepan; simmer 5 minutes over low heat. Add stuffing, peaches and pecans; lightly toss mixture. Place stuffing alongside boneless breast. Cover stuffing with foil. Bake in preheated 325°F oven 1 hour and 45 minutes or until internal temperature reaches 170°F. Let boneless breast stand 10 minutes for easy carving. Prepare gravy according to package directions. Serve turkey with gravy and stuffing.

Makes 6 servings

Preparation Time: 15 minutes plus roasting time

FRANCO-AMERICAN® HOT TURKEY SANDWICHES

1 jar (12 ounces) FRANCO-AMERICAN®
   Slow Roast™ Turkey Gravy
2 servings sliced roasted *or* deli turkey
   (about 6 ounces)
4 slices PEPPERIDGE FARM® Original
   White Bread
   Cranberry sauce

1. In medium skillet over medium heat, heat gravy to a boil.

2. Add turkey. Reduce heat to low and heat through. Place turkey on 2 bread slices and top with remaining bread slices. Spoon gravy over sandwiches. Serve with cranberry sauce.

Makes 2 servings

Hot Roast Beef Sandwiches: Substitute FRANCO-AMERICAN® Slow Roast™ Beef Gravy for the turkey gravy and slices of cooked beef for the turkey.

Prep Time: 5 minutes
Cook Time: 15 minutes

ROAST STUFFED TURKEY

2 packages (6 ounces each) STOVE TOP®
   Stuffing Mix, any variety
½ cup (1 stick) butter or margarine, cut
   into pieces
3 cups hot water
1 (8- to 10-pound) turkey

Prepare stuffing by placing contents of vegetable/seasoning packets and butter in a large bowl. Add hot water; stir just to partially melt butter. Add stuffing crumbs. Stir just to moisten. Do not stuff bird until ready to roast.

Rinse turkey with cold water; pat dry. Do not rub cavity with salt. Lightly stuff neck and body cavities with prepared stuffing. Skewer neck skin to back. Tie legs to tail and twist wing tips under. Place turkey, breast side up, in roasting pan. Roast at 325°F for 3 to 4 hours or as directed on poultry wrapper. Bake any remaining stuffing at 325°F for 30 minutes. Cover baking dish for moist stuffing. If drier stuffing is desired, bake uncovered.

Makes 8 to 10 servings

TURKEY WITH CHILI CRANBERRY SAUCE

1 pound ground raw turkey
¼ cup seasoned dry bread crumbs
¼ cup thinly sliced green onions
1 egg, slightly beaten
¼ teaspoon salt
¼ teaspoon pepper
1 tablespoon vegetable oil
⅔ cup whole berry cranberry sauce
⅓ cup HEINZ® Chili Sauce
2 tablespoons water
⅛ teaspoon ground cinnamon

Combine turkey, bread crumbs, green onions, egg, salt and pepper. Shape into 4 patties, about ½ inch thick. Slowly sauté patties in oil, about 4 to 5 minutes per side or until cooked through. Stir in cranberry sauce, chili sauce, water and cinnamon. Simmer, uncovered, 1 minute.

Makes 4 servings

Franco-American® Hot Turkey Sandwich

SEAFOOD TREASURES

SWORDFISH MESSINA STYLE

2 tablespoons olive or vegetable oil
½ cup chopped fresh parsley
2 tablespoons chopped fresh basil *or*
    2 teaspoons dried basil leaves, crushed
2 cloves garlic, minced
1 can (8 ounces) CONTADINA® Tomato Sauce
¾ cup sliced fresh mushrooms
1 tablespoon capers
1 tablespoon lemon juice
⅛ teaspoon ground black pepper
3 pounds swordfish or halibut steaks

1. Heat oil in small saucepan. Add parsley, basil and garlic; sauté for 1 minute. Reduce heat to low. Add tomato sauce, mushrooms and capers; simmer, uncovered, for 5 minutes.

2. Stir in lemon juice and pepper. Place swordfish in single layer in greased 13×9-inch baking dish; cover with sauce.

3. Bake in preheated 400°F oven for 20 minutes or until fish flakes easily when tested with fork.   *Makes 8 servings*

Prep Time: 5 minutes
Cook Time: 26 minutes

Swordfish Messina Style

LEMON-GARLIC SHRIMP

1 package (6.2 ounces) RICE-A-RONI®
    With 1/3 Less Salt Broccoli Au Gratin
1 tablespoon margarine or butter
1 pound raw medium shrimp, shelled and
    deveined, or large scallops, cut into
    halves
1 medium red or green bell pepper, cut
    into short thin strips
2 cloves garlic, minced
1/2 teaspoon Italian seasoning
1/2 cup reduced-sodium or regular chicken
    broth
1 tablespoon lemon juice
1 tablespoon cornstarch
3 medium green onions, cut into 1/2-inch
    pieces
1 teaspoon grated lemon peel

1. Prepare Rice-A-Roni® Mix as package
directs.

2. While Rice-A-Roni® is simmering, heat
margarine in second large skillet or wok over
medium-high heat. Add shrimp, red pepper,
garlic and Italian seasoning. Stir-fry 3 to 4
minutes or until seafood is opaque.

3. Combine chicken broth, lemon juice and
cornstarch, mixing until smooth. Add broth
mixture and onions to skillet. Stir-fry 2 to 3
minutes or until sauce thickens.

4. Stir 1/2 teaspoon lemon peel into rice. Serve
rice topped with shrimp mixture; sprinkle with
remaining 1/2 teaspoon lemon peel.

Makes 4 servings

FESTIVE STUFFED FISH

2 whole red snappers, about 2 1/2 pounds
    each (or substitute any firm white
    fish), cleaned
  Lemon and lime wedges
2 cloves garlic, minced
2 tablespoons olive oil
2 medium onions, finely chopped
1 cup seeded and chopped medium-hot
    pepper (such as poblano, serrano,
    Anaheim or green bell variety)
1 cup chopped red bell pepper
8 ounces JARLSBERG or JARLSBERG LITE™
    Cheese, shredded
12 tomatillos, thinly sliced, then chopped
    (about 2 cups)
1 cup dry white wine or unsweetened
    apple juice
  Additional lemon and lime wedges

Score flesh on each fish 1/4 inch deep on the
diagonal every 1 1/2 inches. Insert lemon
wedges, peel side out. Cook garlic in olive
oil in medium skillet over medium-high heat.
Add onions and cook until translucent. Add
peppers; cook 2 minutes. Place in large bowl;
stir in cheese and tomatillos. Stuff fish cavity
with cheese mixture. Use kitchen string to tie
each fish closed every 2 inches (3 or 4 ties).
Set aside. Preheat oven to 375°F.

In same skillet, bring wine to a boil. Place fish
in large glass or enamel baking dish. Pour hot
wine over fish and cover tightly. Bake 30
minutes or until fish is opaque. Transfer to
serving platter and remove string. Garnish with
additional lemon and lime wedges.

Makes 4 to 6 servings

Lemon-Garlic Shrimp

CIOPPINO

2 tablespoons olive or vegetable oil
1½ cups chopped onion
1 cup chopped celery
½ cup chopped green bell pepper
1 large clove garlic, minced
1 can (28 ounces) CONTADINA® Whole Peeled Tomatoes, undrained
1 can (6 ounces) CONTADINA® Tomato Paste
1 teaspoon Italian herb seasoning
1 teaspoon salt
½ teaspoon ground black pepper
2 cups water
1 cup dry red wine or chicken broth
3 pounds white fish, shrimp, scallops, cooked crab, cooked lobster, clams and/or oysters (in any proportion)

1. Heat oil in large saucepan. Add onion, celery, bell pepper and garlic; sauté until vegetables are tender. Add tomatoes and juice, tomato paste, Italian seasoning, salt, black pepper, water and wine. Break up tomatoes with spoon.

2. Bring to a boil. Reduce heat to low; simmer, uncovered, for 15 minutes.

3. To prepare fish and seafood: scrub clams and oysters under running water. Place in ½-inch boiling water in separate large saucepan; cover. Bring to a boil. Reduce heat to low; simmer just until shells open, about 3 minutes. Set aside.

4. Cut crab, lobster, fish and scallops into bite-size pieces.

5. Shell and devein shrimp. Add fish to tomato mixture; simmer 5 minutes. Add scallops and shrimp; simmer 5 minutes.

6. Add crab, lobster and reserved clams; simmer until heated through.

Makes about 14 cups

Prep Time: 30 minutes
Cook Time: 35 minutes

BAKED COD WITH TOMATOES AND OLIVES

1 pound cod fillets (about 4 fillets), cut into 2-inch-wide pieces
1 can (14½ ounces) diced Italian-style tomatoes, drained
2 tablespoons chopped pitted ripe olives
1 teaspoon bottled minced garlic
2 tablespoons chopped fresh parsley

1. Preheat oven to 400°F. Spray 13×9-inch baking dish with nonstick olive oil-flavored cooking spray. Arrange cod fillets in pan; season to taste with salt and pepper.

2. Combine tomatoes, olives and garlic in medium bowl. Spoon over fish.

3. Bake 20 minutes or until fish flakes when tested with a fork. Sprinkle with parsley.

Makes 4 servings

Serving Suggestion: For a great accompaniment to this dish, spread French bread with softened butter, sprinkle with paprika and oregano, and broil until lightly toasted.

Prep and Cook Time: 25 minutes

Cioppino

BAKED STUFFED SNAPPER

1 red snapper (1½ pounds)
2 cups hot cooked rice
1 can (4 ounces) sliced mushrooms,
    drained
½ cup diced water chestnuts
¼ cup thinly sliced green onions
¼ cup diced pimiento
2 tablespoons chopped parsley
1 tablespoon finely shredded lemon peel
½ teaspoon salt
⅛ teaspoon black pepper
1 tablespoon margarine, melted

Preheat oven to 400°F. Clean and butterfly fish. Combine rice, mushrooms, water chestnuts, onions, pimiento, parsley, lemon peel, salt and pepper; toss lightly. Fill cavity of fish with rice mixture; close with wooden toothpicks soaked in water. Place fish in 13×9-inch baking dish coated with nonstick cooking spray; brush fish with margarine. Bake 18 to 20 minutes or until fish flakes easily when tested with fork. Wrap any remaining rice in foil and bake in oven with fish.

Makes 4 servings

Favorite recipe from **USA Rice Federation**

The USA Rice Federation is a national industry association representing producers, millers and allied businesses. Working on their behalf, the USA Rice Federation conducts programs to advance the use and consumption of U.S.-grown rice in domestic and international markets.

Plan your holiday meal in advance so you won't be short on time or oven space. If your main dish requires the oven, choose several side dishes that can be cooked elsewhere, such as broccoli or green beans steamed in the microwave, or mashed potatoes or grains cooked on the stove. Whenever possible, choose a few recipes that can be made ahead of time, so you'll have more time to visit with your guests and attend to any last-minute details.

Baked Stuffed Snapper

Trout with Apples and Toasted Hazelnuts

⅓ cup whole hazelnuts
5 tablespoons butter or margarine, divided
1 large Red Delicious apple, cored and cut into 16 wedges
2 butterflied rainbow trout fillets (about 8 ounces each)
Salt and black pepper
3 tablespoons all-purpose flour
1 tablespoon lemon juice
1 tablespoon snipped fresh chives
Lemon slices and fresh chives for garnish

Preheat oven to 350°F. To toast hazelnuts, spread in single layer on baking sheet. Bake 8 to 10 minutes or until skins split.

Wrap hazelnuts in kitchen towel; set aside 5 minutes to cool slightly. Rub nuts in towel to remove as much of the papery skins as possible. Process hazelnuts in food processor until coarsely chopped; set aside.

Melt 3 tablespoons butter in medium skillet over medium-high heat. Add apple; cook 4 to 5 minutes or until crisp-tender. Remove from skillet with slotted spoon; set aside.

Rinse trout and pat dry with paper towels. Sprinkle fish with salt and pepper, then coat in flour. Place fish in skillet. Cook 4 minutes or until golden and fish flakes easily when tested with fork, turning halfway through cooking time. Return apple to skillet. Reduce heat to low and keep warm.

Melt remaining 2 tablespoons butter in small saucepan over low heat. Stir in lemon juice, chives and hazelnuts. Sprinkle fish and apple with hazelnut mixture. Garnish, if desired.

Makes 2 servings

Dijon-Crusted Fish Fillets

¼ cup GREY POUPON® Dijon Mustard, divided
2 tablespoons margarine or butter, melted
½ cup plain dry bread crumbs
2 tablespoons grated Parmesan cheese
2 tablespoons chopped parsley
4 (4- to 6-ounce) firm fish fillets (salmon, cod or catfish)

In small bowl, blend 2 tablespoons mustard and margarine; stir in bread crumbs, cheese and parsley. Place fish fillets on baking sheet; spread fillets with remaining mustard and top with crumb mixture. Bake at 400°F for 10 to 12 minutes or until fish is golden and flakes easily when tested with fork.

Makes 4 servings

Trout with Apples and Toasted Hazelnuts

SNAPPER VERACRUZ

Nonstick cooking spray
1 teaspoon olive oil
¼ large onion, thinly sliced
⅓ cup low sodium fish or vegetable broth, defatted and divided
2 cloves garlic, minced
1 cup GUILTLESS GOURMET® Salsa
20 ounces fresh red snapper, tilapia, sea bass or halibut fillets

Preheat oven to 400°F. Coat baking dish with cooking spray. (Dish needs to be large enough for fish to fit snugly together.) Heat oil in large nonstick skillet over medium heat until hot. Add onion; cook and stir until onion is translucent. Stir in 3 tablespoons broth. Add garlic; cook and stir 1 minute more. Stir in remaining broth and salsa. Bring mixture to a boil. Reduce heat to low; simmer about 2 minutes or until heated through.

Wash fish thoroughly; pat dry with paper towels. Place in prepared baking dish, overlapping thin edges to obtain an overall equal thickness. Pour and spread salsa mixture over fish.

Bake 15 minutes or until fish turns opaque and flakes easily when tested with fork. Serve hot.

Makes 4 servings

CAMPBELL'S® SEAFOOD & MUSHROOM SHELLS

1 package (10 ounces) PEPPERIDGE FARM® Frozen Puff Pastry Shells
4 tablespoons unsalted butter
2½ cups thinly sliced mushrooms (about 8 ounces)
1 can (10¾ ounces) CAMPBELL'S® Condensed Cream of Mushroom Soup *or* 98% Fat Free Cream of Mushroom Soup
½ cup dry white wine *or* vermouth
1 tablespoon lemon juice
1 pound firm white fish (cod, haddock or halibut), cut into 1-inch pieces
½ cup grated Parmesan cheese

1. Bake pastry shells according to package directions.

2. In medium skillet over medium heat, heat butter. Add mushrooms and cook until tender.

3. Add soup, wine, lemon juice and fish. Cook 5 minutes or until fish flakes easily when tested with a fork.

4. Serve in pastry shells. Sprinkle with cheese.

Makes 4 servings

Bake Time: 30 minutes (Bake pastry shells while preparing fish mixture.)
Prep/Cook Time: 20 minutes

Snapper Veracruz

SALMON ON A BED OF LEEKS

3 to 4 leeks
2 teaspoons butter or margarine
½ cup dry white wine or vermouth
2 salmon fillets (6 to 8 ounces)
Salt and black pepper to taste
2 tablespoons grated Gruyère cheese

Trim green tops and root ends from leeks; cut lengthwise into quarters, leaving ⅓ inch together at root end. Separate sections. Rinse under cold running water; drain well.

In 10-inch skillet, melt butter over medium heat. Add leeks; cook 2 to 3 minutes, stirring often, until leeks are wilted. Stir in wine; arrange salmon on leeks. Sprinkle with salt and pepper. Reduce heat to low. Cover; cook 5 minutes. Sprinkle cheese over salmon. Cover; cook another 3 to 5 minutes or until salmon is firm and opaque around edges and cheese is melted. Transfer to warm dinner plate with broad spatula; serve immediately.

Makes 2 servings

Favorite recipe from **National Fisheries Institute**

PENNE PASTA WITH SHRIMP & ROASTED RED PEPPER SAUCE

12 ounces uncooked penne pasta
1 cup low-sodium chicken or vegetable broth, defatted
1 cup GUILTLESS GOURMET® Roasted Red Pepper Salsa
1 cup chopped fresh or low-sodium canned and drained tomatoes
12 ounces medium raw shrimp, peeled and deveined
Fresh Italian parsley sprigs (optional)

Cook pasta according to package directions; drain and keep warm.

Meanwhile, combine broth, salsa and tomatoes in 1-quart saucepan. Bring to a boil over medium-high heat. Reduce heat to medium; simmer about 5 minutes or until hot. Allow to cool slightly.

Pour broth mixture into food processor or blender; process until smooth. Return to saucepan; bring back to a simmer. Add shrimp; simmer 2 minutes or just until shrimp turn pink and opaque. Do not overcook. To serve, divide pasta among 4 warm serving plates. Cover each serving with sauce, dividing shrimp equally among each serving. Garnish with parsley, if desired.   *Makes 4 servings*

Salmon on a Bed of Leeks

MARYLAND CRAB CAKES

1¼ pounds lump crab meat, picked over and
    flaked
¾ cup plain dry bread crumbs, divided
1 cup (4 ounces) shredded ALPINE LACE®
    Reduced Fat Swiss Cheese
⅓ cup finely chopped green onions
¼ cup plain low fat yogurt
¼ cup minced fresh parsley
2 tablespoons fresh lemon juice
1 teaspoon minced garlic
½ teaspoon hot red pepper sauce
¼ cup egg substitute or 1 large egg, beaten
    Butter-flavor nonstick cooking spray
2 large lemons, thinly sliced

1. In a large bowl, lightly toss the crab with
¼ cup of the bread crumbs, the cheese, green
onions, yogurt, parsley, lemon juice, garlic and
hot pepper sauce. Gently stir in the egg
substitute (or the whole egg).

2. Form the mixture into twelve 3-inch patties,
using about ¼ cup of crab mixture for each.
Spray both sides of the patties with the
cooking spray.

3. On wax paper, spread out the remaining
½ cup of bread crumbs. Coat each patty with
the crumb mixture, pressing lightly, then
refrigerate for 1 hour.

4. Preheat the oven to 400°F. Spray a baking
sheet with the cooking spray. Place the crab
cakes on the baking sheet and bake for 20
minutes or until golden brown and crispy,
turning once halfway through. Serve
immediately with the lemon slices.

Makes 6 servings (2 crab cakes each)

BAKED FISH WITH MUSHROOMS

2 pounds fish fillets (whitefish, haddock or
    perch)
2 tablespoons FILIPPO BERIO® Olive Oil
½ cup halved mushroom caps
1 carrot, diced
2 tablespoons chopped leek or onion
1 cup dry white wine
½ cup water or fish stock
¼ teaspoon dried thyme leaves
¼ teaspoon dried marjoram leaves
¼ teaspoon salt
¼ teaspoon freshly ground black pepper

Preheat oven to 350°F. Grease 13×9-inch
baking pan with olive oil. Add fish. In medium
skillet, heat olive oil over medium heat until
hot. Add mushrooms, carrot and leek; cook
and stir 5 minutes or until leek is tender. Add
wine, water, thyme, marjoram, salt and pepper.
Simmer 10 minutes or until vegetables are
tender-crisp. Spoon vegetables over fish,
reserving liquid remaining in skillet. Cover pan
with foil.

Bake 15 to 20 minutes or until fish flakes
easily when tested with fork. Meanwhile,
transfer reserved liquid from skillet to small
saucepan. Bring to a boil over high heat.
Reduce heat to low; simmer, uncovered, 10
minutes or until liquid is reduced by half. Pour
over fish just before serving.

Makes 6 servings

Maryland Crab Cakes

GOLDEN APPLE STUFFED FILLETS

1 cup grated, peeled Washington Golden
   Delicious apple
½ cup grated carrot
½ cup minced green onions
2 tablespoons fresh lemon juice
¼ teaspoon ground ginger
¼ teaspoon ground mustard
¼ teaspoon salt
¼ teaspoon ground black pepper
⅛ teaspoon dried thyme
4 sole, cod or other white fish fillets
   (4 to 5 ounces each)
¼ cup chicken broth or water

1. Heat oven to 400°F; lightly oil small roasting pan. In medium bowl, combine apple, carrot, green onions, lemon juice, ginger, mustard, salt, pepper and thyme; mix well.

2. Spread apple mixture evenly over length of fillets; carefully roll up from shorter ends. Place stuffed fillets, seam side down, in oiled pan. Pour broth over rolled fillets; cover with aluminum foil and bake 10 to 15 minutes or until fish is opaque and barely flakes.

Makes 4 servings

Microwave Directions: Prepare apple stuffing mixture and roll up fillets as above. Place stuffed fillets, seam side down, in oiled microwave-safe dish. Pour broth over rolled fillets; cover with waxed paper and microwave on HIGH (100% power) 5 to 7 minutes or until fish is opaque and barely flakes. (If microwave does not have carousel, rotate dish halfway through cooking.)

Favorite recipe from **Washington Apple Commission**

The image of Washington as one of the top apple-growing regions of the world, and of Washington apples as an international standard of excellence is due to the Washington Apple Commission. Founded in 1937 and headquartered in Wenatchee, Washington, the Commission promotes Washington apples through marketing, public relations and health and food communications.

SUPERB FILLET OF SOLE & VEGETABLES

1 can (10¾ ounces) condensed cream of
   celery soup
½ cup milk
1 cup (4 ounces) shredded Swiss cheese
½ teaspoon dried basil, crumbled
¼ teaspoon seasoned salt
¼ teaspoon pepper
1 package (10 ounces) frozen baby carrots,
   thawed and drained
1 package (10 ounces) frozen asparagus
   cuts, thawed and drained
1⅓ cups FRENCH'S® French Fried Onions,
   divided
1 pound unbreaded sole fillets, thawed if
   frozen

Preheat oven to 375°F. In small bowl, combine soup, milk, ½ cup cheese and the seasonings; set aside. In 12×8-inch baking dish, combine carrots, asparagus and ⅔ cup French Fried Onions. Roll up fish fillets. (If fillets are wide, fold in half lengthwise before rolling.) Place fish rolls upright along center of vegetable mixture. Pour soup mixture over fish and vegetables. Bake, covered, at 375°F for 30 minutes or until fish flakes easily with fork. Stir vegetables; top fish with remaining cheese and ⅔ cup onions. Bake, uncovered, 3 minutes or until onions are golden brown.

Makes 3 to 4 servings

Microwave Directions: Prepare soup mixture as above; set aside. In 12×8-inch microwave-safe dish, combine vegetables as above. Roll up fish fillets as above; place upright around edges of dish. Pour soup mixture over fish and vegetables. Cook, covered, on HIGH 14 to 16 minutes or until fish flakes easily with fork. Stir vegetables and rotate dish halfway through cooking time. Top fish with remaining cheese and onions; cook, uncovered, 1 minute or until cheese melts. Let stand 5 minutes.

FRESH TUNA WITH ISLAND FRUIT SAUCE

4 tuna or halibut steaks (about 1½ pounds)
    Vegetable cooking spray
2¼ cups DOLE® Pineapple Juice or Pine-
    Orange-Banana Juice, divided
1 teaspoon dried basil leaves, crushed
1 can (8 ounces) DOLE® Crushed
    Pineapple
2 teaspoons cornstarch
1 teaspoon grated orange peel

• Place fish in large, nonstick skillet sprayed with vegetable cooking spray. Add 1½ cups juice, basil and enough water to cover fish by 1 inch. Cover; bring to simmer over medium heat.

• Cook fish in simmering liquid (do not boil) 10 to 15 minutes or until fish flakes easily with fork. Meanwhile, combine remaining ¾ cup juice, undrained pineapple, cornstarch and orange peel in small saucepan. Bring to boil, stirring occasionally. Reduce heat to low; cook 2 minutes or until sauce is slightly thickened.

• Remove fish carefully with slotted spatula to serving platter. Garnish with orange slices, if desired. Serve with sauce.

Makes 4 servings

Prep Time: 5 minutes
Cook Time: 20 minutes

Fresh out of Harvard, Jim Dole arrived in Hawaii in 1899 and two years later began growing 60 acres of pineapple. Since fresh pineapple would not withstand the long ocean voyages of that day, Dole had to build a cannery to pack the fruit. By 1905, the cannery was producing an amazing 25,000 cases of canned pineapple.

RED SNAPPER SCAMPI

¼ cup margarine or butter, softened
1 tablespoon white wine
1½ teaspoons minced garlic
½ teaspoon grated lemon peel
⅛ teaspoon black pepper
1½ pounds red snapper, orange roughy or grouper fillets (about 4 to 5 ounces each)

1. Preheat oven to 450°F. Combine margarine, wine, garlic, lemon peel and pepper in small bowl; stir to blend.

2. Place fish on foil-lined shallow baking pan. Top with seasoned margarine. Bake 10 to 12 minutes or until fish begins to flake easily when tested with fork. *Makes 4 servings*

Tip: Add sliced carrots, zucchini and bell pepper cut into matchstick-size strips to the baking pan for an easy vegetable side dish.

Prep and Cook Time: 12 minutes

SHRIMP MILANO

1 pound frozen cleaned shrimp, cooked, drained
2 cups mushroom slices
1 cup green or red pepper strips
1 garlic clove, minced
¼ cup (½ sticks) butter or margarine
¾ pound (12 ounces) VELVEETA® Pasteurized Prepared Cheese Product, cut up
¾ cup whipping cream
½ teaspoon dill weed
⅓ cup (1½ ounces) KRAFT® 100% Grated Parmesan Cheese
8 ounces fettucini, cooked, drained

• In large skillet, sauté shrimp, vegetables and garlic in butter. Reduce heat to low.

• Add prepared cheese product, cream and dill. Stir until prepared cheese product is melted.

• Stir in Parmesan cheese. Add fettucini; toss lightly. *Makes 4 to 6 servings*

Prep Time: 20 minutes
Cook Time: 15 minutes

Red Snapper Scampi

CAMPBELL'S® HEALTHY REQUEST® PRIMAVERA FISH FILLETS

1 large carrot, cut into matchstick-thin strips (about 1 cup)
2 stalks celery, cut into matchstick-thin strips (about 1 cup)
1 small onion, diced (about ¼ cup)
¼ cup water
2 tablespoons Chablis *or* other dry white wine
½ teaspoon dried thyme leaves, crushed
Generous dash pepper
1 can (10¾ ounces) CAMPBELL'S® HEALTHY REQUEST® Condensed Cream of Mushroom Soup
1 pound firm white fish fillets (cod, haddock or halibut)

1. In medium skillet mix carrot, celery, onion, water, wine, thyme and pepper. Over medium-high heat, heat to a boil. Reduce heat to low. Cover and cook 5 minutes or until vegetables are tender-crisp.

2. Stir in soup. Over medium heat, heat to a boil.

3. Place fish in soup mixture. Reduce heat to low. Cover and cook 5 minutes or until fish flakes easily when tested with a fork.

Makes 4 servings

Note: In this recipe, CAMPBELL'S® HEALTHY REQUEST® creates a lower fat alternative to a traditional Newburg-style sauce made with butter and cream.

Prep Time: 10 minutes
Cook Time: 20 minutes

COMPANY CRAB

1 pound Florida blue crabmeat, fresh, frozen or pasteurized
1 can (15 ounces) artichoke hearts, drained
1 can (4 ounces) sliced mushrooms, drained
2 tablespoons butter or margarine
2½ tablespoons all-purpose flour
½ teaspoon salt
⅛ teaspoon ground red pepper
1 cup half-and-half
2 tablespoons dry sherry
2 tablespoons crushed corn flakes
1 tablespoon grated Parmesan cheese
Paprika

Preheat oven to 450°F. Thaw crabmeat if frozen. Remove any pieces of shell or cartilage. Cut artichoke hearts in half; place artichokes in well-greased, shallow 1½-quart casserole. Add crabmeat and mushrooms; cover and set aside.

Melt butter in small saucepan over medium heat. Stir in flour, salt and ground red pepper. Gradually stir in half-and-half. Continue cooking until sauce thickens, stirring constantly. Stir in sherry. Pour sauce over crabmeat. Combine corn flakes and cheese in small bowl; sprinkle over casserole. Sprinkle with paprika. Bake 12 to 15 minutes or until bubbly.

Makes 6 servings

Favorite recipe from **Florida Department of Agriculture and Consumer Services, Bureau of Seafood and Aquaculture**

Campbell's® Healthy Request®
Primavera Fish Fillet

SHRIMP CURRY

1¼ pounds raw large shrimp
1 large onion, chopped
½ cup canned light coconut milk
3 cloves garlic, minced
2 tablespoons finely chopped fresh ginger
2 to 3 teaspoons hot curry powder
¼ teaspoon salt
1 can (14½ ounces) diced tomatoes
1 teaspoon cornstarch
2 tablespoons chopped fresh cilantro
3 cups hot cooked rice

1. Peel shrimp, leaving tails attached and reserving shells. Place shells in large saucepan; cover with water. Bring to a boil over high heat. Reduce heat to low; simmer 15 to 20 minutes. Strain shrimp stock and set aside. Discard shells.

2. Spray large skillet with nonstick cooking spray; heat over medium heat. Add onion; cover and cook 5 minutes. Add coconut milk, garlic, ginger, curry powder, salt and ½ cup shrimp stock; bring to a boil. Reduce heat to low and simmer 10 to 15 minutes or until onion is tender.

3. Add shrimp and tomatoes to skillet; return mixture to a simmer. Cook 3 minutes.

4. Stir cornstarch into 1 tablespoon cooled shrimp stock until dissolved. Add mixture to skillet with cilantro; simmer 1 to 2 minutes or just until slightly thickened, stirring occasionally. Serve over rice. Garnish with carrot and lime slices, if desired.

Makes 6 servings

SAUMON AU FOUR (BAKED SALMON)

5 tablespoons butter, divided
1½ pounds salmon steaks
15 frozen artichoke hearts, cooked, halved
Juice of 1 large lemon
Salt and pepper
1 (4-ounce) package ALOUETTE® Garlic et Herbes Cheese
1 teaspoon dried basil leaves, crushed

Preheat oven to 375°F. Grease casserole dish with 1 tablespoon butter. Arrange salmon steaks and artichoke hearts in dish; sprinkle with lemon juice. Melt remaining 4 tablespoons butter; pour over salmon and artichokes. Season with salt and pepper.

Spread Alouette® generously over salmon and artichokes; sprinkle with basil. Bake about 20 minutes or until fish flakes easily when tested with fork and cheese is melted.

Makes 4 servings

Shrimp Curry

Tuna with Peppercorns on a Bed of Greens

- 4 tuna steaks (about 1½ pounds)
  Salt
- 2 teaspoons coarsely ground black pepper
- 1 tablespoon butter or margarine
- 1 large onion, thinly sliced
- ¼ cup dry white wine
- ½ pound fresh kale or spinach, washed
- 1 tablespoon olive oil
- ½ teaspoon sugar
- ¼ teaspoon black pepper
- 12 julienne strips carrot
  Lemon slices and purple kale for garnish

Preheat oven to 325°F. Rinse tuna and pat dry with paper towels. Lightly sprinkle fish with salt, then press coarsely ground pepper into both sides of steaks; set aside.

Melt butter in large skillet over medium heat. Add onion; cook and stir 5 minutes or until crisp-tender. Add wine and remove from heat. Spread onion mixture on bottom of 13×9-inch glass baking dish. Top with fish. Bake 15 minutes. Spoon liquid over fish and bake 15 minutes more or until fish flakes easily when tested with fork.

Meanwhile, trim away tough stems from kale; cut leaves into 1-inch strips. Heat oil in medium skillet over medium-high heat. Add kale, sugar and black pepper. Cook and stir 2 to 3 minutes or until tender. Place kale on plates. Top with fish and onion mixture. Top fish with carrot strips. Garnish, if desired. Serve immediately.   *Makes 4 servings*

Apricot Lemon Sole

Fish Fillets

- 1 egg
- 1 tablespoon water
- ½ cup corn flake crumbs
- ¼ teaspoon salt
- ¼ teaspoon paprika
- ⅛ teaspoon pepper
- 4 small fillets of sole or flounder

Apricot Lemon Sauce

- ⅔ cup SMUCKER'S® Low Sugar Apricot Preserves
- 1 tablespoon lemon juice
- 1 teaspoon prepared mustard
- ½ teaspoon grated lemon peel
- ⅛ teaspoon salt

Coat baking sheet with nonstick cooking spray. In pie plate, combine egg and water. In plastic bag, combine crumbs, salt, paprika and pepper. Dip each fish fillet into egg mixture; drop into bag and shake to coat with crumbs. Arrange fish in single layer on baking sheet.

Bake at 425°F for 10 minutes or until fish flakes easily with a fork. (Do not turn fish.)

Meanwhile, in small saucepan combine all sauce ingredients; heat until bubbly. Serve sauce with fish.   *Makes 4 servings*

Tuna with Peppercorns on a Bed of Greens

HAZELNUT COATED SALMON STEAKS

¼ cup hazelnuts
4 salmon steaks, about 5 ounces each
1 tablespoon apple butter
1 tablespoon Dijon mustard
¼ teaspoon dry thyme leaves
⅛ teaspoon ground black pepper
2 cups cooked white rice

1. Preheat oven to 375°F. Place hazelnuts on baking sheet; bake 8 minutes or until lightly browned. Quickly transfer nuts to clean dry dish towel. Fold towel; rub vigorously to remove as much of the skins as possible. Finely chop hazelnuts using food processor, nut grinder or chef's knife.

2. Increase oven temperature to 450°F. Place salmon in baking dish. Combine apple butter, mustard, thyme and pepper in small bowl. Brush on salmon; top each with nuts. Bake, nut side up, 14 to 16 minutes or until fish flakes easily with fork. Serve over rice.

Makes 4 servings

The National Pasta Association is the trade association for the U.S. pasta industry. Founded in 1904, the member companies provide a variety of pasta products. For more recipes, visit the NPA website at www.ilovepasta.org.

WINTER PESTO PASTA WITH SHRIMP

12 ounces fettuccine, uncooked
1 cup chopped fresh kale, washed, stems removed
½ cup fresh basil
¼ cup grated Parmesan cheese
2 cloves garlic, cut into halves
⅛ teaspoon salt
1 cup plain nonfat yogurt
1 teaspoon vegetable oil
1 pound medium shrimp, peeled, deveined
1 medium red bell pepper, cut into bite-sized pieces

Cook pasta according to package directions. While pasta is cooking, purée kale, basil, Parmesan cheese, garlic and salt in food processor or blender until smooth. Stir in yogurt.

Heat oil in large skillet over medium-low heat. Sauté shrimp and bell pepper 4 minutes or until shrimp are opaque.

When pasta is done, drain and transfer to serving bowl. Add kale mixture; mix well. Add shrimp and bell pepper; toss gently. Serve immediately. *Makes 4 servings*

Favorite recipe from **National Pasta Association**

Hazelnut Coated Salmon Steak

OVEN-ROASTED BOSTON SCROD

½ cup seasoned dry bread crumbs
1 teaspoon paprika
1 teaspoon grated fresh lemon peel
1 teaspoon dried dill weed
3 tablespoons all-purpose flour
2 egg whites
1 tablespoon water
1½ pounds Boston scrod or orange roughy
    fillets, cut into 6 (4-ounce) pieces
2 tablespoons margarine, melted
    Tartar Sauce (recipe follows)
    Lemon wedges

1. Preheat oven to 400°F. Spray 15×10-inch jelly-roll pan with nonstick cooking spray. Combine bread crumbs, paprika, lemon peel and dill in shallow bowl or pie plate. Place flour in resealable plastic food storage bag. Beat egg whites and water together in another shallow bowl or pie plate.

2. Add fish, one fillet at a time, to bag. Seal bag; turn to coat fish lightly. Dip fish into egg white mixture letting excess drip off. Roll fish in bread crumb mixture. Place in prepared jelly-roll pan. Repeat with remaining fish fillets. Drizzle margarine evenly over fish. Bake 15 to 18 minutes or until fish begins to flake when tested with fork.

3. Prepare Tartar Sauce while fish is baking. Serve fish with lemon wedges and Tartar Sauce. *Makes 6 servings*

TARTAR SAUCE

½ cup mayonnaise
¼ cup sweet pickle relish
2 teaspoons Dijon mustard
¼ teaspoon hot pepper sauce (optional)

Combine all ingredients in small bowl, mix well.

CREAMY SHRIMP & VEGETABLE CASSEROLE

1 can (10¾ ounces) reduced-fat condensed
    cream of celery soup
1 pound fresh or thawed frozen shrimp,
    shelled and deveined
½ cup asparagus (fresh or thawed frozen),
    cut diagonally into 1-inch pieces
½ cup sliced mushrooms
¼ cup sliced green onions
¼ cup diced red bell pepper
1 clove garlic, minced
½ teaspoon dried thyme
½ teaspoon salt
    Hot cooked rice or orzo

Preheat oven to 375°F. Combine soup, shrimp, asparagus, mushrooms, green onions, bell pepper, garlic, thyme and salt in large bowl; mix well. Place in 2-quart baking dish sprayed with nonstick cooking spray. Cover and bake 30 minutes. Serve over rice.

Makes 4 servings

Oven-Roasted Boston Scrod

Vegetables & Sides

VEGETABLES & SIDES

HOLIDAY VEGETABLE BAKE

1 package (16 ounces) frozen vegetable combination
1 can (10¾ ounces) condensed cream of broccoli soup
⅓ cup milk
1⅓ cups FRENCH'S® French Fried Onions, divided

MICROWAVE DIRECTIONS

Combine vegetables, soup, milk and ⅔ *cup* French Fried Onions in 2-quart microwavable casserole. Microwave,* uncovered, on HIGH 10 to 12 minutes or until vegetables are crisp-tender, stirring halfway through cooking time. Sprinkle with remaining ⅔ *cup* onions. Microwave 1 minute or until onions are golden.

Makes 4 to 6 servings

*Or, bake in preheated 375°F oven 30 to 35 minutes.

Prep Time: 5 minutes
Cook Time: 10 minutes

Holiday Vegetable Bake

Spinach-Feta Rice & Ham

1 cup uncooked rice
1 cup reduced-sodium chicken broth
1 onion, chopped
1 cup sliced fresh mushrooms
2 cloves garlic, minced
1 tablespoon lemon juice
2 teaspoons chopped fresh oregano
6 cups (about ¼ pound) shredded fresh
spinach leaves
1 cup chopped HILLSHIRE FARM® Ham
3 ounces feta cheese, crumbled
Freshly ground black pepper

Combine rice, chicken broth and 1 cup water in medium saucepan over high heat. Bring to a boil; stir once or twice. Reduce heat; simmer, covered, 15 minutes or until rice is tender and liquid is absorbed. Spray large skillet with nonstick cooking spray. Sauté onion, mushrooms and garlic over medium-high heat until onion is tender. Stir in lemon juice and oregano. Add rice, spinach, Ham, cheese and pepper; toss lightly until spinach is wilted. *Makes 6 to 8 servings*

Vegetable Sauté

3 medium zucchini (1 pound)
1 medium onion
1 tablespoon vegetable oil
1 tomato, diced
1 tablespoon KIKKOMAN® Soy Sauce
½ teaspoon dried basil leaves, crumbled

Cut zucchini and onion into ¼-inch-wide strips. Heat oil in large skillet over high heat. Add onion; cook and stir 1 minute. Add zucchini; cook and stir 1 minute. Stir in tomato, soy sauce and basil; cook only until tomato is heated through. *Makes 6 servings*

Pine Nut Dressing

1 bag SUCCESS® White or Brown Rice
1 tablespoon reduced-calorie margarine
½ cup chopped onion
½ cup chopped celery
½ cup low sodium chicken broth
¼ cup pine nuts, toasted
1 tablespoon chopped fresh parsley
¾ teaspoon poultry seasoning
¼ teaspoon celery salt
¼ teaspoon pepper

Prepare rice according to package directions.

Melt margarine in large saucepan over medium heat. Add onion and celery; cook and stir until crisp-tender. Stir in rice and remaining ingredients. Reduce heat to low; simmer 10 minutes, stirring occasionally. *Makes 6 servings*

Spinach-Feta Rice & Ham

ZUCCHINI BAKE

²/₃ cup **QUAKER® Oat Bran hot cereal,**
  uncooked
½ **teaspoon Italian seasoning**
¼ **teaspoon black pepper**
1 **egg white**
1 **tablespoon water**
2 **medium zucchini, sliced** ¾ **inch thick,**
  quartered (about 3 cups)
1 **small onion, chopped**
²/₃ **cup low-sodium tomato sauce**
2 **teaspoons olive oil**
2 **teaspoons grated Parmesan cheese**
¼ **cup (1 ounce) shredded part-skim**
  mozzarella cheese

Heat oven to 375°F. Lightly spray 8-inch
square baking dish with nonstick cooking
spray or oil lightly. In large plastic food storage
bag, combine oat bran, Italian seasoning and
pepper; mix well. In shallow dish, lightly beat
egg white and water. Coat zucchini with oat
bran mixture; shake off excess. Dip into egg
mixture, then coat again with oat bran
mixture. Place zucchini in prepared dish;
sprinkle with onion. Spoon combined tomato
sauce and oil over vegetables. Sprinkle with
Parmesan cheese. Bake 30 minutes or until
zucchini is crisp-tender; top with mozzarella
cheese. Serve warm.   *Makes 9 servings*

Microwave Directions: In large plastic food
bag, combine oat bran, Italian seasoning and
pepper; mix well. In shallow dish, lightly beat
egg white and water. Coat zucchini with oat
bran mixture; shake off excess. Dip into egg
mixture, then coat again with oat bran
mixture. Place zucchini in 8-inch square
microwavable dish; sprinkle with onion. Spoon
combined tomato sauce and oil over

vegetables. Sprinkle with Parmesan cheese.
Microwave at HIGH (100% power) 5½ to 6½
minutes or until zucchini is crisp-tender,
rotating dish ½ turn after 3 minutes. Sprinkle
with mozzarella cheese. Let stand 3 minutes
before serving. Serve warm.

ORANGE WILD RICE

¾ **cup wild rice, rinsed well**
1 **small onion, chopped**
2 **tablespoons margarine**
  Finely grated rind of 1 small orange
½ **teaspoon LAWRY'S® Seasoned Pepper**
¼ **teaspoon LAWRY'S® Garlic Powder with**
  Parsley
  Juice of 1 medium orange plus chicken
  broth to equal 1¼ cups
1 **package (10 ounces) frozen peas, thawed**
⅓ **cup chopped pecans**
  Mandarin orange sections (garnish)

In large saucepan, sauté rice and onion in
margarine, stirring frequently. Add orange
rind, Seasoned Pepper, Garlic Powder with
Parsley, orange juice and chicken broth. Bring
to a boil; reduce heat, cover and simmer 35
minutes until liquid is absorbed. Stir in peas
and pecans; simmer 3 to 5 minutes longer.
               Makes 4 to 6 servings

Presentation: Serve with roast pork. Garnish
with Mandarin orange sections.

HONEY KISSED WINTER VEGETABLES

2 to 2½ cups pared seeded ½-inch winter
    squash cubes
1 turnip, pared and cut into ½-inch cubes
2 carrots, pared and cut into ½-inch slices
1 small onion, cut into quarters
¼ cup honey
2 tablespoons butter or margarine, melted
1 teaspoon grated orange peel
¼ teaspoon ground nutmeg

Steam squash, turnip, carrots and onion on
rack over 1 inch of boiling water in large
covered skillet about 5 minutes or until tender.
Drain. Combine honey, butter, orange peel
and nutmeg in small bowl. Drizzle over
vegetables and toss to coat in heated serving
dish. *Makes 4 to 6 servings*

Favorite recipe from **National Honey Board**

HERBED CORN BREAD DRESSING

1 pound bulk pork sausage
1½ cups chopped onion
1 cup chopped celery
4 teaspoons LAWRY'S® Pinch of Herbs
6 cups coarsely crumbled corn bread
¼ cup dry sherry
¼ cup half-and-half

In large skillet, cook sausage until brown and
crumbly; add onion and celery and continue
cooking until tender. Drain fat; add Pinch of
Herbs, corn bread, sherry and half-and-half.
Mix lightly; pack dressing lightly into turkey
cavities. Leftover dressing may be baked in
covered casserole.
*Makes 9 cups dressing, enough for
14- to 16-pound turkey*

Hint: Use a sausage that is lightly seasoned
and a corn bread mix with a minimum amount
of sugar.

® © National Honey Board

*The honey bee is the only insect
that produces food eaten by man.
Bees have been producing honey
for 15 million years; man has
harvested honey for three million
years. Honey is also the only
natural sweetener that needs no
additional refining or processing to
be utilized. Honey bees must tap
two million flowers, flying over
55,000 miles, to make one pound
of honey.*

FESTIVE SWEET POTATO COMBO

2 cans (16 ounces each) sweet potatoes, drained
1⅓ cups FRENCH'S® French Fried Onions, divided
1 large apple, sliced into thin wedges
2 cans (8 ounces each) crushed pineapple, undrained
3 tablespoons packed light brown sugar
¾ teaspoon ground cinnamon

Preheat oven to 375°F. Grease 2-quart shallow baking dish. Layer sweet potatoes, ⅔ cup French Fried Onions and half of the apple wedges in prepared baking dish.

Stir together pineapple with liquid, sugar and cinnamon in medium bowl. Spoon pineapple mixture over sweet potato mixture. Arrange remaining apple wedges over pineapple layer.

Cover; bake 35 minutes or until heated through. Uncover; sprinkle with remaining ⅔ cup onions. Bake 3 minutes or until onions are golden.   *Makes 6 servings*

Prep Time: 10 minutes
Cook Time: 38 minutes

FENNEL WITH BLACK OLIVE DRESSING

1¼ pounds (about 2 medium-size heads) fennel
⅓ cup lemon juice
¼ cup olive or salad oil
⅔ cup pitted California ripe olives, coarsely chopped
Salt and pepper

Trim stems and root end from fennel; core. Reserve feathery wisps of fennel for garnish, if desired. Slice fennel crosswise into ¼-inch-thick pieces. In 4- to 5-quart pan, bring 3 to 4 quarts water to a boil over high heat. Add fennel and cook, uncovered, just until tender to bite, about 5 minutes. Drain; immerse fennel in ice water until cold. Drain well again. In small bowl, beat lemon juice and oil; stir in olives and add salt and pepper to taste. To serve, divide fennel among 6 salad plates and spoon dressing over fennel. Garnish with reserved feathery wisps of fennel, if desired.

Makes 6 servings

Prep Time: 10 minutes
Cook Time: About 5 minutes

Favorite recipe from **California Olive Industry**

Festive Sweet Potato Combo

Broccoli-Cheese Rice Pilaf

¼ cup minced onion
¼ cup diced red bell pepper
2 cups instant rice
1⅓ cups water
1 can (10¾ ounces) condensed broccoli
    and cheese soup
1 tablespoon minced fresh parsley
½ teaspoon salt

Lightly coat medium saucepan with nonstick vegetable cooking spray. Add onion and pepper; cook and stir until tender. Stir in rice. Add water, soup, parsley and salt; mix well. Bring to a boil; reduce heat. Cover and cook 10 minutes or until liquid is absorbed and rice is tender. *Makes 6 servings*

Herb Sauced Vegetables

3 cups fresh vegetables, such as broccoli
    flowerets, cauliflowerets, sliced yellow
    squash, green beans, carrots and snow
    peas
1 cup chicken broth
½ cup prepared HIDDEN VALLEY® Original
    Ranch® Salad Dressing
¼ cup chopped fresh parsley

In large saucepan, steam vegetables separately over boiling chicken broth until crisp-tender, about 5 minutes for each batch. Transfer to heated serving dish. Warm salad dressing and spoon over vegetables. Sprinkle with parsley.
Makes 4 servings

BelGioioso® Parmesan Polenta

Nonstick vegetable oil spray
4 cups canned vegetable broth
1½ cups yellow cornmeal
¾ cups grated BELGIOIOSO® Parmesan
    (about 2 ounces)

Preheat oven to 375°F. Spray 8×8×2-inch glass baking dish with vegetable oil spray. Bring vegetable broth to a boil in medium heavy saucepan over medium heat. Gradually whisk in cornmeal. Continue to whisk until mixture is very thick, about 3 minutes. Mix in BelGioioso® Parmesan and pour mixture into prepared dish. Bake polenta until top begins to brown, about 30 minutes. Serve hot.
Makes 4 to 6 servings

Broccoli-Cheese Rice Pilaf

SESAME GREEN BEANS AND RED PEPPER

1 tablespoon sesame seeds
3 tablespoons FRANK'S® REDHOT® Hot
   Sauce
1 tablespoon olive oil
1 tablespoon soy sauce
2 teaspoons grated peeled fresh ginger
¼ teaspoon Oriental sesame oil
1 clove garlic, minced
1 pound fresh green beans, washed,
   trimmed and cut in half crosswise
¼ teaspoon salt
½ red bell pepper, seeded and cut into very
   thin strips
   Lettuce (optional)

1. Heat large nonstick skillet over medium heat. Add sesame seeds. Cook 1 to 2 minutes or until golden; shaking skillet often. Transfer to small bowl. Whisk in REDHOT sauce, olive oil, soy sauce, ginger, sesame oil and garlic; set aside.

2. Bring 1 cup water to a boil in large saucepan over high heat. Place green beans and salt in steamer basket; set into saucepan. Do not let water touch beans. Cover; steam 5 to 6 minutes or until beans are crisp-tender. Rinse with cold water; drain well.

3. Combine beans and bell pepper in large bowl. Pour sesame dressing over vegetables; toss to coat evenly. Cover; refrigerate 1 hour. Toss just before serving. Serve on lettuce-lined plates, if desired. *Makes 6 servings*

VEGETABLE GRATIN

2 tablespoons olive oil
3 small *or* 1 large zucchini, sliced into
   ¼-inch slices
⅛ teaspoon *each* salt, thyme, rosemary and
   freshly ground black pepper, divided
2 (4-ounce) packages ALOUETTE® Light
   Vegetable Jardin
2 cups fresh broccoli florets
2 small yellow squash, sliced
1 small onion, sliced
1 cup crushed BRETON® Wheat Crackers

• Preheat oven to 350°F. Place oil in medium sized gratin or shallow baking dish.

• Layer zucchini in prepared dish.

• Sprinkle zucchini lightly with half each of salt, thyme, rosemary and pepper.

• Place 3 tablespoons Alouette on top of zucchini.

• Layer with broccoli, yellow squash, onion remaining spices and Alouette until dish is filled.

• Sprinkle with cracker crumbs; cover with foil and bake 20 minutes.

• Remove foil and bake another 20 minutes. Brown lightly under broiler 1 to 2 minutes.

• Serve hot or at room temperature.
Makes 6 to 8 servings

Sesame Green Beans and Red Pepper

RAISIN BREAD STUFFING WITH ORANGE WALNUTS

6 cups cubed raisin bread
1 cup chopped onion
1 cup sliced celery
2 tablespoons butter or margarine
²⁄₃ cup walnut pieces
1 orange
1 teaspoon dried basil
⅛ teaspoon ground allspice
⅛ teaspoon black pepper
  Salt

Preheat oven to 300°F. Spread bread cubes on baking sheet and bake 20 minutes until dry.

Meanwhile, in 3-quart saucepan cook and stir onion and celery in butter over medium-high heat 5 minutes. Add walnuts. Cook and stir 2 minutes; set aside. Grate enough orange peel to equal 2 teaspoons. Squeeze orange juice into measuring cup. Add enough water to juice to equal ¾ cup; stir in orange peel, basil, allspice and pepper. Stir juice mixture into saucepan. Add bread cubes; toss over low heat to blend flavors and heat through. Season with salt. Serve with pork or poultry, or use to stuff chicken or duck before roasting.

Makes 6 servings

Favorite recipe from **Walnut Marketing Board**

In late August, boughs of California walnut trees hang heavy with full, plump walnuts, protected by nature in thick green hulls. When these protective hulls split, the nuts are ready to be harvested. The harvest season usually continues until late November. The California walnut is America's number one consumer ingredient nut, representing over half of all supermarket sales of shelled cooking nuts. Walnuts are a good source of protein and key vitamins. They are rich in Omega-3's, a "good" kind of polyunsaturated fat. Research at Loma Linda University showed that substituting walnuts for saturated fats in your diet can reduce your cholesterol level.

ARABIAN VEGETABLE MEDLEY

**2 pounds eggplant, unpeeled, cut into
  1½-inch cubes**
2 tablespoons olive oil, divided
4 cups sliced onions
2 teaspoons minced garlic
1 teaspoon salt
**½ teaspoon *each* ground cinnamon and
  black pepper**
**2 cans (16 ounces each) tomatoes,
  undrained and coarsely chopped**
**1 can (16 ounces) chick peas, rinsed and
  drained**

1. In large nonstick skillet, over medium-high heat, sauté eggplant in 1 tablespoon oil 10 to 12 minutes or until lightly browned and crisp-tender. Remove eggplant from pan; set aside.

2. In same skillet, over medium-high heat, sauté onions in remaining oil 6 to 8 minutes or until lightly browned and tender. Stir in garlic, salt, cinnamon and pepper and cook 2 to 3 minutes.

3. Stir in eggplant, tomatoes and chick peas; bring to boil. Reduce heat to low; cover and simmer 30 minutes or until eggplant is tender. Remove cover and cook 15 minutes or until most of liquid is absorbed.

Makes 16 servings

Favorite recipe from **National Turkey Federation**

YORKSHIRE PUDDING

2 eggs
1 cup all-purpose flour
½ teaspoon salt
¾ cup milk
¼ cup water
**1 package (1.0 ounce) LAWRY'S®
  Seasoning Blend for Au Jus Gravy**
1½ cups water
½ cup port wine
Dash LAWRY'S® Seasoned Pepper
Vegetable oil

In medium bowl, beat eggs with electric mixer until frothy. Reduce speed and gradually add flour and salt, beating until smooth. Slowly add milk and ¼ cup water, beating until blended. Increase speed to high and continue beating 10 minutes. Let stand 1 hour. In medium saucepan, prepare Seasoning Blend for Au Jus Gravy with 1½ cups water, wine and Seasoned Pepper according to package directions. Set aside. Preheat oven to 400°F. Coat 5-inch ovenproof omelette pan with oil and place in oven. When pan is very hot, remove and pour off excess oil. Add 1 tablespoon Au Jus Gravy mixture and ½ cup batter to pan. Bake 20 to 30 minutes or until puffed and brown. Remove pudding and wrap in foil. Keep warm. Repeat with remaining batter.

Makes 4 Yorkshire Puddings (8 servings)

Serving Suggestion: Cut each pudding into quarters and serve with prime rib or roast beef. Serve remaining Au Jus Gravy over meat.

Tip: To make ahead, wrap each cooked pudding in foil; refrigerate. When ready to serve, reheat wrapped puddings individually in warm oven.

PEPPERIDGE FARM® SAUSAGE CORN BREAD STUFFING

¼ pound bulk pork sausage
1¼ cups water
½ cup cooked whole kernel corn
½ cup shredded Cheddar cheese (2 ounces)
1 tablespoon chopped fresh parsley *or*
   1 teaspoon dried parsley flakes
4 cups PEPPERIDGE FARM® Corn Bread
   Stuffing

1. In large saucepan over medium-high heat, cook sausage until browned, stirring to separate meat. Pour off fat.

2. Stir in water, corn, cheese and parsley. Add stuffing. Mix lightly. Spoon into greased 1½-quart casserole.

3. Cover and bake at 350°F. for 25 minutes or until hot.   *Makes 6 servings*

Tip: This stuffing bake brings a new flavor to the traditional holiday meal—and is easy enough for an everyday meal!

Prep Time: 15 minutes
Cook Time: 25 minutes

PEPPERIDGE FARM® SCALLOPED APPLE BAKE

¼ cup margarine *or* butter, melted
¼ cup sugar
2 teaspoons grated orange peel
1 teaspoon ground cinnamon
1½ cups PEPPERIDGE FARM® Corn Bread
   Stuffing
½ cup coarsely chopped pecans
1 can (16 ounces) whole berry cranberry
   sauce
⅓ cup orange juice *or* water
4 large cooking apples, cored and thinly
   sliced (about 6 cups)

1. Lightly mix margarine, sugar, orange peel, cinnamon, stuffing and pecans and set aside.

2. Mix cranberry sauce, juice and apples. Add **half** the stuffing mixture. Mix lightly. Spoon into 8-inch square baking dish. Sprinkle remaining stuffing mixture over apple mixture.

3. Bake at 375°F. for 40 minutes or until apples are tender.   *Makes 6 servings*

Tip: To melt margarine, remove wrapper and place in microwave-safe cup. Cover and microwave on HIGH 45 seconds.

Prep Time: 25 minutes
Cook Time: 40 minutes

Top to bottom: Pepperidge Farm® Corn Bread
Stuffing and Pepperidge Farm®
Scalloped Apple Bake

GUILTLESS ZUCCHINI

Nonstick cooking spray
4 medium zucchini, sliced
⅓ cup chopped onion
4 cloves garlic, minced
¼ teaspoon dried oregano leaves
½ cup GUILTLESS GOURMET® Salsa
¼ cup (1 ounce) shredded low-fat mozzarella cheese

Coat large nonstick skillet with cooking spray; heat over medium heat until hot. Add zucchini; cook and stir 5 minutes. Add onion, garlic and oregano; cook 5 minutes more or until zucchini and onion are lightly browned. Stir in salsa. Bring just to a boil. Reduce heat to low; simmer 5 minutes more or until zucchini is crisp-tender. Sprinkle cheese on top; cover and cook 1 to 2 minutes or until cheese melts. Serve hot.   *Makes 4 servings*

CORN PUDDING

1 bag (20 ounces) frozen whole kernel corn, thawed
1 small onion, quartered
2 cups milk
2 eggs, beaten
1 package (8½ ounces) corn muffin mix
½ teaspoon salt
1 cup shredded Cheddar cheese
1 cup thinly sliced romaine lettuce
½ cup julienned radishes

Preheat oven to 325°F. Combine corn and onion in food processor; cover and process using on/off pulse until corn is broken but not puréed, scraping side of bowl as necessary. Add milk and eggs; pulse until just blended. Add muffin mix and salt; pulse only until mixed. Pour mixture into greased 11¾×7½-inch baking dish. Bake 45 to 50 minutes or until outside crust is golden brown. Sprinkle pudding with cheese; place under broiler 3 to 4 inches from heat. Broil until cheese is melted and top is crusty. To serve, top with romaine lettuce and radishes.

Makes 8 to 10 servings

Favorite recipe from **National Cattlemen's Beef Association**

PINEAPPLE YAM CASSEROLE

4 medium yams, cooked, peeled and mashed, *or* 2 (16- or 17-ounce) cans yams, drained and mashed
⅓ cup SMUCKER'S® Pineapple Topping
4 tablespoons butter or margarine, melted, divided
1 tablespoon lemon juice

Combine yams, pineapple topping, 3 tablespoons butter and lemon juice; mix well. Brush 1-quart casserole with remaining 1 tablespoon butter. Spoon yam mixture into casserole.

Bake at 350°F for 25 minutes or until heated through.   *Makes 4 servings*

Guiltless Zucchini

APPLE-POTATO PANCAKES

1¼ cups unpeeled, finely chopped apples
1 cup peeled, grated potatoes
½ cup MOTT'S® Natural Apple Sauce
½ cup all-purpose flour
2 egg whites
1 teaspoon salt
   Additional MOTT'S® Natural Apple Sauce
   or apple slices (optional)

1. Preheat oven to 475°F. Spray cookie sheet with nonstick cooking spray.

2. In medium bowl, combine apples, potatoes, ½ cup apple sauce, flour, egg whites and salt.

3. Spray large nonstick skillet with nonstick cooking spray; heat over medium heat until hot. Drop rounded tablespoonfuls of batter 2 inches apart into skillet. Cook 2 to 3 minutes on each side or until lightly browned. Place pancakes on prepared cookie sheet.

4. Bake 10 to 15 minutes or until crisp. Serve with additional apple sauce or apple slices, if desired. Refrigerate leftovers.

Makes 12 servings

SPICED COUSCOUS MOLDS

¾ cup water
⅓ cup chopped red onion
1 large clove garlic, minced
1 tablespoon brown sugar
½ cup uncooked couscous
½ teaspoon curry powder
1 medium red apple, chopped
2 tablespoons walnut pieces
¼ teaspoon salt

Combine water, onion, garlic and sugar in medium microwavable bowl. Microwave on HIGH (100% power) 2 to 4 minutes or until mixture comes to a boil. Remove from microwave; stir in couscous and curry powder. Cover and let stand 5 minutes. Fluff with fork.

Stir in remaining ingredients. Spoon into six 6-ounce custard cups; pack lightly. To serve, invert cups onto dinner plates.

Makes 6 servings

Favorite recipe from **The Sugar Association, Inc.**

The Mott Company was founded in 1842 by Samuel R. Mott, who made cider with the help of hitched horses that plodded in a circle, crushing apples between two large stone drums at the center of the circle. With an increase in demand and mill size, the horses were replaced with water power and steam, and Mott's cider and vinegar were distributed around the country.

Apple-Potato Pancakes

ASIAN SESAME RICE

1 tablespoon low-sodium soy sauce
1 tablespoon rice vinegar
1 tablespoon Dijon mustard
1 tablespoon honey
1 tablespoon chopped fresh cilantro
¼ teaspoon salt
¼ teaspoon ground black pepper
1 tablespoon dark sesame oil
2 carrots, cut into julienned strips
1 cup fresh snow peas, cut diagonally in
    half
4 green onions, sliced
1 clove garlic, minced
3 cups cooked rice
1 tablespoon sesame seeds, toasted*
    Grilled chicken (optional)

*To toast sesame seeds, place in small skillet. Cook
over medium-high heat 1 to 3 minutes or until
lightly browned, stirring constantly.

Combine soy sauce, vinegar, mustard, honey,
cilantro, salt and pepper in small bowl; set
aside. Heat oil in large skillet over medium-
high heat until hot. Add carrots, peas, onions
and garlic; cook and stir 3 to 5 minutes or
until carrots are tender-crisp. Add rice and soy
sauce mixture. Stir until well blended; heat
thoroughly. Sprinkle with sesame seeds. Serve
with chicken.   *Makes 6 servings*

Favorite recipe from **USA Rice Federation**

*During World War II, the demand
for almonds increased greatly in
order to supply the Armed Forces
with the popular chocolate and
almond candy bars.*

SWEET POTATO GRATIN

3 tablespoons olive oil, divided
2 cloves garlic, finely chopped
1½ pounds sweet potatoes (yam variety),
    peeled and sliced ¼ inch thick
⅔ cup chicken broth
    Salt and white pepper
½ cup BLUE DIAMOND® Blanched Whole
    Almonds, chopped
½ cup fresh white bread crumbs
½ cup (2 ounces) shredded Swiss cheese
2 tablespoons chopped fresh parsley

Grease 8-inch square baking pan with
1 tablespoon oil. Sprinkle pan with garlic.
Layer sweet potatoes in pan. Pour in broth.
Season with salt and pepper to taste. Cover
and bake at 375°F 30 minutes. Combine
almonds, bread crumbs, cheese, parsley, ¼
teaspoon salt and ⅛ teaspoon pepper. Toss
with remaining 2 tablespoons oil. Sprinkle
over hot potatoes and bake, uncovered, 20
minutes longer or until golden.

Makes 4 to 6 servings

APPLE BUTTERED SWEET POTATOES

1 pound sweet potatoes, cooked, peeled
   and sliced
1 cup (11-ounce jar) SMUCKER'S® Cider
   Apple Butter
⅓ cup SMUCKER'S® Pineapple Topping
2 tablespoons butter or margarine, melted
½ teaspoon salt
¼ teaspoon ground cinnamon
¼ teaspoon paprika

Arrange sliced sweet potatoes in ungreased shallow baking dish. Combine apple butter and remaining ingredients; mix well. Drizzle mixture over sweet potatoes.

Bake at 350°F for 20 to 30 minutes or until heated through. *Makes 6 servings*

BROWN RICE AND GREEN ONION PILAF

2 tablespoons FILIPPO BERIO® Olive Oil
¾ cup chopped green onions, white part
   and about 2 inches of green part
1 cup uncooked brown rice
2½ cups chicken broth, defatted (see note)
   or water
½ teaspoon salt
   Additional green onion, green part sliced
   into matchstick-size strips (optional)

In heavy medium saucepan, heat olive oil over medium heat until hot. Add chopped green onions; cook and stir 3 to 4 minutes or until wilted. Add rice; cook and stir 3 to 4 minutes to coat rice with oil. Add chicken broth and salt; stir well. Bring to a boil. Cover; reduce heat to low and simmer 40 minutes or until rice is tender and liquid is absorbed. Garnish with additional green onion, if desired.

Makes 4 to 5 servings

Note: To defat chicken broth, refrigerate can of broth for at least 1 hour. Open can; use a spoon to lift out any solid fat floating on surface of broth.

In 1897, Jerome M. Smucker opened a small custom apple cider mill in Orrville, Ohio. As word of his cider spread, he expanded his operation and began making apple butter using a family recipe passed on from his Pennsylvania Dutch grandfather. The apple butter sold well, and in the 1920s, a full line of preserves and jellies was added. Today, the J.M. Smucker Company is the number one producer of jellies, jams, preserves and ice cream toppings in the United States.

MEDITERRANEAN-STYLE ROASTED VEGETABLES

1½ pounds red potatoes
1 tablespoon plus 1½ teaspoons olive oil, divided
1 red bell pepper
1 yellow or orange bell pepper
1 small red onion
2 cloves garlic, minced
½ teaspoon salt
¼ teaspoon black pepper
1 tablespoon balsamic vinegar
¼ cup chopped fresh basil leaves

1. Preheat oven to 425°F. Spray large shallow metal roasting pan with nonstick cooking spray. Cut potatoes into 1½-inch chunks; place in pan. Drizzle 1 tablespoon oil over potatoes; toss to coat. Bake 10 minutes.

2. Cut bell peppers into 1½-inch chunks. Cut onion through the core into ½-inch wedges. Add bell peppers and onion to pan. Drizzle remaining 1½ teaspoons oil over vegetables; sprinkle with garlic, salt and black pepper. Toss well to coat. Return to oven; bake 18 to 20 minutes or until vegetables are brown and tender, stirring once.

3. Transfer to large serving bowl. Drizzle vinegar over vegetables; toss to coat. Add basil; toss again. Serve warm or at room temperature with additional black pepper, if desired.　　　*Makes 6 servings*

SCALLOPED POTATOES WITH GORGONZOLA

1 (14½-ounce) can chicken broth
1½ cups whipping cream
4 teaspoons minced garlic
1½ teaspoons dried sage leaves
1 cup BELGIOIOSO® Gorgonzola
2¼ pounds russet potatoes, peeled, halved and thinly sliced
Salt and pepper to taste

Preheat oven to 375°F. Simmer chicken broth, whipping cream, garlic and sage in medium heavy saucepan 5 minutes or until slightly thickened. Add BelGioioso® Gorgonzola and stir until melted. Remove from heat.

Toss potatoes with salt and pepper in large bowl. Arrange half of potatoes in 13×9×2-inch glass baking dish. Pour half of cream mixture over top of potatoes. Repeat layers with remaining potatoes and cream mixture. Bake until potatoes are tender, about 1¼ hours. Let stand 15 minutes before serving.
Makes 8 servings

Mediterranean-Style Roasted Vegetables

CAMPBELL'S® GREEN BEAN BAKE

1 can (10¾ ounces) CAMPBELL'S®
    Condensed Cream of Mushroom Soup
    or 98% Fat Free Cream of Mushroom
    Soup
½ cup milk
1 teaspoon soy sauce
    Dash pepper
4 cups cooked cut green beans
1 can (2.8 ounces) French fried onions
    (1⅓ cups)

1. In 1½-quart casserole mix soup, milk, soy sauce, pepper, beans and ½ *can* onions.

2. Bake at 350°F. for 25 minutes or until hot.

3. Stir. Sprinkle remaining onions over bean mixture. Bake 5 minutes more or until onions are golden.   *Makes 6 servings*

Tip: Use 1 bag (16 to 20 ounces) frozen green beans, 2 packages (9 ounces *each*) frozen green beans, 2 cans (about 16 ounces *each*) green beans *or* about 1½ pounds fresh green beans for this recipe.

Prep Time: 10 minutes
Cook Time: 30 minutes

APRICOT AND WALNUT BROWN RICE STUFFING

½ cup chopped onion
½ cup chopped celery
1 teaspoon margarine
3 cups cooked brown rice
⅔ cup coarsely chopped dried apricots
½ cup chicken broth
¼ cup coarsely chopped walnuts
¼ cup raisins, plumped
2 tablespoons snipped parsley
½ teaspoon dried thyme leaves
¼ teaspoon salt
¼ teaspoon rubbed sage
¼ teaspoon ground black pepper

Cook onion and celery in margarine in large skillet over medium-high heat until tender-crisp. Add rice, apricots, broth, walnuts, raisins, parsley, thyme, salt, sage and pepper; transfer to 2-quart baking dish. Bake in covered baking dish at 375°F for 15 to 20 minutes. (Stuffing may be baked inside poultry.)   *Makes 6 servings*

Tip: To plump raisins, cover with 1 cup boiling water. Let stand 1 to 2 minutes; drain.

Favorite recipe from **USA Rice Federation**

Campbell's® Green Bean Bake

CARROT AND PARSNIP PURÉE

1 pound carrots, peeled
1 pound parsnips, peeled
1 cup chopped onion
1 cup vegetable broth
1 tablespoon margarine
$\frac{1}{8}$ teaspoon nutmeg

1. Cut carrots and parsnips crosswise into $\frac{1}{2}$-inch pieces.

2. Combine carrots, parsnips, onions and vegetable broth in medium saucepan. Cover; bring to a boil over high heat. Reduce heat; simmer covered 20 to 22 minutes or until vegetables are very tender.

3. Drain vegetables, reserving broth. Combine vegetables, margarine, nutmeg and $\frac{1}{4}$ cup reserved broth in food processor. Process until smooth. Serve immediately or transfer to microwave-safe casserole and chill up to 24 hours.

4. To reheat, microwave covered at HIGH 6 to 7 minutes, stirring after 4 minutes of cooking.

Makes 6 servings

MINI NOODLE KUGELS WITH RASPBERRY FILLING

4 ounces medium or wide egg noodles, uncooked
$\frac{1}{2}$ cup egg substitute
3 tablespoon sugar
$\frac{1}{4}$ teaspoon ground cinnamon
 Pinch nutmeg
$\frac{1}{2}$ cup low-fat cottage cheese
$\frac{1}{3}$ cup applesauce
$\frac{1}{4}$ cup chopped dried apples or raisins
 Vegetable oil cooking spray
6 tablespoons raspberry jam

Preheat oven to 350°F. Prepare egg noodles according to package directions. While noodles are cooking, beat egg substitute, sugar, cinnamon and nutmeg in large bowl until sugar is dissolved and mixture is foamy. Fold in cottage cheese, applesauce and apples. Lightly spray muffin tin (preferably nonstick) with cooking spray. (Do not use baking cups.)

Drain noodles and immediately add to egg mixture. Fill each muffin tin half full. Add 2 teaspoons raspberry jam to each, then fill muffin cups to full. Bake until firm and tops are golden brown, about 45 minutes. Serve warm.

Makes 9 servings

Favorite recipe from **National Pasta Association**

Carrot and Parsnip Purée

Roasted Vegetables Provençal

8 ounces medium or large mushrooms, halved
1 large zucchini, cut into 1-inch pieces, halved
1 large yellow squash or additional zucchini, cut into 1-inch pieces, quartered
1 large red or green bell pepper, cut into 1-inch pieces
1 small red onion, cut into ¼-inch slices, separated into rings
3 tablespoons olive oil
2 cloves garlic, minced
1 teaspoon dried basil leaves
1 teaspoon dried thyme leaves
½ teaspoon salt (optional)
¼ teaspoon freshly ground black pepper
4 large plum tomatoes, quartered
⅔ cup milk
2 tablespoons margarine or butter
1 package (5.1 ounces) PASTA RONI® Angel Hair Pasta with Parmesan Cheese

1. Preheat oven to 425°F. In 15×10-inch jelly-roll pan, combine mushrooms, zucchini, squash, bell pepper and onion. In small bowl, combine oil, garlic, basil, thyme, salt and black pepper. Add to vegetable mixture; toss to coat. Bake 15 minutes; stir in tomatoes. Continue baking 5 to 10 minutes or until vegetables are tender.

2. While vegetables are roasting, combine 1⅓ cups water, milk and margarine in medium saucepan; bring just to a boil. Gradually add pasta while stirring. Stir in contents of seasoning packet. Reduce heat to medium.

3. Boil, uncovered, stirring frequently, 4 minutes. Sauce will be very thin, but will thicken upon standing. Remove from heat.

4. Let stand 3 minutes or until desired consistency. Stir before serving. Serve pasta topped with vegetables.   *Makes 4 servings*

Green Beans with Blue Cheese

1 box (9 ounces) BIRDS EYE® frozen Cut Green Beans
2 tablespoons walnut pieces (toasted, if desired)
1 heaping tablespoon Roquefort or other blue cheese
1 tablespoon butter or margarine, melted (optional)

• Cook beans according to package directions.

• Combine with remaining ingredients; mix well.

• Serve hot.   *Makes 3 servings*

Prep Time: 2 to 3 minutes
Cook Time: 4 to 6 minutes

QUICK 'N' EASY FRESH ORANGE CRANBERRY SAUCE

1 small SUNKIST® orange, unpeeled, cut
   into chunks
2 cans (16 ounces each) whole cranberry
   sauce
¼ teaspoon ground cinnamon
⅛ teaspoon ground allspice
⅛ teaspoon ground nutmeg
   Orange Shells (recipe follows)

In food processor or blender, finely chop
orange chunks. In large bowl, combine finely
chopped orange with remaining ingredients.
Chill well to blend flavors. Serve in Orange
Shells as accompaniment to Rock Cornish
game hens, turkey, chicken or ham.

Makes about 1 quart sauce

Orange Shells: Cut 1 small SUNKIST® orange
in half crosswise. Carefully ream out juice or
cut out "meat" with curved grapefruit knife.
Scrape shells clean with spoon. Edges may be
notched with kitchen shears or paring knife;
for scallops, use coin to outline pattern, then
cut around pattern. To prevent tipping, cut thin
slice from bottom of shell. Shells may be
placed in plastic bag, sealed and stored in
refrigerator or freezer until ready to use.

Note: For a quick, tasty and colorful dessert,
layer Fresh Orange Cranberry Sauce and
frozen vanilla yogurt in parfait glasses. Garnish
with half-cartwheel orange slices and sprigs of
mint.

Sunkist historical crate label

POTATO 'N' ONION BAKE

1 pound all-purpose or baking potatoes,
   thinly sliced
2 medium onions, thinly sliced
2 tablespoons olive or vegetable oil
½ teaspoon salt
½ teaspoon ground black pepper
2 cups RAGÚ® Chunky Gardenstyle Pasta
   Sauce
3 tablespoons grated Parmesan cheese

Preheat oven to 400°F. In 2-quart baking dish,
layer ½ each of the potatoes, onions, oil, salt
and pepper; repeat layer. Bake covered 20
minutes or until potatoes are tender. Remove
cover; pour Ragú® Chunky Gardenstyle Pasta
Sauce over potato mixture; sprinkle with
Parmesan cheese. Bake an additional 10
minutes or until heated through.

Makes 4 servings

FRIED RICE CAKES

1 package (6 ounces) COUNTRY INN®
    Brand Homestyle Chicken &
    Vegetables Rice Dishes
⅓ cup thinly sliced green onions, including
    tops
2 eggs, beaten
2 tablespoons minced fresh cilantro
2 tablespoons soy sauce
1 teaspoon minced fresh ginger
2 to 3 tablespoons vegetable oil, divided

1. Prepare rice according to package
directions, omitting butter. Cover; refrigerate
until completely chilled. Stir remaining
ingredients, except oil, into cold rice.

2. In 12-inch skillet, heat 1 tablespoon oil
over medium heat until hot. For each rice
cake, place ⅓ cup rice mixture into skillet;
flatten slightly to 3-inch diameter. Cook 4
cakes at a time 3 to 4 minutes on each side or
until golden brown. Add more oil to skillet as
needed.   *Makes 4 to 6 servings*

Cook's Tip: Rice cakes may be cooked in
advance, covered and refrigerated. When
ready to serve, place in single layer on baking
sheet. Bake, uncovered, in preheated 350°F
oven for 10 to 15 minutes or until heated
through.

GRANDMA'S NOODLE KUGEL

¼ cup margarine, softened
3 eggs
1½ cups reduced-fat cottage cheese
1 cup reduced-fat sour cream
1 can (20 ounces) crushed pineapple in
    juice, drained
½ cup dark raisins
5½ teaspoons EQUAL® FOR RECIPES *or*
    18 packets EQUAL® sweetener *or*
    ¾ cup EQUAL® SPOONFUL™
½ teaspoon ground cinnamon
1 package (12 ounces) cholesterol-free
    wide noodles, cooked

• Mix margarine and eggs in large bowl until
smooth; blend in cottage cheese, sour cream,
pineapple, raisins, Equal® and cinnamon. Mix
in noodles.

• Spoon mixture evenly into lightly greased
13×9×2-inch baking dish. Bake kugel,
uncovered, in preheated 325°F oven until
heated through, 45 to 55 minutes. Cut into
squares.   *Makes 12 servings*

Fried Rice Cakes

GLAZED MAPLE ACORN SQUASH

1 large acorn or golden acorn squash
1/4 cup water
2 tablespoons pure maple syrup
1 tablespoon margarine or butter, melted
1/4 teaspoon cinnamon

1. Preheat oven to 375°F.

2. Cut stem and blossom ends from squash. Cut squash crosswise into four equal slices. Discard seeds and membrane. Place water in 13×9-inch baking dish. Arrange squash in dish; cover with foil. Bake 30 minutes or until tender.

3. Combine syrup, margarine and cinnamon in small bowl; mix well. Uncover squash; pour off water. Brush squash with syrup mixture, letting excess pool in center of squash.

4. Return to oven; bake 10 minutes or until syrup mixture is bubbly.   *Makes 4 servings*

CREAMED SPINACH CASSEROLE

2 packages (10 ounces each) frozen chopped spinach, thawed, well drained
2 packages (8 ounces each) PHILADELPHIA® Cream Cheese, softened
1 teaspoon lemon and pepper seasoning salt
1/3 cup crushed seasoned croutons

MIX spinach, cream cheese and seasoning salt until well blended.

SPOON mixture into 1-quart casserole. Sprinkle with crushed croutons.

BAKE at 350°F for 25 to 30 minutes or until thoroughly heated.   *Makes 6 to 8 servings*

Prep Time: 10 minutes
Baking Time: 30 minutes

SUCCESS WALDORF DRESSING

1 box SUCCESS® Long Grain & Wild Rice Mix
3 strips bacon
1/2 cup chopped celery
1 medium red apple, chopped
1 medium green apple, chopped
1/2 cup chopped walnuts
1/2 cup raisins
2 tablespoons honey
2 tablespoons lemon juice

Prepare rice mix according to package directions.

Meanwhile, cook bacon in skillet until crisp. Remove bacon and crumble. Cook and stir celery in same skillet until tender. Add remaining ingredients. Fold in cooked rice. Top with crumbled bacon.

Makes 4 to 6 servings

Glazed Maple Acorn Squash

SAUSAGE & RED PEPPER RISOTTO

4½ cups chicken broth
   8 ounces sweet Italian sausage links, removed from casing
   1 tablespoon olive or vegetable oil
   1 large onion, chopped
   1 medium red bell pepper, chopped
   1 clove garlic, finely chopped
1½ cups arborio or regular rice
   ⅓ cup dry white wine or chicken broth
   ⅛ teaspoon dried oregano leaves, crushed
   1 cup RAGÚ® Light Pasta Sauce
   ¼ cup grated Parmesan cheese
   ⅛ teaspoon ground black pepper

In 2-quart saucepan, heat chicken broth; set aside. In heavy-duty 3-quart saucepan, brown sausage over medium-high heat 4 minutes or until sausage is no longer pink; remove sausage. In same 3-quart saucepan, add oil and cook onion over medium heat, stirring occasionally, 3 minutes. Stir in bell pepper and garlic and cook 1 minute. Add rice and cook, stirring occasionally, 1 minute. Slowly add 1 cup broth, wine and oregano and cook, stirring constantly, until liquid is absorbed. Continue adding 2 cups broth, 1 cup at a time, stirring frequently, until liquid is absorbed.

Meanwhile, stir Ragú® Light Pasta Sauce into remaining 1½ cups broth; heat through. Continue adding broth mixture, 1 cup at a time, stirring frequently, until rice is slightly creamy and just tender. Return sausage to saucepan and stir in cheese and black pepper. Serve immediately.   *Makes 4 main-dish or 8 side-dish servings*

ORIGINAL GREEN BEAN CASSEROLE

   1 can (10¾ ounces) condensed cream of mushroom soup
   ¾ cup milk
   ⅛ teaspoon ground black pepper
   2 packages (9 ounces each) frozen cut green beans, thawed and drained *or* 2 cans (14.5 ounces each) cut green beans, drained
1⅓ cups FRENCH'S® French Fried Onions, divided

Preheat oven to 350°F. Combine soup, milk and ground pepper in 1½ quart casserole; stir until well blended. Stir in beans and ⅔ *cup* French Fried Onions.

Bake, uncovered, 30 minutes or until hot. Stir; sprinkle with remaining ⅔ *cup* onions. Bake 5 minutes or until onions are golden.
Makes 6 servings

Microwave Directions: Prepare green bean mixture as above; pour into 1½-quart microwave-safe casserole. Cook, covered, on HIGH 8 to 10 minutes or until heated through. Stir beans halfway through cooking time. Top with remaining onions; cook, uncovered, 1 minute. Let stand 5 minutes.

Prep Time: 5 minutes
Cook Time: 35 minutes

Sausage & Red Pepper Risotto

Broccoli-Rice Casserole

½ cup chopped onion
½ cup chopped celery
⅓ cup chopped red bell pepper
1 can (10¾ ounces) condensed broccoli
    and cheese soup
¼ cup reduced-fat sour cream
1 (10-ounce) package frozen chopped
    broccoli, thawed and drained
2 cups cooked rice
1 tomato, cut into ¼-inch slices

Preheat oven to 350°F. Coat large skillet with nonstick cooking spray. Add onion, celery and pepper; cook and stir until crisp-tender. Stir in soup and sour cream. Layer broccoli and rice in 1½-quart baking dish sprayed with cooking spray. Top rice with soup mixture, spreading evenly.

Cover and bake 20 minutes. Top with tomato; bake, uncovered, 10 minutes.

Makes 6 servings

Hot Sweet Potatoes

4 small sweet potatoes (4 ounces each)
2 tablespoons margarine *or* unsalted
    butter, softened
½ teaspoon TABASCO® brand Pepper Sauce
¼ teaspoon dried savory leaves, crushed

Cover potatoes with water in large saucepan. Cover and cook over high heat 20 to 25 minutes or until potatoes are tender. Drain potatoes and cut in half lengthwise. Preheat broiler. Combine margarine and TABASCO®

Sauce in small bowl. Spread ¾ teaspoon margarine mixture over cut side of each potato half. Season each with pinch of savory. Place on foil-lined broiler pan and broil, watching carefully, about 5 minutes or until lightly browned. Serve hot.

Makes 4 servings

Edmund McIlhenny, founder of McIlhenny Company and creator of Tabasco® brand Pepper Sauce.

Broccoli-Rice Casserole

CAKES & PIES

LEMON SOUFFLÉ CHEESECAKE

1 graham cracker, crushed, or 2 tablespoons graham cracker
   crumbs, divided
2/3 cup boiling water
1 package (4-serving size) JELL-O® Brand Lemon Flavor
   Sugar Free Low Calorie Gelatin Dessert or JELL-O®
   Brand Lemon Flavor Gelatin Dessert
1 cup LIGHT N' LIVELY® 1% Lowfat Cottage Cheese with Calcium
1 tub (8 ounces) PHILADELPHIA® LIGHT® Light Cream Cheese
2 cups thawed COOL WHIP FREE® or COOL WHIP LITE®
   Whipped Topping

SPRINKLE ½ of the crumbs onto side of 8- or 9-inch springform pan or 9-inch pie plate sprayed with nonstick cooking spray.

STIR boiling water into gelatin in large bowl at least 2 minutes until completely dissolved. Pour into blender. Add cheeses; blend on medium speed until smooth.

POUR into large bowl. Gently stir in whipped topping. Pour into prepared pan; smooth top. Sprinkle remaining crumbs around outside edge. Refrigerate 4 hours or until set. Remove side of pan just before serving. Garnish as desired.   *Makes 8 servings*

Lemon Soufflé Cheesecake

"PERFECTLY CHOCOLATE" CHOCOLATE CAKE

2 cups sugar
1¾ cups all-purpose flour
¾ cup HERSHEY'S Cocoa
1½ teaspoons baking powder
1½ teaspoons baking soda
1 teaspoon salt
2 eggs
1 cup milk
½ cup vegetable oil
2 teaspoons vanilla extract
1 cup boiling water
"Perfectly Chocolate" Chocolate Frosting
(recipe follows)

Heat oven to 350°F. Grease and flour two 9-inch round baking pans.

Stir together sugar, flour, cocoa, baking powder, baking soda and salt in large bowl. Add eggs, milk, oil and vanilla; beat on medium speed of electric mixer 2 minutes. Stir in boiling water (batter will be thin). Pour batter into prepared pans.

Bake 30 to 35 minutes or until wooden pick inserted in center comes out clean. Cool 10 minutes; remove from pans to wire racks. Cool completely. Frost with "Perfectly Chocolate" Chocolate Frosting.

Makes 10 to 12 servings

One-Pan Cake: Grease and flour 13×9×2-inch baking pan. Heat oven to 350°F. Pour batter into prepared pan. Bake 35 to 40 minutes. Cool completely. Frost.

Three-Layer Cake: Grease and flour three 8-inch round baking pans. Heat oven to 350°F. Pour batter into prepared pans. Bake 30 to 35 minutes. Cool 10 minutes; remove from pans to wire racks. Cool completely. Frost.

Bundt Cake: Grease and flour 12-cup Bundt pan. Heat oven to 350°F. Pour batter into prepared pan. Bake 50 to 55 minutes. Cool 15 minutes; remove from pan to wire rack. Cool completely. Frost.

Cupcakes: Line muffin cups (2½ inches in diameter) with paper bake cups. Heat oven to 350°F. Fill cups ⅔ full with batter. Bake 22 to 25 minutes. Cool completely. Frost. Makes about 30 cupcakes

"PERFECTLY CHOCOLATE" CHOCOLATE FROSTING

1 stick (½ cup) butter or margarine
⅔ cup HERSHEY'S Cocoa
3 cups powdered sugar
⅓ cup milk
1 teaspoon vanilla extract

Melt butter. Stir in cocoa. Alternately add powdered sugar and milk, beating to spreading consistency. Add small amount additional milk, if needed. Stir in vanilla.

Makes about 2 cups frosting

"Perfectly Chocolate" Chocolate Cake

Fresh Lemon Sunshine Cake

1½ cups sifted cake flour
¼ teaspoon salt
6 eggs, separated
¼ teaspoon cream of tartar
1½ cups sugar, divided
5 tablespoons water
    Grated peel and juice of 1 SUNKIST®
    Lemon (3 tablespoons juice)
    Hint O' Lemon Glaze (recipe follows)

Sift together flour and salt. In large bowl, with electric mixer, beat egg whites and cream of tartar at high speed until soft peaks form. Gradually add ½ cup sugar, beating until medium-stiff peaks form; set aside. With same beaters, in medium bowl, beat egg yolks 2 minutes. Gradually add remaining 1 cup sugar, beating at high speed until egg yolk mixture is very thick. Beat in water and lemon juice; stir in lemon peel. Add flour mixture all at once; gently fold, then lightly stir until well-blended. Carefully fold yolk mixture into beaten egg whites. Pour batter into *ungreased* 10-inch tube pan with removable bottom. Smooth top and cut through batter with table knife to remove any large air bubbles. Bake at 325°F for 45 to 55 minutes or until cake springs back when lightly touched. Immediately invert onto neck of bottle or wire rack; cool completely upside-down. With narrow spatula or knife, loosen around tube and sides. Lift out tube and cake; loosen cake around bottom. Invert onto cake plate. Glaze top with Hint O' Lemon Glaze, allowing some to drizzle over sides.* Garnish each serving with lemon cartwheel twists, fresh berries and fresh mint leaves, if desired.   *Makes 16 servings*

*Or, cover top of cake with thin layer of Hint O' Lemon Glaze; let dry. Cover remaining glaze with damp paper towels and plastic wrap. When top of cake is dry, drizzle or pipe remaining glaze (thinned with a few drops of lemon juice, if necessary) over top of cake in decorative pattern.

Hint O' Lemon Glaze: In small bowl combine 1½ cups sifted confectioners' sugar and 1½ to 2 tablespoons fresh squeezed lemon juice.

One medium lemon will yield about 3 tablespoons juice and 2 to 3 teaspoons grated peel. Store lemons in the refrigerator for 2 to 3 weeks, but bring them to room temperature before juicing to extract more juice. It also helps to roll the lemon on a countertop before juicing, pressing down on the fruit with the palm of your hand—this breaks some of the inner membranes and helps release more juice.

Fresh Lemon Sunshine Cake

ALMOND FUDGE BANANA CAKE

3 extra-ripe, medium DOLE® Bananas, peeled
1½ cups sugar
½ cup margarine, softened
3 eggs
3 tablespoons amaretto liqueur *or*
    ½ to 1 teaspoon almond extract
1 teaspoon vanilla extract
1½ cups all-purpose flour
½ cup unsweetened cocoa powder
1 teaspoon baking soda
½ teaspoon salt
½ cup DOLE® Chopped Almonds, toasted, ground
    Banana Chocolate Glaze (recipe follows)

• Mash bananas; set aside.

• Beat sugar and margarine until light and fluffy. Beat in eggs, liqueur and vanilla.

• Combine dry ingredients. Stir in almonds. Add to sugar mixture alternately with bananas. Beat well.

• Pour batter into greased 10-inch Bundt pan. Bake in preheated 350°F oven 45 to 50 minutes or until toothpick inserted in center comes out almost clean and cake pulls away from side of pan. Cool 10 minutes. Remove cake from pan to wire rack to cool completely. Drizzle glaze over top and down side of cake.

Makes 16 to 20 servings

BANANA CHOCOLATE GLAZE

1 extra-ripe, small DOLE® Banana, puréed
1 square (1 ounce) semisweet chocolate, melted

• With wire whisk, beat puréed banana into melted chocolate.

NO BAKE CAPPUCCINO CHEESECAKE

1 package (11.1 ounces) JELL-O® No Bake Real Cheesecake
2 tablespoons sugar
⅓ cup butter or margarine, melted
2 teaspoons MAXWELL HOUSE® Instant Coffee
1½ cups cold milk
¼ teaspoon ground cinnamon

MIX crumbs, sugar and butter thoroughly with fork in 9-inch pie plate until crumbs are well moistened. Press firmly against side of pie plate first, using finger or large spoon to shape edge. Press remaining crumbs firmly onto bottom using measuring cup.

DISSOLVE coffee in milk. Beat milk mixture, filling mix and cinnamon with electric mixer on low speed until blended. Beat on medium speed 3 minutes. (Filling will be thick.) Spoon into crust.

REFRIGERATE at least 1 hour.

Makes 8 servings

Preparation Time: 15 minutes
Refrigerating Time: 1 hour

ANGEL FOOD CAKE WITH PINEAPPLE SAUCE

1 can (20 ounces) DOLE® Crushed
    Pineapple
1 tablespoon orange marmalade, peach or
    apricot fruit spread
2 tablespoons sugar
1 tablespoon cornstarch
1 prepared angel food cake

• Combine undrained pineapple, orange marmalade, sugar and cornstarch in small saucepan. Bring to boil. Reduce heat to low; cook 2 minutes, stirring constantly, or until sauce thickens. Cool slightly. Sauce can be served warm or chilled.

• Cut angel food cake into 12 slices. To serve, spoon sauce over each slice.

Makes 12 servings

Prep Time: 10 minutes
Cook Time: 5 minutes

FUDGY PEANUT BUTTER CAKE

1 (18.25-ounce) box chocolate fudge
    cake mix
2 eggs
1½ cups plus ⅔ cup water, divided
1 (16-ounce) package chocolate fudge
    frosting mix
1¼ cups SMUCKER'S® Chunky Natural
    Peanut Butter or LAURA SCUDDER'S®
    Nutty Old-Fashioned Peanut Butter

Grease and flour 10-inch tube pan. In large bowl, blend cake mix, eggs and 1½ cups water until moistened; mix as directed on cake package. Pour batter into pan.

In medium bowl, combine frosting mix, peanut butter and ⅔ cup water; blend until smooth. Spoon over batter in pan.

Bake in preheated 350°F oven 35 to 45 minutes or until top springs back when touched lightly in center. Cool upright in pan 1 hour; remove from pan. Cool completely.

Makes 12 to 15 servings

In 1897, Jerome M. Smucker first pressed cider at a mill he opened in Ohio. He later prepared apple butter as well, offering his product in crocks bearing a hand-signed seal as a personal guarantee of quality. J.M. Smucker's name became well-known throughout the region and the nation for wholesome, flavorful fruit products.

TOFFEE BITS CHEESECAKE

Chocolate Crumb Crust (recipe follows)
3 packages (8 ounces each) cream cheese, softened
¾ cup sugar
3 eggs
1¾ cups (10-ounce package) SKOR® English Toffee Bits or 1¾ cups HEATH® Bits 'O Brickle, divided
1 teaspoon vanilla extract
Sweetened whipped cream

1. Prepare Chocolate Crumb Crust; set aside. Heat oven to 350°F.

2. Beat cream cheese and sugar in large bowl until smooth. Add eggs, one at a time, beating well after each addition. Set aside 1 tablespoon toffee bits. Gently stir remaining toffee bits and vanilla into batter; pour into prepared crust.

3. Bake 45 to 50 minutes or until almost set. Remove from oven to wire rack. With knife, loosen cake from side of pan. Cool completely; remove side of pan. Cover; refrigerate. Just before serving, garnish with sweetened whipped cream and reserved toffee bits. Cover; refrigerate leftover cheesecake.

Makes 10 to 12 servings

Chocolate Crumb Crust: Heat oven to 350°F. Stir together 1¼ cups (about 40 wafers) vanilla wafer crumbs, ⅓ cup powdered sugar and ⅓ cup HERSHEY'S Cocoa in medium bowl; stir in ¼ cup (½ stick) melted butter or margarine. Press mixture firmly onto bottom and ½ inch up side of 9-inch springform pan. Bake 8 minutes; cool slightly.

SPICY APPLESAUCE CAKE

2¼ cups all-purpose flour
2 teaspoons baking soda
1 teaspoon ground cinnamon
1 teaspoon ground nutmeg
½ teaspoon ground cloves
1 cup firmly packed brown sugar
½ cup FILIPPO BERIO® Olive Oil
1½ cups applesauce
1 cup raisins
1 cup coarsely chopped walnuts
Powdered sugar or sweetened whipped cream (optional)

Preheat oven to 375°F. Grease 9-inch square pan with olive oil. In medium bowl, combine flour, baking soda, cinnamon, nutmeg and cloves.

In large bowl, beat brown sugar and olive oil with electric mixer at medium speed until blended. Add applesauce; mix well. Add flour mixture all at once; beat on low speed until well blended. Stir in raisins and nuts. Spoon batter into prepared pan.

Bake 20 to 25 minutes or until lightly browned. Cool completely on wire rack. Cut into squares. Serve plain, dusted with powdered sugar or frosted with whipped cream, if desired.

Makes 9 servings

Toffee Bits Cheesecake

MOCHA MARBLE POUND CAKE

2 cups all-purpose flour
2 teaspoons baking powder
1 teaspoon baking soda
½ teaspoon salt
1 cup sugar
¼ cup FLEISCHMANN'S® Original Margarine, softened
1 teaspoon vanilla extract
½ cup EGG BEATERS® Healthy Real Egg Substitute
1 (8-ounce) container low-fat coffee yogurt
¼ cup unsweetened cocoa Mocha Yogurt Glaze (recipe follows)

In small bowl, combine flour, baking powder, baking soda and salt; set aside.

In large bowl, with electric mixer at medium speed, beat sugar, margarine and vanilla until creamy. Add Egg Beaters®; beat until smooth. With mixer at low speed, add yogurt alternately with flour mixture, beating well after each addition. Remove half of batter to medium bowl. Add cocoa to batter remaining in large bowl; beat until blended. Alternately spoon coffee and chocolate batters into greased 9×5×3-inch loaf pan. With knife, cut through batters to create marbled effect.

Bake at 325°F for 60 to 65 minutes or until toothpick inserted in center comes out clean. Cool in pan on wire rack for 10 minutes. Remove from pan; cool completely on wire rack. Frost with Mocha Yogurt Glaze.

Makes 16 servings

Mocha Yogurt Glaze: In small bowl, combine ½ cup powdered sugar, 1 tablespoon unsweetened cocoa and 1 tablespoon low-fat coffee yogurt until smooth; add more yogurt if necessary to make spreading consistency.

Prep Time: 20 minutes
Cook Time: 65 minutes

Holiday gifts from the kitchen are always welcome and appreciated. In addition to labeling your gift and adding festive packaging, it's nice to pair your gifts of food with complementary items: cake pans or a cake server with your favorite cake, a new wooden bread board with a crusty loaf of homemade bread, or a set of oven mitts with a tin of Christmas cookies.

Mocha Marble Pound Cake

PHILLY 3-STEP® CRANBERRY CHEESECAKE

2 packages (8 ounces each)
   PHILADELPHIA® Cream Cheese,
   softened
½ cup sugar
½ teaspoon grated orange peel
½ teaspoon vanilla
2 eggs
¾ cup chopped cranberries, divided
1 ready-to-use graham cracker crumb crust
   (6 ounces or 9 inches)

1. MIX cream cheese, sugar, peel and vanilla with electric mixer on medium speed until well blended. Add eggs; mix until blended. Stir in ½ cup of the cranberries.

2. POUR into crust. Sprinkle with remaining ¼ cup cranberries.

3. BAKE at 350°F for 40 minutes or until center is almost set. Cool. Refrigerate 3 hours or overnight. Garnish with additional cranberries, mint leaves and orange peel.

Makes 8 servings

Prep Time: 10 minutes
Baking Time: 40 minutes

GINGERBREAD UPSIDE-DOWN CAKE

1 can (20 ounces) DOLE® Pineapple Slices
½ cup margarine, softened, divided
1 cup packed brown sugar, divided
10 maraschino cherries
1 egg
½ cup dark molasses
1½ cups all-purpose flour
1 teaspoon baking soda
1 teaspoon ground ginger
½ teaspoon ground cinnamon
½ teaspoon salt

• Preheat oven to 350°F. Drain pineapple; reserve ½ cup syrup. In 10-inch cast iron skillet, melt ¼ cup margarine. Remove from heat. Add ½ cup brown sugar and stir until blended. Arrange pineapple slices in skillet. Place 1 cherry in center of each slice.

• In large mixer bowl, beat remaining ¼ cup margarine and ½ cup brown sugar until light and fluffy. Beat in egg and molasses. In small bowl, combine flour, baking soda, ginger, cinnamon and salt.

• In small saucepan, bring reserved pineapple syrup to a boil. Add dry ingredients to creamed mixture alternately with hot syrup. Spread evenly over pineapple in skillet. Bake 30 to 40 minutes or until wooden pick inserted in center comes out clean. Let stand in skillet on wire rack 5 minutes. Invert onto serving plate. *Makes 8 to 10 servings*

Philly 3-Step® Cranberry Cheesecake

CHOCOLATE RASPBERRY AVALANCHE CAKE

2 cups all-purpose flour
2 cups granulated sugar
6 tablespoons unsweetened cocoa
1½ teaspoons baking soda
1 teaspoon salt
1 cup hot coffee
¾ cup Butter Flavor* CRISCO® all-vegetable shortening plus additional for greasing
½ cup milk
3 eggs
¼ cup raspberry-flavored liqueur
Confectioners' sugar
1 cup fresh raspberries

*Butter Flavor Crisco® is artificially flavored.

1. Heat oven to 350°F. Grease 10-inch (12-cup) Bundt pan with shortening. Flour lightly. Place wire rack on counter for cooling cake.

2. Combine flour, granulated sugar, cocoa, baking soda and salt in large bowl. Add coffee and ¾ cup shortening. Beat at low speed of electric mixer until dry ingredients are moistened. Add milk. Beat at medium speed 1½ minutes. Add eggs, 1 at a time, beating well after each addition. Pour into prepared pan.

3. Bake at 350°F for 40 to 45 minutes, or until toothpick inserted in center comes out clean. *Do not overbake.* Cool 10 minutes before removing from pan. Place cake, fluted side up, on wire rack. Cool 10 minutes. Brush top and side with liqueur. Cool completely. Dust top with confectioners' sugar.

4. Place cake on serving plate. Fill center with raspberries. *Makes 1 (10-inch) cake (12 to 16 servings)*

Crisco® was packaged in glass jars during World War II because of metal shortages.

Chocolate Raspberry Avalanche Cake

COUNTRY OVEN
CARROT CAKE

CAKE

1 package DUNCAN HINES® Moist
   Deluxe® Yellow Cake Mix
4 eggs
½ cup canola oil plus additional for
   greasing
3 cups grated carrots
1 cup finely chopped nuts
2 teaspoons ground cinnamon

CREAM CHEESE FROSTING

4 ounces (half of 8-ounce package) cream
   cheese, softened
2 tablespoons butter or margarine,
   softened
1 teaspoon vanilla extract
2 cups confectioners' sugar

1. Preheat oven to 350°F. Grease and flour
13×9×2-inch pan (see Variation).

2. For cake, combine cake mix, eggs, oil,
carrots, nuts and cinnamon in large bowl.
Beat at low speed with electric mixer until
moistened. Beat at medium speed for 2
minutes. Pour into pan. Bake at 350°F for
40 to 45 minutes or until toothpick inserted
in center comes out clean. Cool completely.

3. For cream cheese frosting, place cream
cheese, butter and vanilla extract in small
bowl. Beat at low speed until smooth and
creamy. Add confectioners' sugar gradually,
beating until smooth. Add more sugar to
thicken or milk or water to thin frosting, as
needed. Spread frosting on cooled cake.

Makes 12 to 16 servings

Carrot Layer Cake: Carrot cake can also be
baked in two 8- or 9-inch round cake pans at
350°F for 35 to 40 minutes or until toothpick
inserted in centers comes out clean. Cool cake
following package directions. To prepare
frosting, double quantity of ingredients and use
large bowl. Prepare following directions
above. Fill and frost cooled cake. Garnish with
whole pecans.

Tip: To save time, use DUNCAN HINES®
Creamy Homestyle Cream Cheese Frosting.

*Duncan Hines® introduced its "New Fudge Marble Cake
Mix" in 1957.*

HOLIDAY FRUIT CAKE

2 cups dark raisins
1 cup golden raisins
1 cup whole candied red cherries
¼ cup candied pineapple chunks
¼ cup mixed candied fruit
2¼ cups all-purpose flour, divided
1 teaspoon baking powder
½ teaspoon ground nutmeg
½ teaspoon ground cardamom
½ teaspoon ground coriander
1¼ cups firmly packed light brown sugar
1 cup MOTT'S® Natural Apple Sauce
8 egg whites
3 tablespoons honey
1 tablespoon grated orange peel
1 tablespoon grated lemon peel
1 teaspoon vanilla extract
½ cup MOTT'S® Apple Juice

1. Preheat oven to 300°F. Spray 9-inch springform pan with nonstick cooking spray. Line pan with waxed paper, extending paper at least 1 inch above rim of pan. Spray waxed paper with nonstick cooking spray.

2. In medium bowl, combine dark raisins, golden raisins, cherries, pineapple and mixed fruit. Toss with ¼ cup flour.

3. In another medium bowl, combine remaining 2 cups flour, baking powder, nutmeg, cardamom and coriander.

4. In large bowl, combine brown sugar, apple sauce, egg whites, honey, orange peel, lemon peel and vanilla.

5. Add flour mixture to apple sauce mixture alternately with apple juice; stir just until blended. Fold in fruit mixture. Pour batter into prepared pan.

6. Bake 2 hours or until toothpick inserted in center comes out clean and cake is firm to the touch. Cool completely on wire rack. Remove cake from pan; peel off waxed paper. Wrap cake tightly in aluminum foil; store in refrigerator up to 2 weeks or in freezer up to 2 months. Cut into 20 slices.

Makes 20 servings

Fruitcakes are baked in a slow oven for a long period of time. To prevent the outer edges from burning before the inside of the cake is done, set the pan containing the fruitcake batter in a larger baking pan filled halfway with hot water. (If a springform pan is used, wrap the bottom and side in foil to prevent leaking before setting it in the water bath.) For a change of pace, make mini fruitcakes by baking the batter in mini loaf pans or foil or paper-lined muffin tins; reduce the baking time by half to two-thirds.

EGGNOG CHEESECAKE

CRUST

2 cups vanilla wafer crumbs
6 tablespoons butter or margarine, melted
½ teaspoon ground nutmeg

FILLING

4 (8-ounce) packages PHILADELPHIA®
   Cream Cheese, softened
1 cup sugar
3 tablespoons all-purpose flour
3 tablespoons rum
1 teaspoon vanilla
2 eggs
1 cup whipping cream
4 egg yolks

CRUST

• **HEAT** oven to 325°F. Mix crumbs, butter and nutmeg; press onto bottom and 1½-inches up sides of 9-inch springform pan. Bake 10 minutes.

FILLING

• **BEAT** cream cheese, sugar, flour, rum and vanilla at medium speed with electric mixer until well blended. Add eggs, 1 at a time, mixing at low speed after each addition, just until blended.

• **BLEND** in cream and egg yolks; pour into crust.

• **BAKE** 1 hour and 10 minutes to 1 hour and 15 minutes or until center is almost set. Run knife or metal spatula around rim of pan to loosen cake; cool before removing rim of pan. Refrigerate 4 hours or overnight. Garnish with COOL WHIP® Whipped Topping and ground nutmeg.   *Makes 12 servings*

PEPPERIDGE FARM®
CARAMEL APPLE TARTS

1 package (10 ounces) PEPPERIDGE
   FARM® Frozen Puff Pastry Shells
6 tablespoons sugar
½ teaspoon ground cinnamon
½ teaspoon ground ginger
3 apples *or* pears, peeled, cored and thinly
   sliced (about 4 cups)
⅔ cup caramel sauce
   Vanilla ice cream

1. Thaw pastry shells at room temperature 30 minutes. Preheat oven to 375°F. Mix sugar, cinnamon and ginger and set aside.

2. Roll pastry shells into 5-inch circles on lightly floured surface. Place on 2 shallow-sided baking sheets. Divide apple slices among pastry circles. Sprinkle each with **1 tablespoon** sugar mixture. Bake 25 minutes or until pastry is golden.

3. In small saucepan over medium heat, heat caramel sauce until warm. Spoon over tarts. Serve with ice cream.   *Makes 6 servings*

Tip: For more delicious PEPPERIDGE FARM® Puff Pastry recipes and ideas, visit our Web site at www.puffpastry.com.

Thaw Time: 30 minutes
Prep Time: 20 minutes
Cook Time: 25 minutes

Eggnog Cheesecake

SPICED PUMPKIN PIE

Reduced-Fat Pie Pastry (recipe follows)
or favorite pastry for 9-inch pie
1 can (16 ounces) pumpkin
1 can (12 ounces) evaporated skim milk
3 eggs
5½ teaspoons EQUAL® FOR RECIPES or
    18 packets EQUAL® sweetener or
    ¾ cup EQUAL® SPOONFUL™
¼ teaspoon salt
1 teaspoon ground cinnamon
½ teaspoon ground ginger
¼ teaspoon ground nutmeg
⅛ teaspoon ground cloves

• Roll pastry on floured surface into circle 1 inch larger than inverted 9-inch pie pan. Ease into pan; trim and flute edge.

• Beat pumpkin, evaporated milk and eggs in medium bowl; beat in remaining ingredients. Pour into pastry shell. Bake in preheated 425°F oven 15 minutes; reduce heat to 350°F and bake until knife inserted near center comes out clean, about 40 minutes. Cool on wire rack.

Makes 8 servings

REDUCED-FAT PIE PASTRY

1¼ cups all-purpose flour
1 teaspoon EQUAL® FOR RECIPES or
    3 packets EQUAL® sweetener or
    2 tablespoons EQUAL® SPOONFUL™
¼ teaspoon salt
4 tablespoons cold margarine, cut into
    pieces
5 to 5½ tablespoons ice water

• Combine flour, Equal® and salt in medium bowl; cut in margarine with pastry blender until mixture resembles coarse crumbs. Mix in water, 1 tablespoon at a time, stirring lightly with fork after each addition until dough is formed. Wrap and refrigerate until ready to use.

• For prebaked crust, roll pastry on lightly floured surface into circle 1 inch larger than inverted 9-inch pie pan. Ease pastry into pan; trim and flute edge. Pierce bottom and side of pastry with fork. Bake in preheated 425°F oven until pastry is browned, 10 to 15 minutes. Cool on wire rack.

Makes pastry for 9-inch pie (8 servings)

Tip: Double recipe for double crust or lattice pies.

A cool kitchen and cold ingredients (any liquids should be ice cold) will help in making a successful pie crust. It's also easier to roll out chilled pie dough than room temperature pie dough. If the crust will not be prebaked, the filling should be poured into the pie shell just before baking to prevent it from getting soggy. Baking the pie on a preheated metal baking sheet will also help prevent a soggy crust.

Spiced Pumpkin Pie

APPLE CRANBERRY PIE

1 package (8 ounces) PHILADELPHIA®
   Cream Cheese, softened
½ cup firmly packed brown sugar, divided
1 egg
1 (9-inch) unbaked pastry shell
2 cups sliced apples
½ cup halved cranberries
1 teaspoon ground cinnamon, divided
⅓ cup flour
⅓ cup old-fashioned or quick-cooking oats,
   uncooked
¼ cup (½ stick) butter or margarine
¼ cup chopped nuts

MIX cream cheese and ¼ cup of the sugar
with electric mixer on medium speed until
well blended. Blend in egg. Pour into pastry
shell.

TOSS apples, cranberries and ½ teaspoon
cinnamon. Spoon over cream cheese mixture.

MIX flour, oats, remaining ¼ cup sugar and
remaining ½ teaspoon cinnamon. Cut in butter
until mixture resembles coarse crumbs. Stir in
nuts. Spoon over fruit mixture.

BAKE at 375°F for 40 to 45 minutes or until
lightly browned. Cool slightly before serving.
Makes 8 to 10 servings

Prep Time: 15 minutes plus cooling
Baking Time: 45 minutes

IRISH COFFEE CREAM PIE

1 package (4 ounces) BAKER'S®
   GERMAN'S® Sweet Chocolate
1 tub (8 ounces) COOL WHIP® Whipped
   Topping, thawed
1 prepared graham cracker crumb or
   chocolate flavor crumb crust
   (6 ounces)
1 cup cold milk
2 tablespoons Irish whiskey (optional)
1 package (4-serving size) JELL-O® Vanilla
   Flavor Instant Pudding & Pie Filling
1 teaspoon MAXWELL HOUSE® Instant
   Coffee

MICROWAVE chocolate in medium
microwavable bowl on HIGH 2 to 3 minutes
or until chocolate is almost melted, stirring
halfway through heating time. Stir until
chocolate is completely melted. Cool 20
minutes or until room temperature.

STIR 1½ cups of the whipped topping into
chocolate with wire whisk until smooth.
Spread onto bottom of crust.

POUR milk and whiskey into medium bowl.
Add pudding mix and instant coffee. Beat with
wire whisk 2 minutes. Gently stir in 1¼ cups
of the whipped topping. Spread over chocolate
layer.

REFRIGERATE 3 hours or freeze 2 hours.
Garnish with remaining whipped topping.
Makes 8 servings

Apple Cranberry Pie

HERSHEY'S COCOA CREAM PIE

½ cup HERSHEY'S Cocoa
1¼ cups sugar
⅓ cup cornstarch
¼ teaspoon salt
3 cups milk
3 tablespoons butter or margarine
1½ teaspoons vanilla extract
1 baked 9-inch pie crust or graham cracker crumb crust, cooled

In medium saucepan, stir together cocoa, sugar, cornstarch and salt. Gradually add milk, stirring until smooth. Cook over medium heat, stirring constantly, until mixture comes to a boil; boil 1 minute. Remove from heat; stir in butter and vanilla. Pour into prepared crust. Press plastic wrap directly onto surface. Cool to room temperature. Refrigerate 6 to 8 hours. Garnish as desired. Cover; refrigerate leftover pie.   *Makes 6 to 8 servings*

CHOCOLATE MACAROON HEATH® PIE

½ cup (1 stick) butter or margarine, melted
3 cups MOUNDS® Sweetened Coconut Flakes
2 tablespoons all-purpose flour
1¼ cups (6-ounce package) HEATH® Bits
½ gallon chocolate ice cream, softened

Heat oven to 375°F.

Combine butter, coconut and flour. Press into 9-inch pie pan. Bake at 375°F for 10 minutes or until edge is light golden brown. Cool completely.

Set aside ¼ cup Heath® Bits. Combine ice cream and remaining Heath® Bits. Spread into cooled crust. Sprinkle with ¼ cup reserved bits. Freeze at least 5 hours. Remove from freezer about 10 minutes before serving.
            Makes 6 to 8 servings

Milton S. Hershey, founder of Hershey Foods, with his wife Catherine.

Hershey's Cocoa Cream Pie

Sweet Potato Meringue Pie

1 (9-inch) graham cracker crust

FILLING

**2 whole sweet potatoes or 1 (29-ounce)
   can sweet potatoes, drained
1 cup (12-ounce jar) SMUCKER'S® Sweet
   Orange Marmalade
2 egg yolks
¼ teaspoon cinnamon
¼ teaspoon ginger
⅛ teaspoon allspice
⅛ teaspoon nutmeg
   Pinch of salt
1 cup evaporated skim milk
3 tablespoons cornstarch**

MERINGUE

**3 egg whites
   Pinch of salt
⅓ cup sugar**

Bake graham cracker crust at 400°F for 10 minutes.

Meanwhile, pierce sweet potatoes with fork and microwave on HIGH for 4 minutes. Combine cooked sweet potatoes, marmalade, egg yolks, cinnamon, ginger, allspice, nutmeg and salt; stir to blend thoroughly. Stir in evaporated milk. Add cornstarch and stir until smooth.

Pour filling into pie crust. Bake at 400°F for 45 to 55 minutes or until knife inserted in center comes out clean. Remove pie from oven and set aside to cool. Reduce oven heat to 350°F.

Beat egg whites and salt with electric mixer until soft peaks form. Gradually add sugar;

beat until egg whites are stiff and shiny. Carefully spread meringue over top of cooled pie. Bake at 350°F for 15 minutes or until meringue is golden brown.

Cool pie on wire rack. Serve at room temperature or refrigerate and serve cold.

Makes 10 servings

Fluffy Cranberry Orange Pie

**⅔ cup boiling water
1 package (4-serving size) JELL-O® Brand
   Cranberry Flavor Gelatin Dessert or
   any other red flavor
½ cup cold water
   Ice cubes
1 tub (8 ounces) COOL WHIP® Whipped
   Topping, thawed
¾ cup cranberry-orange relish
1 prepared graham cracker crumb crust
   (6 ounces)
   Sugared Cranberries (recipe follows)
   Orange slices, cut into small wedges**

STIR boiling water into gelatin in large bowl 2 minutes or until completely dissolved. Mix cold water and ice cubes to make 1 cup. Add to gelatin; stir until slightly thickened (consistency of unbeaten egg whites). Remove any remaining ice. Gently stir in 2½ cups of the whipped topping with wire whisk until blended. Gently stir in relish. Refrigerate 20 minutes or until mixture is very thick and will mound. Spoon into pie crust.

REFRIGERATE 2 hours or until firm. Garnish with remaining whipped topping, Sugared Cranberries and orange slices.

Makes 8 servings

Sugared Cranberries: Dip fresh cranberries into 1 lightly beaten egg white. (Note: Use only clean eggs with no cracks in shells.) Hold to permit excess egg white to drain off; roll in sugar in flat plate to coat well. Place on tray covered with waxed paper. Let stand until dry.

CHOCOLATE BANANA PUDDING PIE

4 squares BAKER'S® Semi-Sweet Baking Chocolate
2 tablespoons milk
1 tablespoon butter or margarine
1 prepared graham cracker crumb crust (6 ounces)
1½ to 2 medium bananas, sliced
2¾ cups cold milk
2 packages (4-serving size) JELL-O® Vanilla or Banana Flavor Instant Pudding & Pie Filling

MICROWAVE chocolate, 2 tablespoons milk and butter in medium microwavable bowl on HIGH 1 to 1½ minutes, stirring every 30 seconds. Stir until chocolate is completely melted. Spread evenly onto bottom of crust. Refrigerate 30 minutes or until chocolate is firm. Arrange banana slices over chocolate.

POUR 2¾ cups milk into large bowl. Add pudding mixes. Beat with wire whisk 1 minute. Spread over banana slices.

REFRIGERATE 4 hours or until set.

Makes 8 servings

Preparation Time: 20 minutes
Refrigerating Time: 4½ hours

In 1852, a new kind of chocolate was introduced, Baker's German's sweet chocolate, named for Samuel German, who helped perfect this delectable sweet chocolate. It is a special blend of chocolate, enriched with cocoa butter and sugar, that retains its rich and mild flavor in recipes.

Pumpkin Apple Tart

Crust

- 1 cup plain dry bread crumbs
- 1 cup crunchy nut-like cereal nuggets
- 1/2 cup sugar
- 1/2 teaspoon ground cinnamon
- 1/2 teaspoon ground nutmeg
- 1/4 cup MOTT'S® Natural Apple Sauce
- 2 tablespoons margarine, melted
- 1 egg white

Filling

- 12 ounces evaporated skim milk
- 1 1/2 cups solid-pack pumpkin
- 2/3 cup sugar
- 1/2 cup MOTT'S® Chunky Apple Sauce
- 1/3 cup GRANDMA'S® Molasses
- 2 egg whites
- 1 whole egg
- 1/2 teaspoon ground ginger
- 1/2 teaspoon ground cinnamon
- 1/2 teaspoon ground nutmeg
- Frozen light nondairy whipped topping, thawed (optional)

1. Preheat oven to 375°F. Spray 9- or 10-inch springform pan with nonstick cooking spray.

2. To prepare Crust, in medium bowl, combine bread crumbs, cereal, 1/2 cup sugar, 1/2 teaspoon cinnamon and 1/2 teaspoon nutmeg.

3. Add 1/4 cup apple sauce, margarine and egg white; mix until moistened. Press onto bottom of prepared pan.

4. Bake 8 minutes.

FILLING

5. To prepare Filling, place evaporated milk in small saucepan. Cook over medium heat until milk almost boils, stirring occasionally.

6. In large bowl, combine evaporated milk, pumpkin, 2/3 cup sugar, 1/2 cup chunky apple sauce, molasses, 2 egg whites, whole egg, ginger, 1/2 teaspoon cinnamon and 1/2 teaspoon nutmeg. Pour into baked crust.

7. Increase oven temperature to 400° F. Bake 35 to 40 minutes or until center is set.

8. Cool 20 minutes on wire rack. Remove side of pan. Spoon or pipe whipped topping onto tart, if desired. Cut into 12 slices. Refrigerate leftovers.   *Makes 12 servings*

Eggnog Pie

- 1 cup cold dairy or canned eggnog
- 1 package (6-serving size) JELL-O® Vanilla Flavor Instant Pudding & Pie Filling
- 1 tablespoon rum*
- 1/4 teaspoon ground nutmeg
- 1 tub (8 ounces) COOL WHIP® Whipped Topping, thawed, divided
- 1 prepared graham cracker crumb crust (6 ounces)

*Or, use 1/4 teaspoon rum extract.

Pour cold eggnog into medium bowl. Add pudding mix, rum and nutmeg. Beat with wire whisk or electric mixer on lowest speed 2 minutes. Let stand 5 minutes.

Fold in 2 cups of the whipped topping. Spoon into crust. Refrigerate 2 hours or until set.

Garnish with remaining whipped topping. Sprinkle with additional nutmeg, if desired.
Makes 1 (9-inch) pie

Pumpkin Apple Tart

QUICK-AND-EASY HOLIDAY TRIFLE

3 cups cold milk
2 packages (4-serving size) JELL-O® Vanilla Flavor Instant
    Pudding & Pie Filling
1 tub (8 ounces) COOL WHIP® Whipped Topping, thawed
1 package (12 ounces) pound cake, cut into ½-inch cubes
¼ cup orange juice
2 cups sliced strawberries

POUR milk into large bowl. Add pudding mixes. Beat with wire whisk 1 minute. Gently stir in 2 cups of the whipped topping.

ARRANGE ½ of the cake cubes in 3½-quart serving bowl. Drizzle with ½ of the orange juice. Spoon ½ of the pudding mixture over cake cubes. Top with strawberries. Layer with remaining cake cubes, orange juice and pudding mixture.

REFRIGERATE until ready to serve. Top with remaining whipped topping and garnish as desired. *Makes 12 servings*

Preparation Time: 20 minutes
Refrigerating Time: 1 hour

Quick-and-Easy Holiday Trifle

PEPPERIDGE FARM® CHOCOLATE MOUSSE NAPOLEONS WITH STRAWBERRIES & CREAM

½ package (17¼-ounce size) PEPPERIDGE
   FARM® Frozen Puff Pastry Sheets
   (1 sheet)
1 cup heavy cream
¼ teaspoon ground cinnamon
1 package (6 ounces) semi-sweet chocolate
   pieces, melted and cooled
2 cups sweetened whipped cream *or*
   whipped topping
1½ cups sliced strawberries
1 square (1 ounce) semi-sweet chocolate,
   melted (optional)
   Confectioners' sugar

1. Thaw pastry sheet at room temperature 30 minutes. Preheat oven to 400°F.

2. Unfold pastry on lightly floured surface. Cut into 3 strips along fold marks. Cut each strip into 6 rectangles.

3. Bake 15 minutes or until golden. Remove from baking sheet and cool on wire rack.

4. In medium bowl place cream and cinnamon. Beat with electric mixer at high speed until stiff peaks form. Fold in melted chocolate pieces. Split pastries into 2 layers. Spread 12 rectangles with chocolate cream. Top with another rectangle. Spread with whipped cream, sliced strawberries and remaining rectangles. Serve immediately or cover and refrigerate up to 4 hours. Just before serving, drizzle with melted chocolate and sprinkle with confectioners' sugar.

Makes 12 napoleons

Thaw Time: 30 minutes
Prep Time: 25 minutes
Cook Time: 15 minutes

A double boiler is the safest method for melting chocolate because it prevents scorching. Place the chocolate in the top of a double boiler or in a heatproof bowl over hot, not boiling water, and stir until smooth. To use the direct heat method, place the chocolate in a heavy saucepan and melt over very low heat, stirring constantly. To melt chocolate in the microwave, place a 1-ounce square or 1 cup (6 ounces) of chips in a small microwavable bowl. Microwave at HIGH 1 to 1½ minutes, stirring after 1 minute. Stir the chocolate at 30-second intervals until smooth. Be sure to stir microwaved chocolate since it may retain its original shape even after melting.

**Pepperidge Farm® Chocolate Mousse
Napoleons with Strawberries & Cream**

TIRAMISU

1½ cups cold 2% lowfat milk, divided
1 container (8 ounces) pasteurized process cream cheese product
2 tablespoons MAXWELL HOUSE® or YUBAN® Instant Coffee or SANKA® Brand 99.7% Caffeine Free Instant Coffee
1 tablespoon hot water
2 tablespoons brandy (optional)
1 package (4-serving size) JELL-O® Vanilla Flavor Sugar Free Instant Pudding & Pie Filling
2 cups thawed COOL WHIP LITE® Whipped Topping
1 package (3 ounces) ladyfingers, split
1 square (1 ounce) BAKER'S® Semi-Sweet Baking Chocolate, grated

• Pour ½ cup of the milk into blender container. Add cream cheese product; cover. Blend until smooth. Blend in the remaining 1 cup milk.

• Dissolve coffee in water; add to blender with brandy. Add pudding mix; cover. Blend until smooth, scraping down sides occasionally; pour into large bowl. Gently stir in whipped topping.

• Cut ladyfingers in half crosswise. Cover bottom of 8-inch springform pan with ladyfinger halves. Place remaining halves, cut-ends down, around sides of pan. Spoon pudding mixture into pan. Chill until firm, about 3 hours. Remove side of pan. Sprinkle with grated chocolate.   *Makes 12 servings*

AMBROSIAL FRUIT DESSERT

1 medium DOLE® Fresh Pineapple
1 medium DOLE® Orange, peeled, sliced
1 red DOLE® Apple, cored, sliced
1 cup seedless DOLE® Grapes
    Fruit Glaze (recipe follows)
4 teaspoons flaked coconut

• Twist crown from pineapple. Cut pineapple in half lengthwise. Refrigerate one half for another use, such as fruit salad. Cut fruit from shell. Cut fruit crosswise into thin slices.

• Arrange fruits on 4 dessert plates. Drizzle with Fruit Glaze. Sprinkle with coconut.
    Makes 4 servings

FRUIT GLAZE

¾ cup DOLE® Pineapple Orange Juice
2 tablespoons orange marmalade
1 tablespoon cornstarch
1 teaspoon rum extract
2 teaspoons grated lime peel

• Combine all ingredients, except lime peel, in saucepan. Cook, stirring, until sauce boils and thickens. Cool. Stir in lime peel.

Tiramisu

TEMPTING APPLE TRIFLES

½ **cup skim milk**
1½ **teaspoons cornstarch**
4½ **teaspoons dark brown sugar**
  1 **egg white**
½ **teaspoon canola oil**
½ **teaspoon vanilla extract**
½ **teaspoon rum extract, divided**
¼ **cup unsweetened apple cider, divided**
  2 **tablespoons raisins**
½ **teaspoon ground cinnamon**
  1 **cup peeled and chopped Golden Delicious apple**
  1 **cup ½-inch angel food cake cubes, divided**

To prepare custard, combine milk and cornstarch in small, heavy saucepan; stir until cornstarch is completely dissolved. Add brown sugar, egg white and oil; blend well. Slowly bring to a boil over medium-low heat until thickened, stirring constantly with whisk. Remove from heat; stir in vanilla and ¼ teaspoon rum extract. Set aside; cool completely.

Combine 2 tablespoons cider, raisins and cinnamon in medium saucepan; bring to a boil over medium-low heat. Add apple and cook until apple is fork-tender and all liquid has been absorbed, stirring frequently. Remove from heat; set aside to cool.

To assemble, place ¼ cup cake cubes in bottom of 2 small trifle or dessert dishes. Combine remaining 2 tablespoons cider and ¼ teaspoon rum extract in small bowl; mix well. Spoon 1½ teaspoons cider mixture over cake in each dish. Top each with ¼ of custard mixture and ¼ cup cooked apple mixture. Repeat layers. Serve immediately. Garnish with fresh mint, if desired.   *Makes 2 servings*

CHERRY ALMOND SUPREME

  1 **can (8 ounces) pitted dark sweet cherries in light syrup, undrained**
  1 **package (4-serving size) JELL-O® Brand Cherry Flavor Sugar Free Gelatin Dessert**
¾ **cup boiling water**
  Ice cubes
  2 **tablespoons chopped toasted almonds**
  1 **cup thawed COOL WHIP® LITE® Whipped Topping**

Drain cherries, reserving syrup. If necessary, add enough water to reserved syrup to measure ½ cup. Cut cherries into quarters. Completely dissolve gelatin in boiling water. Combine measured syrup and enough ice to measure 1¼ cups. Add to gelatin; stir until slightly thickened. Remove any unmelted ice. Chill until thickened. Measure 1¼ cups gelatin; stir in half the cherries and half the nuts. Set aside.

Gently stir whipped topping into remaining gelatin. Add remaining cherries and nuts; spoon into 6 dessert glasses. Chill until set but not firm, about 15 minutes. Top with clear gelatin mixture. Chill until set, about 1 hour.
      Makes 6 servings (about 3 cups)

Tempting Apple Trifles

CHOCOLATE MOUSSE

1 teaspoon unflavored gelatin
1 tablespoon cold water
2 tablespoons boiling water
½ cup sugar
¼ cup HERSHEY'S Cocoa
1 cup chilled whipping cream
1 teaspoon vanilla extract

In small bowl sprinkle gelatin over cold water; let stand 1 minute to soften. Add boiling water; stir until gelatin is completely dissolved and mixture is clear. Cool slightly. In small mixer bowl stir together sugar and cocoa; add whipping cream and vanilla. Beat at medium speed, scraping bottom of bowl occasionally, until mixture is stiff; pour in gelatin mixture and beat until well blended. Spoon into serving dishes. Refrigerate about 30 minutes.
Makes four ½-cup servings

Chocolate Mousse Filled Croissants: Prepare Chocolate Mousse according to directions. Cut 6 bakery croissants horizontally in half. Spread about ⅓ cup mousse onto each bottom half; replace with top half of croissant. Refrigerate about 30 minutes. Makes 6 servings

Chocolate Mousse Parfaits: Prepare Chocolate Mousse according to directions. Alternately spoon mousse and sliced fresh fruit into parfait glasses. Refrigerate about 1 hour. Makes 5 to 6 servings

Senior Hall of Milton Hershey School, c. 1940. Milton Hershey and his wife Catherine founded this home and school for orphan boys in 1909.

Clockwise from top left: Chocolate Mousse Filled Croissants, Chocolate Mousse Parfaits and Chocolate Mousse

ALMOND-PEAR STRUDEL

¾ cup slivered almonds, divided
5 to 6 cups thinly sliced crisp pears
    (4 to 5 medium pears)
1 tablespoon grated lemon peel
1 tablespoon lemon juice
⅓ cup plus 1 teaspoon sugar, divided
2 teaspoons ground cinnamon
1 teaspoon ground nutmeg
4 tablespoons butter or margarine, divided
6 sheets (¼ pound) phyllo dough
½ teaspoon almond extract

1. Preheat oven to 300°F. Spread almonds in shallow baking pan. Bake 10 to 12 minutes or until lightly browned, stirring frequently; cool and cover. Place sliced pears in large microwavable container. Stir in lemon peel and lemon juice. Microwave on HIGH 6 minutes or until tender; cool. Combine ⅓ cup sugar, cinnamon and nutmeg in small bowl; cover. Cover pears and refrigerate overnight.

2. Place butter in microwavable container. Microwave on HIGH 20 seconds or until melted. Lay 2 sheets plastic wrap on work surface to make 20-inch square. Place 1 phyllo sheet in middle of plastic wrap. (Cover remaining phyllo dough with damp kitchen towel to prevent dough from drying out.). Brush 1 teaspoon melted butter onto phyllo sheet. Place second phyllo sheet over first; brush with 1 teaspoon butter. Repeat layering with remaining sheets of phyllo. Cover with plastic wrap. Cover remaining butter. Refrigerate phyllo dough and butter overnight or up to 1 day.

3. Preheat oven to 400°F. Drain reserved pears in colander. Toss pears with reserved sugar mixture and almond extract. Melt reserved butter. Uncover phyllo dough and spread pear mixture evenly over phyllo, leaving 3-inch strip on far long side. Sprinkle pear mixture with ½ cup toasted almonds. Brush strip with 2 teaspoons melted butter. Beginning at long side of phyllo opposite 3-inch strip, carefully roll up jelly-roll style, using plastic wrap to gently lift, forming strudel. Place strudel, seam-side down, onto buttered baking sheet. Brush top with 1 teaspoon butter. Bake 20 minutes or until deep golden. Brush again with 1 teaspoon butter. Combine remaining ¼ cup toasted almonds with remaining butter; sprinkle on top of strudel. Sprinkle with remaining 1 teaspoon sugar. Bake an additional 5 minutes. Cool 10 minutes; sprinkle with powdered sugar, if desired.

Makes 8 servings

Almond-Pear Strudel

FLAN

2 cups sugar, divided
½ cup water
1 package (8 ounces) PHILADELPHIA®
  Cream Cheese, softened
1 can (13 ounces) evaporated milk
4 eggs
1 teaspoon vanilla
  Dash salt

STIR 1 cup of the sugar and water in heavy saucepan on medium high heat. Boil until syrup turns deep golden brown. Remove from heat; immediately pour into 8- or 9-inch round cake pan, tilting pan to distribute syrup evenly on bottom.

MIX cream cheese and remaining 1 cup sugar with electric mixer on medium speed until well blended. Gradually add milk. Blend in eggs, vanilla and salt. Pour mixture into pan.

PLACE pan in large baking pan; place in oven. Pour boiling water into pan to about ¾ of the way up sides of cake pan.

BAKE at 350°F for 1 hour and 20 minutes or until knife inserted near center comes out clean. Remove cake pan from water; cool. Cover. Refrigerate several hours. To serve, run metal spatula around edge of pan. Unmold onto serving plate.   *Makes 8 to 10 servings*

Prep Time: 30 minutes plus refrigerating
Baking Time: 1 hour 20 minutes

KAHLÚA® CHOCOLATE-MINT TRIFLE

1 chocolate cake mix (without pudding)
1 cup KAHLÚA®
2 boxes (4-serving size) instant chocolate
  pudding
3½ cups milk
3 cups whipped topping
  Peppermint candy, crushed

Prepare, bake and cool cake in 13×9-inch baking pan according to package directions. Poke holes in cake with fork; pour Kahlúa® over top. Refrigerate overnight. Cut cake into cubes.

Prepare pudding mix with milk in large bowl according to package directions. Layer in large clear glass trifle dish or glass bowl ⅓ each of cake cubes, pudding, whipped topping and candy. Repeat layers two more times. Refrigerate leftovers.

Makes about 18 servings

Flan

CRANBERRY CREAM CHEESE DESSERT

1½ cups boiling water
 1 package (8-serving size) or 2 packages (4-serving size) JELL-O® Brand Cranberry Flavor Gelatin Dessert, or any red flavor
1½ cups cold water
 1 can (16 ounces) whole berry cranberry sauce
1½ cups graham cracker crumbs
 ½ cup sugar, divided
 ½ cup (1 stick) butter or margarine, melted
 1 package (8 ounces) PHILADELPHIA® Cream Cheese, softened
 2 tablespoons milk
 1 tub (8 ounces) COOL WHIP® Whipped Topping, thawed

STIR boiling water into gelatin in large bowl at least 2 minutes until completely dissolved. Stir in cold water and cranberry sauce. Refrigerate about 1¼ hours or until slightly thickened (consistency of unbeaten egg whites).

MEANWHILE, mix crumbs, ¼ cup of the sugar and butter in 13×9-inch pan. Press firmly onto bottom of pan. Refrigerate until ready to fill.

BEAT cream cheese, remaining ¼ cup sugar and milk in large bowl until smooth. Gently stir in 2 cups of the whipped topping. Spread evenly over crust. Spoon gelatin mixture over cream cheese layer.

REFRIGERATE 3 hours or until firm. Serve with remaining whipped topping.

Makes 15 servings

Preparation Time: 25 minutes
Refrigerating Time: 4¼ hours

SPICED APPLE & CRANBERRY COMPOTE

2½ cups cranberry juice cocktail
 1 package (6 ounces) dried apples
 ½ cup (2 ounces) dried cranberries
 ½ cup Rhine wine or apple juice
 ½ cup honey
 2 cinnamon sticks, broken into halves
 Frozen yogurt or ice cream (optional)
 Additional cinnamon sticks (optional)

SLOW COOKER DIRECTIONS

Mix juice, apples, cranberries, wine, honey and cinnamon stick halves in slow cooker. Cover and cook on LOW 4 to 5 hours or until liquid is absorbed and fruit is tender. Remove and discard cinnamon stick halves. Ladle compote into bowls. Serve warm, at room temperature or chilled with scoop of frozen yogurt or ice cream and garnish with additional cinnamon sticks, if desired.

Makes 6 servings

Spiced Apple & Cranberry Compote

SPARKLING DESSERT

1½ cups boiling water
1 package (8-serving size) or 2 packages
   (4-serving size) JELL-O® Brand
   Sparkling White Grape or Lemon
   Flavor Gelatin Dessert
2½ cups cold seltzer or club soda
1 cup sliced strawberries

STIR boiling water into gelatin in large bowl at least 2 minutes until completely dissolved. Stir in cold seltzer. Refrigerate about 1½ hours or until thickened (spoon drawn through leaves definite impression).

MEASURE 1 cup thickened gelatin into medium bowl; set aside. Stir strawberries into remaining gelatin. Spoon into champagne glasses or dessert dishes.

BEAT reserved gelatin with electric mixer on high speed until fluffy and about doubled in volume. Spoon over clear gelatin in glasses. Refrigerate 2 hours or until firm.

Makes 8 servings

Preparation Time: 15 minutes
Refrigerating Time: 3½ hours

Historical ad for the "dessert that can be made in a minute."

Sparkling Dessert

COLD CHERRY MOUSSE WITH VANILLA SAUCE

1 envelope whipped topping mix
½ cup skim milk
½ teaspoon vanilla extract
2 envelopes unflavored gelatin
½ cup sugar
½ cup cold water
1 package (16 ounces) frozen unsweetened cherries, thawed, undrained and divided
1 tablespoon fresh lemon juice
½ teaspoon almond extract
Vanilla Sauce (recipe follows)

Prepare whipped topping according to package directions using milk and vanilla; set aside. Combine gelatin and sugar in small saucepan; stir in water. Let stand 5 minutes to soften. Heat over low heat until gelatin is completely dissolved. Cool to room temperature. Set aside 1 cup cherries without juice for garnish. Place remaining cherries and juice in blender. Add lemon juice, almond extract and gelatin mixture; process until blended. Fold cherry purée into whipped topping. Pour mixture into Bundt pan or ring mold. Refrigerate 4 hours or overnight until jelled.

To serve, unmold mousse onto large serving plate. Spoon remaining 1 cup cherries into center of mousse. Serve with Vanilla Sauce. Garnish with fresh mint, if desired.

Makes 6 servings

VANILLA SAUCE

4½ teaspoons cherry brandy *or* 1 teaspoon vanilla extract plus ½ teaspoon cherry extract
¾ cup melted vanilla ice milk or low-fat ice cream, cooled

Stir brandy into ice milk in small bowl; blend well.
Makes ¾ cup

Powdered gelatin will last indefinitely if it is wrapped airtight and stored in a cool, dry place. It is important to soak gelatin in cold liquid for several minutes (as the recipe directs) before dissolving it, so the gelatin granules soften, swell and dissolve smoothly when heated. When heated, gelatin mixtures should never be brought to a boil, or the ability of the gelatin to set will be destroyed. Once the gelatin mixture is ready to pour into a mold, rinse the mold first with cold water. This will make it easier to remove the food from the mold after it has set.

Cold Cherry Mousse with Vanilla Sauce

ALL-AMERICAN PINEAPPLE & FRUIT TRIFLE

1 DOLE® Fresh Pineapple
1 cup frozen sliced peaches, thawed
1 cup frozen strawberries, thawed, sliced
1 cup frozen raspberries, thawed
1 (10-inch) angel food cake
1 package (4-serving size) vanilla flavor
   sugar free instant pudding and pie
   filling mix
⅓ cup cream sherry
½ cup thawed frozen whipped topping

• Twist crown from pineapple. Cut pineapple in half lengthwise. Refrigerate one half for another use, such as fruit salad. Cut fruit from shell. Cut fruit into thin wedges. Reserve 3 wedges for garnish; combine remaining pineapple with peaches and berries.

• Cut cake in half. Freeze one half for another use. Tear remaining cake into chunks.

• Prepare mix according to package directions.

• In 2-quart glass serving bowl, arrange half of cake chunks; sprinkle with half of sherry. Top with half each fruit mixture and pudding. Repeat layers. Cover; chill 1 hour or overnight.

• Just before serving, garnish with whipped topping and reserved pineapple wedges.

Makes 8 to 10 servings

LEMON BERRY TERRINE

1 package (12 ounces) pound cake
1 package (8 ounces) PHILADELPHIA®
   Cream Cheese, softened
1½ cups cold milk, divided
1 package (4-serving size) JELL-O® Lemon
   Flavor Instant Pudding & Pie Filling
1 teaspoon grated lemon peel
1 tub (8 ounces) COOL WHIP® Whipped
   Topping, thawed
1 pint strawberries, hulled, divided

LINE bottom and sides of 8×4-inch loaf pan with waxed paper.

CUT rounded top of cake and trim edges of cake; reserve for another use. Cut cake horizontally into 5 slices. Line bottom and long sides of pan with 3 cake slices. Cut another cake slice in half; place on short sides of pan.

BEAT cream cheese and ½ cup of the milk in large bowl with electric mixer on low speed until smooth. Add remaining milk, pudding mix and lemon peel; beat 2 minutes. Gently stir in 1 cup of the whipped topping.

SPOON ½ of the filling into cake-lined pan. Arrange ½ of the strawberries, stem-side up, in filling, pressing down slightly. Top with remaining filling. Place remaining cake slice on top of filling.

REFRIGERATE 3 hours or until firm. Invert pan onto serving plate; remove waxed paper. Garnish with remaining whipped topping and strawberries.   *Makes 16 servings*

Preparation Time: 30 minutes
Refrigerating Time: 3 hours

All-American Pineapple & Fruit Trifle

COCOA KISS COOKIES

- 1 cup (2 sticks) butter or margarine, softened
- ⅔ cup sugar
- 1 teaspoon vanilla extract
- 1⅔ cups all-purpose flour
- ¼ cup HERSHEY'S Cocoa
- 1 cup finely chopped pecans
- 1 bag (9 ounces) HERSHEY'S KISSES® Milk Chocolates
- Powdered sugar

In large bowl, beat butter, sugar and vanilla until creamy. Stir together flour and cocoa; gradually add to butter mixture, beating until blended. Add pecans; beat until well blended. Refrigerate dough about 1 hour or until firm enough to handle. Heat oven to 375°F. Remove wrappers from chocolate pieces. Mold scant tablespoon of dough around each chocolate piece, covering completely. Shape into balls. Place on ungreased cookie sheet. Bake 10 to 12 minutes or until set. Cool slightly, about 1 minute; remove from cookie sheet to wire rack. Cool completely. Roll in powdered sugar. Roll in sugar again just before serving, if desired.

Makes about 4½ dozen cookies

Top to bottom: Cocoa Kiss Cookies, Hershey's Great American Chocolate Chip Cookies (page 308)

HERSHEY'S GREAT AMERICAN CHOCOLATE CHIP COOKIES

- 1 cup (2 sticks) butter, softened
- ¾ cup granulated sugar
- ¾ cup packed light brown sugar
- 1 teaspoon vanilla extract
- 2 eggs
- 2¼ cups all-purpose flour
- 1 teaspoon baking soda
- ½ teaspoon salt
- 2 cups (12-ounce package) HERSHEY'S Semi-Sweet Chocolate Chips
- 1 cup chopped nuts (optional)

Heat oven to 375°F. In large mixer bowl, beat butter, granulated sugar, brown sugar and vanilla until creamy. Add eggs; beat well. Stir together flour, baking soda and salt; gradually add to butter mixture, beating well. Stir in chocolate chips and nuts, if desired. Drop dough by rounded teaspoonfuls onto ungreased cookie sheet. Bake 8 to 10 minutes or until lightly browned. Cool slightly; remove from cookie sheet to wire rack. Cool completely.   *Makes about 6 dozen cookies*

Hershey's Great American Chocolate Chip Pan Cookies: Spread dough into greased 15½×10½×1-inch jelly-roll pan. Bake at 375°F for 20 minutes or until lightly browned. Cool completely in pan on wire rack. Cut into bars. Makes about 4 dozen bars.

Skor® & Chocolate Chip Cookies: Omit 1 cup HERSHEY'S Semi-Sweet Chocolate Chips and nuts; replace with 1 cup finely chopped SKOR® bars. Drop onto cookie sheets and bake as directed.

PUMPKIN HARVEST BARS

- 1¾ cups all-purpose flour
- 2 teaspoons baking powder
- 1 teaspoon grated orange peel
- 1 teaspoon ground cinnamon
- ½ teaspoon salt
- ½ teaspoon ground nutmeg
- ¼ teaspoon ground ginger
- ¼ teaspoon ground cloves
- ¾ cup sugar
- ½ cup MOTT'S® Natural Apple Sauce
- ½ cup solid-pack pumpkin
- 1 whole egg
- 1 egg white
- 2 tablespoons vegetable oil
- ½ cup raisins

1. Preheat oven to 350°F. Spray 13×9-inch baking pan with nonstick cooking spray.

2. In small bowl, combine flour, baking powder, orange peel, cinnamon, salt, nutmeg, ginger and cloves.

3. In large bowl, combine sugar, apple sauce, pumpkin, whole egg, egg white and oil.

4. Add flour mixture to apple sauce mixture; stir until well blended. Stir in raisins. Spread batter into prepared pan.

5. Bake 25 to 30 minutes or until toothpick inserted in center comes out clean. Cool on wire rack 15 minutes; cut into 16 bars.
Makes 16 servings

Pumpkin Harvest Bars

CHUNKY BUTTER CHRISTMAS COOKIES

1¼ cups butter, softened
1 cup packed brown sugar
½ cup dairy sour cream
1 egg
2 teaspoons vanilla
1½ cups all-purpose flour
1 teaspoon baking soda
1 teaspoon salt
1½ cups old fashioned or quick oats, uncooked
1 (10-ounce) package white chocolate pieces
1 cup flaked coconut
1 (3½-ounce) jar macadamia nuts, coarsely chopped

Beat butter and sugar in large bowl until light and fluffy. Blend in sour cream, egg and vanilla. Add combined flour, baking soda and salt; mix well. Stir in oats, white chocolate pieces, coconut and nuts. Drop rounded teaspoonfuls of dough, 2 inches apart, onto ungreased cookie sheet. Bake in preheated 375°F oven 10 to 12 minutes or until edges are lightly browned. Cool 1 minute; remove to cooling rack. *Makes 5 dozen*

Favorite recipe from **Wisconsin Milk Marketing Board**

ALMOND FUDGE TOPPED SHORTBREAD

1 cup (2 sticks) margarine or butter, softened
½ cup powdered sugar
¼ teaspoon salt
1¼ cups all-purpose flour
1 (12-ounce) package HERSHEY'S Semi-Sweet Chocolate Chips
1 (14-ounce) can sweetened condensed milk (NOT evaporated milk)
½ teaspoon almond extract
Sliced almonds, toasted

Preheat oven to 350°F. In large bowl, beat margarine, sugar and salt until fluffy. Add flour; mix well. With floured hands, press evenly into greased 13×9-inch baking pan. Bake 20 to 25 minutes or until lightly browned.

In heavy saucepan, over low heat, melt chips and sweetened condensed milk, stirring constantly. Remove from heat; stir in extract. Spread evenly over baked shortbread. Garnish with almonds; press down firmly. Cool. Chill 3 hours or until firm. Cut into bars. Store covered at room temperature.

Makes 24 to 36 bars

CHEWY CHOCOLATE NO-BAKES

1 cup (6 ounces) semisweet chocolate
    pieces
16 large marshmallows
⅓ cup (5 tablespoons plus 1 teaspoon)
    margarine or butter
1 teaspoon vanilla
2 cups QUAKER® Oats (quick or old
    fashioned, uncooked)
1 cup (any combination of) raisins, diced
    dried mixed fruit, flaked coconut,
    miniature marshmallows or chopped
    nuts

In large saucepan over low heat, melt
chocolate pieces, marshmallows and
margarine, stirring until smooth. Remove
from heat; cool slightly. Stir in remaining
ingredients. Drop by rounded teaspoonfuls
onto wax paper. Chill 2 to 3 hours. Let stand
at room temperature about 15 minutes before
serving. Store in tightly covered container in
refrigerator. *Makes 3 dozen*

Microwave Directions: Place chocolate pieces,
margarine and marshmallows in large
microwavable bowl. Microwave on HIGH
1 to 2 minutes or until mixture is melted
and smooth, stirring every 30 seconds.
Proceed as recipe directs.

Early Quaker® Oats canister

CHEWY OATMEAL-APRICOT-DATE BARS

COOKIES

1¼ cups firmly packed brown sugar
¾ cup plus 4 teaspoons Butter Flavor* CRISCO® all-vegetable shortening plus additional for greasing
3 eggs
2 teaspoons vanilla
2 cups quick oats, uncooked, divided
½ cup all-purpose flour
2 teaspoons baking powder
1 teaspoon cinnamon
¼ teaspoon nutmeg
¼ teaspoon salt
1 cup finely grated carrots
1 cup finely minced dried apricots
1 cup minced dates
1 cup finely chopped walnuts
⅔ cup vanilla chips

FROSTING

2½ cups confectioners sugar
1 (3-ounce) package cream cheese, softened
¼ cup Butter Flavor* CRISCO® all-vegetable shortening
1 to 2 teaspoons milk
¾ teaspoon lemon extract
½ teaspoon vanilla
½ teaspoon finely grated lemon peel
⅓ cup finely chopped walnuts

* Butter Flavor Crisco® is artificially flavored.

1. Preheat oven to 350°F. Grease 13×9-inch baking pan with shortening. Flour lightly.

2. For cookies, combine brown sugar and ¾ cup plus 4 teaspoons shortening in large bowl. Beat at medium speed of electric mixer until fluffy. Add eggs, 1 at a time, and 2 teaspoons vanilla. Beat until well blended and fluffy.

3. Process ½ cup oats in food processor or blender until finely ground. Combine ground oats with flour, baking powder, cinnamon, nutmeg and salt in medium bowl. Add oat mixture gradually to creamed mixture at low speed. Add remaining 1½ cups oats, carrots, apricots, dates, 1 cup nuts and vanilla chips. Mix until partially blended. Finish mixing with spoon. Spread in prepared pan.

4. Bake 35 to 45 minutes or until center is set and cookie starts to pull away from sides of pan. Toothpick inserted in center should come out clean. *Do not overbake.* Cool completely.

5. For frosting, combine confectioners sugar, cream cheese, ¼ cup shortening, milk, lemon extract, vanilla and lemon peel in medium bowl. Beat at low speed until blended. Increase speed to medium-high. Beat until fluffy. Stir in ⅓ cup nuts. Spread on baked surface. Cut into bars about 2¼×2 inches. Refrigerate.   *Makes about 24 bars*

Chewy Oatmeal-Apricot-Date Bars

SNOW-COVERED ALMOND CRESCENTS

1 cup (2 sticks) margarine or butter, softened
¾ cup powdered sugar
½ teaspoon almond extract *or* 2 teaspoons vanilla extract
2 cups all-purpose flour
¼ teaspoon salt (optional)
1 cup QUAKER® Oats (quick or old-fashioned, uncooked)
½ cup finely chopped almonds
Additional powdered sugar

Preheat oven to 325°F. Beat margarine, ¾ cup powdered sugar and almond extract until fluffy. Add flour and salt; mix until well blended. Stir in oats and almonds. Shape level measuring tablespoonfuls of dough into crescents. Place on ungreased cookie sheet about 2 inches apart.

Bake 14 to 17 minutes or until bottoms are light golden brown. Remove to wire rack. Sift additional powdered sugar generously over warm cookies. Cool completely. Store tightly covered.   *Makes about 4 dozen cookies*

BLACK RUSSIAN BROWNIES

4 squares (1 ounce each) unsweetened chocolate
1 cup butter
¾ teaspoon ground black pepper
4 eggs, lightly beaten
1½ cups granulated sugar
1½ teaspoons vanilla
⅓ cup KAHLUA®
2 tablespoons vodka
1⅓ cups all-purpose flour
½ teaspoon salt
¼ teaspoon baking powder
1 cup chopped walnuts or toasted sliced almonds
Powdered sugar (optional)

Preheat oven to 350°F. Line bottom of 13×9-inch baking pan with waxed paper. Melt chocolate and butter with pepper in small saucepan over low heat, stirring until smooth. Remove from heat; cool.

Combine eggs, granulated sugar and vanilla in large bowl; beat well. Stir in cooled chocolate mixture, Kahlua and vodka. Combine flour, salt and baking powder; add to chocolate mixture and stir until blended. Add walnuts. Spread evenly in prepared pan.

Bake just until wooden toothpick inserted into center comes out clean, about 25 minutes. *Do not overbake.* Cool in pan on wire rack. Cut into bars. Sprinkle with powdered sugar.
Makes about 2½ dozen brownies

Snow-Covered Almond Crescents

PINWHEELS

3 to 3¼ cups all-purpose flour, divided
1 package RED STAR® Active Dry Yeast or
    Quick•Rise™ Yeast
⅓ cup sugar
1 teaspoon salt
½ cup water
⅓ cup shortening
2 eggs
    Cherry or raspberry preserves
1 egg, slightly beaten, plus 1 tablespoon
    water, for egg wash mixture
    Candied cherries and confectioners'
    sugar for garnish

In large mixer bowl, combine 1½ cups flour, yeast, sugar and salt; mix well. Heat water and shortening until very warm (120° to 130°F). Add shortening mixture to flour mixture. Blend in 2 eggs at low speed until moistened; beat 3 minutes at medium speed. By hand, gradually stir in enough remaining flour to make soft dough. Cover dough with plastic wrap. Refrigerate 6 to 12 hours. While dough is chilling, punch down several times.

Allow dough to come to room temperature. Divide dough in half. Roll each half into 14×10½-inch rectangle. Cut into 3½-inch squares. Place on greased baking sheets. Cut each square diagonally from each corner to ½ inch from center so there are 2 points at each corner. Place rounded teaspoonful preserves in center of each square. Lightly brush every other point with egg wash mixture. Bring moistened points toward center; gently twist and pinch to fasten together. Top each center with small piece of dough (about ½ inch in diameter), or use candied cherry for garnish.

Lightly cover pinwheels; let rise at room temperature until almost doubled, 15 to 20 minutes (10 to 15 minutes for Quick•Rise™ Yeast). Bake at 350°F for 15 minutes or until golden brown. Remove to wire rack to cool slightly. Sprinkle with confectioners' sugar.
Makes 2 dozen cookies

OATMEAL RAISIN COOKIES

¼ cup (4 tablespoons) margarine, softened
3 tablespoons granulated sugar *or*
    1¼ teaspoons EQUAL® Measure
    (5 packets) *or* 2 tablespoons fructose
¼ cup egg substitute *or* 2 egg whites
¾ cup unsweetened applesauce
¼ cup frozen unsweetened apple juice
    concentrate, thawed
1 teaspoon vanilla
1 cup all-purpose flour
1 teaspoon baking soda
½ teaspoon ground cinnamon
¼ teaspoon salt (optional)
1½ cups QUAKER® Oats (quick or old
    fashioned, uncooked)
⅓ cup raisins, chopped

Heat oven to 350°F. Lightly spray large cookie sheet with cooking spray. Beat margarine and sugar until creamy. Beat in egg substitute. Add applesauce, apple juice concentrate and vanilla; beat well. Blend in combined flour, baking soda, cinnamon and salt. Stir in oats and raisins. Drop by rounded teaspoonfuls onto prepared cookie sheet. Bake 15 to 17 minutes or until cookies are firm to the touch and lightly browned. Cool 1 minute; transfer to wire rack. Cool completely. Store in airtight container. *Makes about 3 dozen*

CHOCOLATE FILLED WALNUT-OATMEAL BARS

2 cups packed light brown sugar
1 cup (2 sticks) butter or margarine, softened
2 eggs, beaten
1 teaspoon vanilla extract
½ teaspoon powdered instant coffee (optional)
3 cups quick oats, uncooked
2½ cups all-purpose flour
1½ cups chopped walnuts, divided
1 teaspoon baking soda
½ teaspoon salt
Chocolate Filling (recipe follows)

Heat oven to 350°F. In large bowl, beat brown sugar and butter until well blended. Add eggs, vanilla and instant coffee; beat until light and fluffy. Stir together oats, flour, 1 cup walnuts, baking soda and salt; with spoon, gradually stir into butter mixture. Set aside 2 cups dough. Press remaining dough onto bottom of ungreased 15½×10½×1-inch jelly-roll pan. Prepare Chocolate Filling; spread over dough. Crumble reserved dough over filling. Sprinkle with remaining ½ cup walnuts. Bake 25 minutes or until top is golden brown (chocolate will be soft). Cool in pan; cut into bars.

Makes about 4 dozen bars

CHOCOLATE FILLING

½ cup (1 stick) butter or margarine
⅔ cup HERSHEY'S Cocoa
¼ cup sugar
1 can (14 ounces) sweetened condensed milk (not evaporated milk)
1½ teaspoons vanilla extract

In medium saucepan over low heat, melt butter. Stir in cocoa and sugar. Add sweetened condensed milk; cook, stirring constantly, until smooth and thick. Remove from heat. Stir in vanilla.

Milton Snavely Hershey, founder of Hershey Foods Corporation

CRANBERRY ORANGE RICOTTA CHEESE BROWNIES

FILLING

1 cup ricotta cheese
3 tablespoons whole-berry cranberry sauce
¼ cup sugar
1 egg
2 tablespoons cornstarch
¼ to ½ teaspoon grated orange peel
4 drops red food color (optional)

BROWNIES

¾ cup sugar
½ cup (1 stick) butter or margarine, melted
1 teaspoon vanilla extract
2 eggs
¾ cup all-purpose flour
½ cup HERSHEY'S Cocoa
½ teaspoon baking powder
½ teaspoon salt

Preheat oven to 350°F. Grease 9-inch square baking pan.

To prepare Filling, in small bowl, beat ricotta cheese, cranberry sauce, ¼ cup sugar, 1 egg and cornstarch until smooth. Stir in orange peel and food color, if desired. Set aside.

To prepare Brownies, in another small bowl, stir together ¾ cup sugar, melted butter and vanilla; add 2 eggs, beating well. Stir together flour, cocoa, baking powder and salt; add to butter mixture, mixing thoroughly. Spread half of chocolate batter in prepared pan. Spread cheese mixture over top. Drop remaining chocolate batter by teaspoonfuls onto cheese mixture.

Bake 40 to 45 minutes or until wooden pick inserted in center comes out clean. Cool completely in pan on wire rack. Cut into squares; refrigerate.

Makes about 16 brownies

Give a new twist to your Christmas by hosting an old-fashioned cookie swap, a delicious way to share the holiday spirit. Each guest should bring a batch of his or her favorite cookies, enough for everyone to take some home. You might ask them to bring copies of their recipe as well, so that any guest who likes what they've tasted can bake the cookies themselves. As the host, you simply provide bags, baskets or plates for collecting and carrying all the cookies, and a few beverages to accompany the cookie feast—hot chocolate and hot apple cider are good choices for this time of year.

Cranberry Orange Ricotta Cheese Brownies

BLACK FOREST OATMEAL FANCIES

1 cup Butter Flavor* CRISCO® all-vegetable shortening
1 cup firmly packed brown sugar
1 cup granulated sugar
2 eggs
2 teaspoons vanilla
1 ⅔ cups all-purpose flour
1 teaspoon baking soda
1 teaspoon salt
½ teaspoon baking powder
3 cups quick oats (not instant or old fashioned), uncooked
1 baking bar (6 ounces) white chocolate, coarsely chopped
6 squares (1 ounce each) semi-sweet chocolate, coarsely chopped
½ cup coarsely chopped red candied cherries
½ cup sliced almonds

*Butter Flavor Crisco® is artificially flavored.

1. Heat oven to 375°F. Place foil on countertop for cooling cookies. Combine shortening, sugars, eggs and vanilla in large bowl. Beat at medium speed until well blended.

2. Combine flour, baking soda, salt and baking powder. Mix into shortening mixture at low speed until well blended. Stir in oats, white chocolate, semi-sweet chocolate, cherries and nuts with spoon. Drop rounded tablespoonfuls of dough 2 inches apart onto ungreased baking sheets.

3. Bake at 375°F for 9 to 11 minutes or until set. Cool 2 minutes on baking sheets. Remove cookies to foil to cool completely.

Makes about 3 dozen cookies

HONEY NUT RUGELACH

1 cup butter or margarine, softened
3 ounces cream cheese, softened
½ cup honey, divided
2 cups flour
1 teaspoon lemon juice
1 teaspoon ground cinnamon, divided
1 cup finely chopped walnuts
½ cup dried cherries or cranberries

Cream butter and cream cheese until fluffy. Add 3 tablespoons honey and mix well. Mix in flour until dough holds together. Form into a ball, wrap and refrigerate 2 hours or longer. Divide dough into 4 equal portions. On floured surface, roll one portion of dough into 9-inch circle. Combine 2 tablespoons honey and lemon juice; mix well. Brush dough with ¼ of honey mixture; sprinkle with ¼ teaspoon cinnamon. Combine walnuts and cherries in small bowl; drizzle with remaining 3 tablespoons honey and mix well. Spread ¼ of walnut mixture onto dough, stopping ½ inch from outer edge. Cut circle into 8 triangular pieces. Roll up dough staring at wide outer edge and rolling toward tip. Gently bend ends to form a crescent. Place on oiled parchment paper-lined baking sheet; refrigerate 20 minutes or longer. Repeat with remaining dough and filling. Bake at 350°F 20 to 25 minutes or until golden brown. Cool on wire racks. *Makes 32 cookies*

Freezing Tip: Unbaked cookies can be placed in freezer-safe containers or bags and frozen until ready to bake.

Favorite recipe from **National Honey Board**

Black Forest Oatmeal Fancies

Mocha Crinkles

1⅓ cups firmly packed light brown sugar
½ cup vegetable oil
¼ cup low-fat sour cream
1 egg
1 teaspoon vanilla
1¾ cups all-purpose flour
¾ cups unsweetened cocoa powder
2 teaspoons instant espresso or coffee granules
1 teaspoon baking soda
¼ teaspoon salt
⅛ teaspoon ground black pepper
½ cup powdered sugar

1. Beat brown sugar and oil in medium bowl with electric mixer. Mix in sour cream, egg and vanilla. Set aside.

2. Mix flour, cocoa, espresso, baking soda, salt and pepper in another medium bowl.

3. Add flour mixture to brown sugar mixture; mix well. Refrigerate dough until firm, 3 to 4 hours.

4. Preheat oven to 350°F. Pour powdered sugar into shallow bowl. Set aside. Cut dough into 1-inch pieces; roll into balls. Roll balls in powdered sugar.

5. Bake on ungreased cookie sheets 10 to 12 minutes or until tops of cookies are firm to touch. (Do not overbake.) Cool on wire racks.

Makes 6 dozen cookies

Chocolate Peanut Butter Bars

2 cups peanut butter
1 cup sugar
2 eggs
1 package (8 ounces) BAKER'S® Semi-Sweet Chocolate
1 cup chopped peanuts

HEAT oven to 350°F.

BEAT peanut butter, sugar and eggs in large bowl until light and fluffy. Reserve 1 cup peanut butter mixture; set aside.

MELT 4 squares chocolate. Add to peanut butter mixture in bowl; mix well. Press into ungreased 13×9-inch pan. Top with reserved peanut butter mixture.

BAKE for 30 minutes or until edges are lightly browned. Melt remaining 4 squares chocolate; spread evenly over entire surface. Sprinkle with peanuts. Cool in pan until chocolate is set. Cut into bars. *Makes about 24 bars*

Prep Time: 15 minutes
Bake Time: 30 minutes

Mocha Crinkles

LEMON COOKIES

²/₃ cup MIRACLE WHIP® Salad Dressing
1 two-layer yellow cake mix
2 eggs
2 teaspoons grated lemon peel
²/₃ cup ready-to-spread vanilla frosting
4 teaspoons lemon juice

• Preheat oven to 375°F.

• Blend salad dressing, cake mix and eggs at low speed with electric mixer until moistened. Add peel. Beat on medium speed 2 minutes. (Dough will be stiff.)

• Drop rounded teaspoonfuls of dough, 2 inches apart, onto greased cookie sheet.

• Bake 9 to 11 minutes or until lightly browned. (Cookies will still appear soft.) Cool 1 minute; remove from cookie sheet. Cool completely on wire rack.

• Stir together frosting and juice until well blended. Spread on cookies.

Makes about 4 dozen cookies

EASY PEANUTTY SNICKERDOODLES

3 tablespoons sugar
3 teaspoons ground cinnamon
1 package (22.3 ounces) golden sugar
    cookie mix
2 eggs
¹/₃ cup vegetable oil
1 teaspoon water
1 cup REESE'S® Peanut Butter Chips

Heat oven to 375°F. Stir together sugar and cinnamon in small bowl; set aside.

Empty cookie mix into large bowl. Break up any lumps. Add eggs, oil and water; stir with spoon or fork until well blended. Stir in peanut butter chips. Shape dough into 1-inch balls. (If dough is too soft, cover and refrigerate about 1 hour.) Roll balls in cinnamon-sugar; place on ungreased cookie sheet.

Bake 9 to 11 minutes or until set. Cool slightly; remove from cookie sheet to wire rack. Cool completely.

Makes about 3¹/₂ dozen cookies

CHEWY RED RASPBERRY BARS

1 cup firmly packed light brown sugar
¹/₂ cup butter or margarine, at room
    temperature
¹/₂ teaspoon almond extract
1 cup all-purpose flour
1 cup quick-cooking or old-fashioned oats
1 teaspoon baking powder
¹/₂ cup SMUCKER'S® Red Raspberry
    Preserves

Combine brown sugar and butter; beat until fluffy. Beat in almond extract. Mix in flour, oats and baking powder until crumbly. Reserve ¹/₄ cup mixture; pat remaining mixture in bottom of greased 8-inch square baking pan. Dot preserves over crumb mixture in pan; sprinkle with reserved crumb mixture.

Bake at 350°F for 30 to 40 minutes or until brown. Cool on wire rack. Cut into bars.

Makes 12 bars

BROWNIE CHEESECAKE BARS

⅔ **cup plus 2 tablespoons margarine or butter**
1½ **cups sugar**
1½ **cups all-purpose flour**
⅔ **cup HERSHEY'S Cocoa**
½ **cup milk**
3 **eggs**
3 **teaspoons vanilla extract, divided**
½ **teaspoon baking powder**
1 **cup chopped nuts, optional**
1 **(8-ounce) package cream cheese, softened**
1 **tablespoon cornstarch**
1 **(14-ounce) can sweetened condensed milk (NOT evaporated milk)**

Preheat oven to 350°F. Melt ⅔ cup margarine. In large bowl, beat melted margarine, sugar, flour, cocoa, milk, 2 eggs, 2 teaspoons vanilla and baking powder until well blended. Stir in nuts if desired. Spread in greased 13×9-inch baking pan.

In small bowl, beat cheese, remaining 2 tablespoons margarine and cornstarch until fluffy. Gradually beat in sweetened condensed milk, remaining 1 egg and 1 teaspoon vanilla. Pour evenly over brownie batter. Bake 40 minutes or until top is lightly browned. Cool. Chill. Cut into bars. Garnish as desired. Store covered in refrigerator.

Makes 24 to 36 bars

HERSHEY'S®

Milton Hershey located his chocolate manufacturing operation in the heart of Pennsylvania's dairy country, so he could obtain the large supplies of fresh milk needed to make fine milk chocolate. He went on to build what is now the world's largest chocolate manufacturing plant, opening in 1905. At the time, milk chocolate was considered an expensive luxury, but Milton Hershey believed that he could mass-produce high quality chocolate. Today the company produces millions of pounds of chocolate every day.

TINY MINI KISSES™ PEANUT BLOSSOMS

¾ cup REESE'S® Creamy Peanut Butter
½ cup shortening
⅓ cup granulated sugar
⅓ cup packed light brown sugar
1 egg
3 tablespoons milk
1 teaspoon vanilla extract
1½ cups all-purpose flour
½ teaspoon baking soda
½ teaspoon salt
   Granulated sugar
   HERSHEY'S MINI KISSES™ Chocolate

1. Heat oven to 350°F.

2. In large bowl, beat peanut butter and shortening with electric mixer until well mixed. Add ⅓ cup granulated sugar and brown sugar; beat well. Add egg, milk and vanilla; beat until fluffy. Stir together flour, baking soda and salt; gradually add to peanut butter mixture, beating until blended. Shape into ½-inch balls. Roll in granulated sugar; place on ungreased cookie sheet.

3. Bake 5 to 6 minutes or until set. Immediately press MINI KISS™ Chocolate into center of each cookie. Remove from cookie sheet to wire rack.

Makes about 14 dozen cookies

Variation: For larger cookies, shape dough into 1-inch balls. Roll in granulated sugar. Place on ungreased cookie sheet. Bake 10 minutes or until set. Immediately place 3 MINI KISSES™ Chocolate in center of each cookie, pressing down slightly. Remove from cookie sheet to wire rack. Cool completely.

CRANBERRY ALMOND SQUARES

3 cups cranberries
1 cup raisins
1 cup chopped peeled apple
1 cup unsweetened apple juice
1 tablespoon granulated sugar
1½ cups whole wheat flour
1 cup regular oats, uncooked
⅓ cup firmly packed brown sugar
1 teaspoon ground cinnamon
⅛ teaspoon salt
½ cup molasses
¼ cup CRISCO® Oil
2 tablespoons slivered almonds, toasted, chopped

Heat oven to 350°F. Lightly oil 13×9-inch pan. Combine cranberries, raisins, apple, apple juice and granulated sugar in saucepan. Bring to a boil. Cook 5 minutes or until cranberry skins pop, stirring occasionally. Reduce heat and simmer, uncovered, 10 minutes. Stir occasionally. Cool.

Combine flour, oats, brown sugar, cinnamon and salt in medium bowl. Combine molasses and oil; add to flour mixture. Toss with fork until mixture resembles coarse meal. Press 2 cups flour mixture in bottom of prepared pan. Top with cranberry mixture. Spread evenly. Combine remaining flour mixture and almonds. Sprinkle over cranberry mixture. Press lightly.

Bake at 350°F for 35 minutes or until golden. Do not overbake. Cool. Cut into squares. Store loosely covered. *Makes 24 servings*

Tiny Mini Kisses™ Peanut Blossoms

BANANA COCOA MARBLED BARS

½ cup uncooked rolled oats
1½ cups all-purpose flour
 2 teaspoons baking powder
½ teaspoon baking soda
½ teaspoon salt
 1 cup sugar
½ cup MOTT'S® Natural Apple Sauce
 1 whole egg
 1 egg white
 2 tablespoons vegetable oil
⅓ cup low-fat buttermilk
 2 tablespoons unsweetened cocoa powder
 1 large ripe banana, mashed (⅔ cup)

1. Preheat oven to 350°F. Spray 9-inch square baking pan with nonstick cooking spray.

2. Place oats in food processor or blender; process until finely ground.

3. In medium bowl, combine oats, flour, baking powder, baking soda and salt.

4. In large bowl, combine sugar, apple sauce, whole egg, egg white and oil.

5. Add flour mixture to apple sauce mixture; stir until well blended. (Mixture will look dry.)

6. Remove 1 cup of batter to small bowl. Add buttermilk and cocoa; mix well.

7. Add banana to remaining batter. Mix well; spread into prepared pan.

8. Drop tablespoonfuls of cocoa batter into pan. Run knife through batters to marble.

9. Bake 35 minutes or until toothpick inserted in center comes out clean. Cool on wire rack 15 minutes; cut into 14 bars.

Makes 14 servings

ORANGE PECAN REFRIGERATOR COOKIES

2⅓ cups all-purpose flour
½ teaspoon baking soda
¼ teaspoon salt
½ cup butter or margarine, softened
½ cup packed brown sugar
½ cup granulated sugar
 1 egg, lightly beaten
   Grated peel of 1 SUNKIST® Orange
 3 tablespoons fresh squeezed orange juice
¾ cup pecan pieces

In bowl, stir together flour, baking soda and salt. In large bowl, blend together butter, brown sugar and granulated sugar. Add egg, orange peel and juice; beat well. Stir in pecans. Gradually beat in flour mixture. (Dough will be stiff.) Divide mixture in half and shape each half (on a long piece of waxed paper) into a roll about 1¼ inches in diameter and 12 inches long. Roll up tightly in waxed paper. Chill several hours or overnight.

Cut into ¼-inch slices and arrange on lightly greased cookie sheets. Bake at 350°F for 10 to 12 minutes or until lightly browned. Cool on wire racks.   *Makes about 6 dozen cookies*

Chocolate Filled Sandwich Cookies: Cut each roll into ⅛-inch slices and bake as above. When cool, to make each sandwich cookie, spread about 1 teaspoon canned chocolate fudge frosting on the bottom side of one cookie; cover with a second cookie of the same shape. Makes about 4 dozen sandwich cookies.

Banana Cocoa Marbled Bars

P.B. CHIPS BROWNIE CUPS

1 cup (2 sticks) butter or margarine
2 cups sugar
2 teaspoons vanilla extract
4 eggs
¾ cup HERSHEY'S Cocoa or HERSHEY'S Dutch Processed Cocoa
1¾ cups all-purpose flour
½ teaspoon baking powder
½ teaspoon salt
1⅔ cups (10-ounce package) REESE'S Peanut Butter Chips, divided

1. Heat oven to 350°F. Line 18 muffin cups (2½ inches in diameter) with paper or foil bake cups.

2. In large microwave-safe bowl, place butter. Microwave at HIGH (100%) 1 to 1½ minutes or until melted. Stir in sugar and vanilla. Add eggs; beat well. Add cocoa; beat until well blended. Add flour, baking powder and salt; beat well. Stir in 1⅓ cups peanut butter chips. Divide batter evenly into muffin cups; sprinkle with remaining ⅓ cup peanut butter chips.

3. Bake 25 to 30 minutes or until surface is firm; cool completely in pan on wire rack.
Makes about 1½ dozen brownie cups

ALMOND TOFFEE BARS

¾ cup butter or margarine, softened
¾ cup packed brown sugar
1½ cups all-purpose flour
½ teaspoon almond extract
½ teaspoon vanilla extract
¼ teaspoon salt
1 package (6 ounces) semi-sweet real chocolate pieces
¾ cup BLUE DIAMOND® Chopped Natural Almonds, toasted

Preheat oven to 350°F. Cream butter and sugar; blend in flour. Add extracts and salt, mixing well. Spread in bottom of ungreased 13×9×2-inch baking pan. Bake in 350°F oven for 15 to 20 minutes or until deep golden brown. Remove from oven and sprinkle with chocolate pieces. When chocolate has melted, spread evenly; sprinkle with almonds. Cut into bars; cool. *Makes about 40 bars*

P.B. Chips Brownie Cups

BAKER'S® HOLIDAY BROWNIES

4 squares BAKER'S® Unsweetened Baking Chocolate
¾ cup (1½ sticks) butter *or* margarine
2 cups sugar
3 eggs
1 teaspoon vanilla
1 cup flour
1 cup coarsely chopped nuts (optional)
White Chocolate Coconut Frosting (recipe follows)

HEAT oven to 350°F (325°F for glass baking dish). Line 13×9-inch baking pan with foil extending over edges to use as handles. Grease foil.

MICROWAVE chocolate and butter in large microwavable bowl on HIGH 2 minutes or until butter is melted. Stir until chocolate is completely melted.

STIR sugar into chocolate until well blended. Mix in eggs and vanilla. Stir in flour and nuts until well blended. Spread batter in prepared pan.

BAKE 30 to 35 minutes or until toothpick inserted in center comes out with fudgy crumbs. DO NOT OVERBAKE. Cool in pan. Run knife around edges of pan to loosen brownies from sides. Lift from pan onto cutting board using foil as handles. Frost with White Chocolate Coconut Frosting.

REFRIGERATE brownies 10 minutes to set frosting. Cut into squares or cut with cookie cutters into holiday shapes. (Press cutter down into brownies to cut. Lift up and push brownie up through cutter to remove.) Decorate with assorted decorating icings, gels and decors.

Makes 24 brownie squares or about 10 (2-inch) brownie cut-outs

White Chocolate Coconut Frosting: Beat 1 stick softened butter, 1 cup powdered sugar and 2 tablespoons milk in medium bowl with electric mixer on low speed until blended. Beat on medium speed 30 seconds until smooth. Beat in 3 squares melted BAKER'S® Premium White Baking Chocolate. Stir in half of a 7-ounce bag (1⅓ cups) BAKER'S® Sweetened Flaked Coconut. Sprinkle remaining coconut over brownies after they are frosted and cut, if desired.

Prep Time: 10 minutes
Bake Time: 35 minutes

DIVINE TRUFFLE BROWNIES

1 package (8 ounces) BAKER'S® Semi-
    Sweet *or* 1 package (6 ounces)
    BAKER'S® Bittersweet Baking
    Chocolate Squares, divided
¼ cup (½ stick) butter *or* margarine
¾ cup sugar, divided
3 eggs, divided
¾ cup flour
⅔ cup heavy *or* whipping cream

HEAT oven to 350°F (325°F for glass baking dish). Line 8-inch baking pan with foil extending over edges to form handles. Grease foil.

MICROWAVE 2 squares chocolate and butter in medium microwavable bowl on HIGH 1½ minutes or until butter is melted. Stir until chocolate is melted. Stir in ½ cup of the sugar. Stir in 1 egg until well blended. Stir in flour. Spread batter in pan.

MICROWAVE remaining chocolate (6 squares if using semi-sweet, 4 squares if using bittersweet) and cream in microwavable bowl on HIGH 1½ minutes; stir until chocolate is melted.

BEAT remaining ¼ cup sugar and 2 eggs in small bowl with electric mixer on high speed 1 minute until thick and lemon yellow colored; beat in chocolate/cream mixture. Pour over batter in pan.

BAKE 35 to 40 minutes or until truffle topping is set and edges begin to pull away from sides of pan. Cool in pan. Run knife around edges of pan to loosen brownies. Lift from pan using foil as handles. Cut into 16 brownies.

Makes 16 brownies

Prep Time: 15 minutes
Bake Time: 35 minutes

In 1765, an Irish immigrant, John Hannon, started milling chocolate in Dorchester, Massachusetts with financial help from Dr. James Baker. Without the expensive import costs, the price went down and chocolate became a popular drink. Dr. Baker eventually took over the mill and it became a family enterprise; his grandson, Walter, took over the company in 1824.

FESTIVE FRUITED WHITE CHIP BLONDIES

½ cup (1 stick) butter or margarine
1⅔ cups (10-ounce package) HERSHEY'S Premier White Chips, divided
2 eggs
¼ cup granulated sugar
1¼ cups all-purpose flour
⅓ cup orange juice
¾ cup cranberries, chopped
¼ cup chopped dried apricots
½ cup coarsely chopped nuts
¼ cup packed light brown sugar

1. Heat oven to 325°F. Grease and flour 9-inch square baking pan.

2. In medium saucepan, melt butter; stir in 1 cup white chips. In large bowl, beat eggs until foamy. Add granulated sugar; beat until thick and pale yellow in color. Add flour, orange juice and white chip mixture; beat just until combined. Spread one-half of batter, about 1¼ cups, into prepared pan.

3. Bake 15 minutes until edges are lightly browned; remove from oven.

4. Stir cranberries, apricots and remaining ⅔ cup white chips into remaining one-half of batter; spread over top of hot baked mixture. Stir together nuts and brown sugar; sprinkle over top.

5. Bake 25 to 30 minutes or until edges are lightly browned. Cool completely in pan on wire rack. Cut into bars.

Makes about 16 bars

GINGERSNAPS

2½ cups all-purpose flour
1½ teaspoons ground ginger
1 teaspoon baking soda
1 teaspoon ground allspice
½ teaspoon salt
1½ cups sugar
2 tablespoons margarine, softened
½ cup MOTT'S® Apple Sauce
¼ cup GRANDMA'S® Molasses

1. Preheat oven to 375°F. Spray cookie sheet with nonstick cooking spray.

2. In medium bowl, sift together flour, ginger, baking soda, allspice and salt.

3. In large bowl, beat sugar and margarine with electric mixer at medium speed until blended. Whisk in apple sauce and molasses.

4. Add flour mixture to apple sauce mixture; stir until well blended.

5. Drop rounded tablespoonfuls of dough 1 inch apart onto prepared cookie sheet. Flatten each slightly with moistened fingertips.

6. Bake 12 to 15 minutes or until firm. Cool completely on wire rack.

Makes 3 dozen cookies

Festive Fruited White Chip Blondies

ESPRESSO CHOCOLATE CHIP KISSES

1¼ cups firmly packed light brown sugar
¾ cup Butter Flavor* CRISCO all-vegetable shortening
2 tablespoons milk
1 teaspoon vanilla
½ teaspoon brandy extract
1 egg
1¾ cups all-purpose flour
1 teaspoon instant coffee
1 teaspoon salt
¾ teaspoon baking soda
⅓ cup milk chocolate chips
⅓ cup semi-sweet chocolate chips
½ cup coarsely chopped walnuts (optional)**
32 chocolate kisses, unwrapped

*Butter Flavor Crisco® is artifically flavored.

**If nuts are omitted, add an additional ½ cup semi-sweet chocolate chips.

1. Heat oven to 375°F. Place sheets of foil on countertop for cooling cookies.

2. Combine brown sugar, ¾ cup shortening, milk, vanilla and brandy extract in large bowl. Beat at medium speed of electric mixer until well blended. Beat egg into creamed mixture.

3. Combine flour, instant coffee, salt and baking soda. Mix into creamed mixture just until blended. Stir in milk chocolate chips and semi-sweet chocolate chips and walnuts.

4. Drop rounded measuring tablespoonfuls of dough 3 inches apart onto ungreased baking sheets.

5. Bake one baking sheet at a time at 375°F for 8 to 10 minutes for chewy cookies, or 11 to 13 minutes for crisp cookies. *Do not overbake.* Place 1 chocolate kiss in center of each cookie. Cool 2 minutes on baking sheet. Remove cookies to foil to cool completely.
Makes about 3 dozen cookies

PLUM OAT SQUARES

1 cup uncooked rolled oats
⅓ cup whole wheat flour
⅓ cup packed brown sugar
1 teaspoon ground cinnamon
¼ teaspoon baking soda
¼ teaspoon ground nutmeg
1 egg, slightly beaten
2 tablespoons unsalted butter, melted
2 tablespoons unsweetened apple juice concentrate, thawed
1 teaspoon vanilla
2 fresh California plums, finely chopped

Preheat oven to 350°F. Grease 11×7-inch baking pan; set aside. Combine oats, flour, sugar, cinnamon, baking soda and nutmeg in large bowl. Combine egg, butter, juice and vanilla in small bowl until well blended. Stir into oat mixture until well blended. Fold in plums. Spread evenly into prepared pan. Bake 25 minutes or until wooden pick inserted in center comes out clean. Cool in pan on wire rack 10 minutes. Cut into squares. Serve warm or cool completely. *Makes 12 squares*

Favorite recipe from **California Tree Fruit Agreement**

Espresso Chocolate Chip Kisses

Rich Chocolate Chip Toffee Bars

2⅓ cups all-purpose flour
⅔ cup packed light brown sugar
¾ cup (1½ sticks) butter or margarine
1 egg, slightly beaten
2 cups (12-ounce package) HERSHEY'S Semi-Sweet Chocolate Chips, divided
1 cup coarsely chopped nuts
1 can (14 ounces) sweetened condensed milk (not evaporated milk)
1¾ cups (10-ounce package) SKOR® English Toffee Bits, divided

1. Heat oven to 350°F. Grease 13×9×2-inch baking pan.

2. In large bowl, stir together flour and brown sugar. Cut in butter with pastry blender until mixture resembles coarse crumbs. Add egg; mix well. Stir in 1½ cups chocolate chips and nuts. Reserve 1½ cups mixture. Press remaining crumb mixture onto bottom of prepared pan.

3. Bake 10 minutes. Pour sweetened condensed milk evenly over hot crust. Top with 1½ cups toffee bits. Sprinkle reserved crumb mixture and remaining ½ cup chips over top.

4. Bake 25 to 30 minutes or until golden brown. Sprinkle with remaining ¼ cup toffee bits. Cool completely in pan on wire rack. Cut into bars.   *Makes about 36 bars*

Frosted Pumpkin Softies

1 cup (2 sticks) margarine or butter, softened
¾ cup firmly packed brown sugar
¾ cup granulated sugar
1 cup canned pumpkin
1 egg
1 teaspoon vanilla
2½ cups QUAKER® Oats (quick or old fashioned, uncooked)
1¾ cups all-purpose flour
1 teaspoon pumpkin pie spice or ground cinnamon
1 teaspoon baking soda
¼ teaspoon salt (optional)

FROSTING

3 ounces cream cheese, softened
1 tablespoon milk
½ teaspoon vanilla
2½ cups powdered sugar
Yellow and red food coloring (optional)

Heat oven to 350°F. Beat together margarine and sugars until creamy. Add pumpkin, egg and vanilla; beat well. Add combined oats, flour, pumpkin pie spice, baking soda and salt; mix well. Drop by rounded tablespoonfuls onto ungreased cookie sheet. Bake 11 to 13 minutes or until light golden brown. Cool 1 minute on cookie sheet; remove to wire rack. Cool completely.

For frosting, beat together cream cheese, milk and vanilla until smooth. Gradually beat in powdered sugar until smooth; tint with food color, if desired. Frost cookies; store covered in refrigerator.   *Makes about 4 dozen*

Rich Chocolate Chip Toffee Bars

KRINGLE'S CUTOUTS

1¼ cups granulated sugar
  1 cup Butter Flavor* CRISCO® all-
    vegetable shortening
  2 eggs
  ¼ cup light corn syrup or regular pancake
    syrup
  1 teaspoon vanilla
  3 cups plus 4 tablespoons all-purpose
    flour, divided
  ¾ teaspoon baking powder
  ½ teaspoon baking soda
  ½ teaspoon salt
    Colored sugar, decors and prepared
    frosting (optional)

*Butter Flavor Crisco® is artificially flavored.

1. Combine sugar and 1 cup shortening in large bowl. Beat at medium speed of electric mixer until well blended. Add eggs, syrup and vanilla. Beat until well blended and fluffy.

2. Combine 3 cups flour, baking powder, baking soda and salt. Add gradually to creamed mixture at low speed. Mix until well blended.

3. Divide dough into 4 quarters. Cover and refrigerate at least two hours or overnight.

4. Heat oven to 375°F. Place sheets of foil on countertop for cooling cookies.

5. Spread 1 tablespoon flour on large sheet of waxed paper. Place one quarter of dough on floured paper. Flatten slightly with hands. Turn dough over. Cover with another large sheet of waxed paper. Roll dough to ¼-inch thickness. Remove top layer of waxed paper. Cut out with seasonal cookie cutters. Place cutouts 2 inches apart on ungreased baking sheets. Roll and cut out remaining dough. Sprinkle with colored sugar and decors or leave plain to frost when cool.

6. Bake at 375°F for 5 to 9 minutes, depending on size of cookies. (Bake small, thin cookies about 5 minutes; larger cookies about 9 minutes.) *Do not overbake.* Cool 2 minutes on baking sheet. Remove cookies to foil sheets to cool completely.

Makes 3 to 4 dozen cookies
(depending on size and shape)

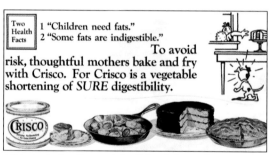

Historical advertisement for Crisco® shortening

BEST BROWNIES

½ cup (1 stick) butter or margarine, melted
1 cup sugar
1 teaspoon vanilla extract
2 eggs
½ cup all-purpose flour
⅓ cup HERSHEY'S Cocoa
¼ teaspoon baking powder
¼ teaspoon salt
½ cup chopped nuts (optional)
   Creamy Brownie Frosting (recipe follows)

Heat oven to 350°F. Grease 8- or 9-inch square baking pan. Stir together butter, sugar and vanilla in large bowl. Add eggs; beat well with spoon. Combine flour, cocoa, baking powder and salt; gradually blend into butter mixture. Stir in nuts.

Spread into prepared pan. Bake 20 to 25 minutes or until brownies begin to pull away from of pan. Cool; frost with Creamy Brownie Frosting. Cut into squares.

Makes about 16 brownies

CREAMY BROWNIE FROSTING

3 tablespoons butter or margarine,
   softened
3 tablespoons HERSHEY'S Cocoa
1 tablespoon light corn syrup or honey
½ teaspoon vanilla extract
1 cup powdered sugar
1 to 2 tablespoons milk

Beat butter, cocoa, corn syrup and vanilla in small bowl. Add powdered sugar and milk; beat to spreading consistency.

Makes about 1 cup frosting

It may sound strange, but brownies can make a great gift! Brownies and bar cookies generally pack well; just avoid those with moist fillings and frostings since they tend to become sticky at room temperature. Soft, moist cookies can survive packing and shipping better than fragile, brittle cookies, and many non-fragile confections, such as caramels and fudge, are good choices as well.

It's best to prepare foods just before packing and mailing, and to choose a speedy method of shipment (but be sure that your cookies and bars and completely cooled before packaging). Wrap each type of cookie separately to retain flavors and textures. Pack wrapped cookies in rows as tightly as possible to prevent breakage during shipping. Wrap all breakable containers in bubble wrap and fill boxes with packing peanuts.

Christmas Candy

CHRISTMAS CANDY

HOLIDAY PEPPERMINT CANDIES

- 4 ounces PHILADELPHIA® Cream Cheese, softened
- 1 tablespoon butter or margarine
- 1 tablespoon light corn syrup
- $1/4$ teaspoon peppermint extract *or* few drops peppermint oil
- 4 cups powdered sugar
  - Green and red food coloring
  - Sifted powdered sugar
  - Green, red and white decorating icing (optional)

MIX cream cheese, butter, corn syrup and extract in large mixing bowl with electric mixer on medium speed until well blended. Gradually add 4 cups powdered sugar; mix well.

DIVIDE mixture into thirds. Knead a few drops green food coloring into first third; repeat with red food coloring and second third. Wrap each third in plastic wrap.

SHAPE into 1-inch balls, working with 1 color mixture at a time. Place on wax paper-lined cookie sheet. Flatten each ball with bottom of glass that has been lightly dipped in sifted powdered sugar.

REPEAT with remaining mixtures. Decorate with icing. Store candies in refrigerator. *Makes 5 dozen*

Holiday Peppermint Candies

MINT TRUFFLES

1 package (10 ounces) mint chocolate
   chips
1/3 cup whipping cream
1/4 cup butter or margarine
1 container (3 1/2 ounces) chocolate
   sprinkles

Line baking sheet with waxed paper; set aside.
Melt chips with whipping cream and butter in
heavy, medium saucepan over low heat,
stirring occasionally. Pour into pie pan.
Refrigerate until mixture is fudgy, but soft,
about 2 hours.

Shape about 1 tablespoonful mixture into
1 1/4-inch ball. To shape, roll mixture between
palms. Repeat procedure with remaining
mixture. Place balls on waxed paper.

Place sprinkles in shallow bowl; roll balls in
sprinkles. Place truffles in petit four or candy
cups. (If sprinkles won't stick because truffle
has set, roll truffle between palms until outside
is soft.) Truffles may be refrigerated 2 to 3 days
or frozen several weeks.

Makes about 24 truffles

Tip: Truffles can also be coated with
unsweetened cocoa, powdered sugar, chopped
nuts, sprinkles or cookie crumbs to add flavor
and prevent the truffle from melting in your
fingers.

HONEY-ROASTED BRIDGE MIX

1/2 cup honey
2 tablespoons butter or margarine
1 teaspoon ground cinnamon, divided
4 cups mixed nuts
2 to 3 tablespoons superfine sugar

Preheat oven to 325°F. Combine honey, butter
and 1/2 teaspoon cinnamon in saucepan. Bring
mixture to a boil; cook 2 minutes, stirring
constantly. Pour honey mixture over nuts; stir
well until nuts are coated. Spread nut mixture
onto foil-lined cookie sheet or jelly-roll pan.

Bake 10 to 15 minutes or until nuts are glazed
and lightly browned. Do not allow nuts to
burn. Cool 20 to 30 minutes; remove from foil.
Combine sugar and remaining 1/2 teaspoon
cinnamon; toss with glazed nuts to coat.

Makes 4 cups

Prep Time: about 15 minutes
Bake Time: about 15 minutes

Favorite recipe from **National Honey Board**

Mint Truffles

BUTTER ALMOND CRUNCH

1½ cups HERSHEY'S Semi-Sweet Chocolate
    Chips, divided
1¾ cups chopped almonds, divided
1½ cups butter or margarine
1¾ cups sugar
  3 tablespoons light corn syrup
  3 tablespoons water

Heat oven to 350°F. Line 13×9×2-inch pan with foil; butter foil. Sprinkle 1 cup chocolate chips into pan; set aside. In shallow baking pan spread chopped almonds. Bake about 7 minutes or until golden brown; set aside. In heavy 3-quart saucepan melt butter; blend in sugar, corn syrup and water. Cook over medium heat, stirring constantly, to 300°F on a candy thermometer (hard-crack stage) or until mixture separates into hard, brittle threads when dropped into very cold water. (Bulb of candy thermometer should not rest on bottom of saucepan.) Remove from heat; stir in 1½ cups toasted almonds. Immediately spread mixture evenly over chocolate chips in prepared pan; do not disturb chips. Sprinkle with remaining ¼ cup toasted almonds and remaining ½ cup chocolate chips; cool slightly. With sharp knife score candy into 1½-inch squares, wiping knife blade after drawing through candy. Cool completely; remove from pan. Remove foil; break candy into pieces. Store in airtight container in cool, dry place.

Makes about 2 pounds candy

Hershey's Milk Chocolate Bar label, 1905

Butter Almond Crunch

WHITE CHOCOLATE-DIPPED APRICOTS

**3 ounces white chocolate, coarsely
   chopped**
20 dried apricot halves

Line baking sheet with waxed paper; set aside.
Melt white chocolate in bowl over hot (not
boiling) water; stir constantly.

Dip half of each apricot piece in chocolate,
coating both sides. Place on prepared baking
sheet. Refrigerate until firm. Store in
refrigerator in container between layers of
waxed paper.   *Makes 20 apricots*

STUFFED PECANS

½ cup semisweet chocolate chips
¼ cup sweetened condensed milk
½ teaspoon vanilla
   Powdered sugar (about ½ cup)
80 large pecan halves

Melt chips in small saucepan over very low
heat, stirring constantly. Remove from heat.
Stir in sweetened condensed milk and vanilla
until smooth. Stir in enough sugar to make stiff
mixture. Refrigerate, if needed.

Place 1 rounded teaspoonful chocolate
mixture on flat side of 1 pecan half. Top with
another pecan half. Repeat with remaining
pecans and chocolate mixture. Store in
refrigerator.   *Makes about 40 candies*

PEANUT BUTTER CUPS

**2 cups (12 ounces) semisweet chocolate
   chips**
1 cup (6 ounces) milk chocolate chips
1½ cups powdered sugar
1 cup crunchy or smooth peanut butter
**½ cup vanilla wafer crumbs (about
   11 wafers)**
**6 tablespoons butter or margarine,
   softened**

Line 12 (2½-inch) muffin cups with double-
thickness paper cups or foil cups; set aside.

Melt both chips in heavy, small saucepan over
very low heat, stirring constantly.

Spoon about 1 tablespoonful of the chocolate
into each cup. With back of spoon, bring
chocolate up side of each cup. Refrigerate
until firm, about 20 minutes.

Combine sugar, peanut butter, crumbs and
butter in medium bowl.

Spoon 2 tablespoons of the peanut butter
mixture into each chocolate cup. Spread with
small spatula.

Spoon about 1 tablespoon remaining
chocolate over each peanut butter cup.
Refrigerate until firm.   *Makes 12 cups*

Note: To remove paper cups, cut slit in bottom
of paper and peel paper up from bottom. Do
not peel paper down from top edge.

*White Chocolate-Dipped Apricots
and Stuffed Pecans*

EASY TURTLE FUDGE

1 package (12 ounces) semisweet
    chocolate chips (2 cups)
2 ounces bittersweet or semisweet
    chocolate, chopped
1 cup sweetened condensed milk
1/4 teaspoon salt
30 individually wrapped caramel candies,
    unwrapped
1 tablespoon water
40 pecan halves

1. Grease 11×7-inch pan; set aside.

2. Melt chips in heavy medium saucepan over very low heat, stirring constantly to prevent scorching. Remove from heat as soon as chocolate is melted; stir in bittersweet chocolate until melted. Stir in sweetened condensed milk and salt until smooth.

3. Spread evenly in prepared pan with narrow metal spatula; cover with foil. Refrigerate until firm.

4. Cut fudge into 40 squares by cutting 5 sections lengthwise and 8 sections crosswise with long thin-bladed knife. Transfer to baking sheet lined with waxed paper, placing squares 1/2 inch apart.

5. Place caramels and water in heavy small saucepan. Heat over low heat until melted, stirring frequently. Drizzle or top fudge pieces with caramel mixture. Top each piece with 1 pecan half.

6. Store candies in airtight container in freezer. Bring to room temperature before serving.

Makes 40 candies

HOLIDAY WREATHS

1/2 cup margarine or butter
1 package (10 ounces, about 40) regular
    marshmallows
1 teaspoon green liquid food coloring
6 cups KELLOGG'S CORN FLAKES® cereal
Red cinnamon candies

1. Melt margarine in large saucepan over low heat. Add marshmallows and cook, stirring constantly, until marshmallows melt and mixture is syrupy. Remove from heat. Stir in food coloring.

2. Add Kellogg's Corn Flakes® cereal. Stir until well coated.

3. Portion warm cereal mixture using 1/4 cup dry measure onto wax paper-lined baking sheet. Using buttered fingers, quickly shape mixture into individual wreaths. Dot with red cinnamon candies.   *Makes 16 wreaths*

Variation: Press warm cereal mixture into buttered 5 1/2-cup ring mold or shape into ring on serving plate. Remove from mold and dot with red candies. Slice to serve.

Easy Turtle Fudge

GIFT BOX

- 1 package (12 ounces) pound cake
- 1 package (8 ounces) PHILADELPHIA® Cream Cheese, cubed, softened
- 1½ cups cold milk, divided
- 1 package (4-serving size) JELL-O® Lemon or Vanilla Flavor Instant Pudding & Pie Filling
- 1 teaspoon grated lemon peel
- 1 tub (8 ounces) COOL WHIP® Whipped Topping, thawed
- 1 can (11 ounces) mandarin orange segments, drained
- Chewy fruit snack rolls
- Assorted small candies

LINE bottom and sides of 8×4-inch loaf pan with wax paper.

CUT rounded top off cake; reserve for snacking or another use. Trim edges of cake. Cut cake horizontally into 5 slices. Line bottom and long sides of pan with 3 cake slices. Cut another cake slice crosswise in half; place on short sides of pan.

BEAT cream cheese and ½ cup of the milk in large bowl with electric mixer on low speed until smooth. Add remaining milk, pudding mix and lemon peel. Beat 1 to 2 minutes or until well blended. Gently stir in 1 cup of the whipped topping and oranges.

SPOON filling into cake-lined pan. Place remaining cake slice on top of filling.

REFRIGERATE 3 hours or until firm. Invert pan onto serving plate; remove pan and wax paper. Frost cake with remaining whipped topping. Decorate with snack roll to form ribbon. Garnish with candies. *Makes 16 servings*

CHOCOLATE "ORNAMENTS"

- 1 package (8 squares) BAKER'S® Semi-Sweet Baking Chocolate
- 4 ounces PHILADELPHIA® Cream Cheese, cubed, softened
- 1 tub (8 ounces) COOL WHIP® Whipped Topping, thawed
- Assorted coatings, such as: powdered sugar, finely chopped nuts, toasted BAKER'S® ANGEL FLAKE Coconut, grated BAKER'S® Semi-Sweet Baking Chocolate, cookie crumbs or multicolored sprinkles

MICROWAVE chocolate in large microwavable bowl on HIGH 2 minutes or until chocolate is almost melted, stirring halfway through heating time. Stir until chocolate is completely melted. Add cream cheese; stir with wire whisk until smooth. Cool 20 minutes or until room temperature. Gently stir in whipped topping with wire whisk until blended.

FREEZE 1 hour; scoop into 1-inch balls. If necessary, freeze balls 30 minutes longer or until firm enough to roll. Roll in assorted coatings as desired. Refrigerate or freeze until ready to serve. *Makes 2½ to 3 dozen*

Cool Tips : When freezing these "ornaments" or delicate cookies, freeze first in a single layer on baking sheet, then pack in plastic boxes with wax paper between layers and store in the freezer.

Top to bottom: Gift Box, Chocolate "Ornaments"

COOKIES AND CREAM CHEESECAKE BONBONS

24 chocolate cream-filled cookies, divided
1 package (8 ounces) cream cheese, softened
1 cup nonfat dry milk
1 teaspoon vanilla
1 package (1 pound) powdered sugar (about 4 cups)
Fresh raspberries and raspberry leaves for garnish

1. Coarsely chop 12 cookies with chef's knife on cutting board; set aside.

2. Place remaining 12 cookies in food processor; process until fine crumbs form. Place crumbs on baking sheet lined with waxed paper; set aside.

3. Beat cream cheese, dry milk and vanilla in medium bowl with electric mixer at medium speed until smooth. Beat in powdered sugar, 1 cup at a time, at low speed until mixture is smooth. Stir in reserved chopped cookies. Refrigerate 2 hours or until firm.

4. Shape rounded tablespoonfuls cream cheese mixture into balls. Roll balls in reserved cookie crumbs. Garnish, if desired. Store in airtight container in refrigerator.

Makes about 3 dozen bonbons

CHOCOLATE PEANUT BUTTER BALLS

1 cup crunchy peanut butter
1 cup powdered sugar
¼ cup margarine or butter, softened
2 cups KELLOGG'S® RICE KRISPIES® cereal
54 mini-muffin cup papers
1½ cups semi-sweet chocolate morsels
2 tablespoons shortening

1. In large mixer bowl, combine peanut butter, sugar and margarine on medium speed. Add Kellogg's® Rice Krispies® cereal, mixing until thoroughly combined. Portion mixture, using rounded measuring teaspoon. Roll into balls. Place each ball in paper cup. Refrigerate.

Melt morsels and shortening in small saucepan, over low heat, stirring constantly. Spoon 1 teaspoon melted chocolate over each peanut butter ball. Refrigerate until firm. Store in airtight container in refrigerator.

Makes 54 peanut butter balls

Cookies and Cream Cheesecake Bonbons

Kahlúa® Kisses

3/4 **teaspoon instant coffee powder**
1/3 **cup water**
 1 **cup plus 2 tablespoons sugar**
1/4 **cup KAHLÚA®**
 3 **egg whites, room temperature**
1/4 **teaspoon cream of tartar**
   Dash salt

In heavy 2-quart saucepan, dissolve coffee powder in water. Add 1 cup sugar; stir over low heat until sugar dissolves. Do not allow to boil. Stir in Kahlúa®. Brush down sides of pan with pastry brush frequently dipped in cold water. Bring mixture to a boil over medium heat. Do not stir. Boil until candy thermometer registers 240° to 242°F, about 15 minutes, adjusting heat if necessary to prevent boiling over. Mixture will be very thick. Remove from heat (temperature will continue to rise).

Immediately beat egg whites with cream of tartar and salt until soft peaks form. Add remaining 2 tablespoons sugar; continue beating until stiff peaks form. Gradually beat hot Kahlua® syrup into egg whites, beating after each addition to thoroughly mix. Continue beating 4 to 5 minutes or until meringue is very thick, firm and cooled to lukewarm.

Line baking sheet with foil, shiny side down. Using pastry bag fitted with large star tip, pipe meringue into kisses about 1½ inches wide at base and 1½ inches high onto baking sheet. Bake on center rack of 200°F oven for 4 hours. Without opening door, turn off oven. Let kisses dry in oven 2 more hours or until crisp. Remove from oven; cool completely on baking sheet. Store in airtight container up to 1 week.

Makes 2½ dozen cookies

Chocolate Brittle Drops

1/2 **package (4 squares) BAKER'S® Semi-Sweet Baking Chocolate**
1½ **cups (½ pound) coarsely crushed peanut brittle**

PLACE unwrapped chocolate in heavy saucepan on very low heat; stir constantly until just melted. Remove from heat; stir in peanut brittle. Drop by teaspoonfuls onto wax paper-lined cookie sheet. Let stand at room temperature or refrigerate until chocolate is firm.

Makes about 2 dozen

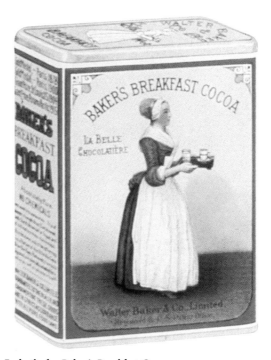

Early tin for Baker's Breakfast Cocoa

TRADITIONAL PEANUT BRITTLE

1½ cups salted peanuts
1 cup sugar
1 cup light corn syrup
¼ cup water
2 tablespoons butter or margarine
¼ teaspoon baking soda

Heavily butter large cookie sheet; set aside. Place peanuts in ungreased 8-inch square baking pan. To warm peanuts, place in oven and heat oven to 250°F.

Meanwhile, place sugar, corn syrup, water and butter in heavy 2-quart saucepan. Stir over medium-low heat until sugar has dissolved and mixture comes to a boil, being careful not to splash sugar mixture on side of pan. Carefully clip candy thermometer to side of pan (do not let bulb touch bottom of pan). Cook over medium-low heat until thermometer registers 280°F, without stirring. Gradually stir in warm peanuts. Cook until thermometer registers 300°F (hard-crack stage), stirring frequently.

Immediately remove from heat; stir in baking soda until thoroughly blended. (Mixture will froth and foam.) Immediately pour onto prepared cookie sheet. Spread mixture to form even layer. Cool about 30 minutes or until set. Break brittle into pieces. Store in airtight container.   *Makes about 1½ pounds candy*

Variation: Use almonds instead of peanuts and stir in ½ teaspoon almond extract with baking soda.

Homemade gifts are made extraordinary when tucked into uniquely decorated packages. Craft, stationery and kitchen supply stores carry a wide variety of supplies that can add a special touch to your gifts.

• *Baskets are available in many sizes, materials and colors, especially around holiday time; the smaller ones are just right for cookies. Wrap them in plain or colored cellophane, gather the ends and tie them with festive ribbons.*

• *Boxes and gift bags also come in a variety of shapes and sizes and are well suited for cookies and candies. Tuck in colorful tissue paper or other decorative paper to add a finishing touch.*

• *Tins or metal containers with tight fitting lids are just the right thing for cookies and candies because they hold up well when sent through the mail. Attach personalized gift tags to use as cards or as labels for your goodies, including storage directions if appropriate.*

TRIPLE LAYER CHOCOLATE MINTS

6 ounces semisweet chocolate, chopped
6 ounces white chocolate, chopped
1 teaspoon peppermint extract
6 ounces milk chocolate, chopped

1. Line 8-inch square pan with foil, leaving 1-inch overhang on sides.

2. Place semisweet chocolate in top of double boiler over simmering water. Stir until melted. Remove from heat.

3. Spread melted chocolate onto bottom of prepared pan. Let stand until firm. (If not firm after 45 minutes, refrigerate 10 minutes.)

4. Melt white chocolate in clean double boiler; stir in peppermint extract. Spread over semisweet chocolate. Shake pan to spread evenly. Let stand 45 minutes or until set.

5. Melt milk chocolate in same double boiler. Spread over white chocolate. Shake pan to spread evenly. Let stand 45 minutes or until set.

6. Cut mints into 16 (2-inch) squares. Remove from pan by lifting mints and foil with foil handles. Place squares on cutting board.

7. Cut each square diagonally into 2 triangles. Cut in half again to make 64 small triangles. Store in airtight container in refrigerator.

Makes 64 mints

HERSHEY'S BUCKEYES

1⅓ cups REESE'S® Crunchy Peanut Butter
¾ cup (1½ sticks) butter or margarine, softened
3 cups powdered sugar
2 cups (12-ounce package) HERSHEY'S Semi-Sweet Chocolate Chips
1 tablespoon shortening (do not use butter, margarine or oil)

1. Beat peanut butter and butter in large bowl until blended. Gradually add powdered sugar, beating until well blended. Cover; refrigerate until firm enough to shape, about 30 minutes.

2. Shape into 1-inch balls. Cover; refrigerate until firm, about 1 hour.

3. Place chocolate chips and shortening in medium microwave-safe bowl. Microwave at HIGH (100%) 1½ minutes; stir. If necessary, microwave at HIGH an additional 15 seconds at a time, stirring after each heating, just until chips are melted when stirred.

4. Dip each ball into chocolate mixture, coating ¾ of ball. Place on wax paper, uncoated side up. Let stand until chocolate hardens. Store, covered, in refrigerator.

Makes about 5 dozen candies

Prep Time: 30 minutes
Chill Time: 1½ hours
Cook Time: 1½ minutes
Cool Time: 1 hour

Triple Layer Chocolate Mints

TROPICAL SUGARPLUMS

½ cup vanilla baking chips
¼ cup light corn syrup
½ cup chopped dates
¼ cup chopped maraschino cherries, well
  drained
1 teaspoon vanilla
¼ teaspoon rum extract
1¼ cups crushed gingersnaps
  Flaked coconut

1. Combine vanilla chips and corn syrup in large skillet. Cook and stir over low heat until melted and smooth.

2. Stir in dates, cherries, vanilla and rum extract until well blended. Add gingersnaps, stirring until well blended. (Mixture will be stiff.)

3. Form mixture into ¾-inch balls; roll in coconut. Place in foil petit four cups, if desired. Serve immediately or let stand overnight to allow flavors to blend.

Makes about 2 dozen candies

Prep Time: 20 minutes

WHITE CHOCOLATE FUDGE

4 cups sifted powdered sugar
1 package (8 ounces) PHILADELPHIA®
  Cream Cheese, softened
2 packages (12 squares) BAKER'S®
  Premium White Baking Chocolate,
  melted
¾ cup chopped dried apricots
¾ cup chopped macadamia nuts
1½ teaspoon vanilla

ADD sugar gradually to cream cheese, beating with electric mixer on medium speed until well blended. Add remaining ingredients; mix well.

SPREAD into greased 8-inch square pan. Refrigerate several hours.

CUT into 1-inch squares.

Makes 64 squares

Prep Time: 15 minutes plus refrigerating

ORANGE-CANDIED WALNUTS

1½ cups sugar
½ cup corn syrup
2 tablespoons butter
4 cups California walnuts
1 teaspoon orange extract

Melt sugar, corn syrup and butter in large, shallow pan over medium-high heat. Add walnuts. Cook and stir about 15 minutes or until sugar mixture begins to caramelize. Stir in extract. Spread walnut mixture evenly onto greased baking sheet, separating walnuts into small clusters. Cool completely.

Makes 4 cups

Favorite recipe from **Walnut Marketing Board**

Tropical Sugarplums

FESTIVE POPCORN TREATS

6 cups popped popcorn
½ cup sugar
½ cup light corn syrup
¼ cup peanut butter
   Green food color
¼ cup red cinnamon candies

Line baking sheet with waxed paper. Pour popcorn into large bowl. Combine sugar and corn syrup in medium saucepan. Bring to a boil over medium heat, stirring constantly; boil 1 minute. Remove from heat. Add peanut butter and green food color; stir until peanut butter is completely melted. Pour over popcorn; stir to coat well. Lightly butter hands and shape popcorn mixture into trees. While trees are still warm, press red cinnamon candies into trees. Place on prepared baking sheet; let stand until firm, about 30 minutes.

Makes 6 servings

TIGER STRIPES

1 package (12 ounces) semisweet
   chocolate chips
3 tablespoons chunky peanut butter,
   divided
2 (2-ounce) white chocolate baking bars

Line 8-inch square pan with foil. Grease lightly. Melt semisweet chocolate and 2 tablespoons peanut butter in small saucepan over low heat; stir well. Pour half of chocolate mixture into prepared pan. Let stand 10 to 15 minutes to cool slightly. Melt white baking bars with remaining 1 tablespoon peanut butter over low heat in small saucepan. Spoon half of white chocolate mixture over dark chocolate mixture. Drop remaining dark and white chocolate mixtures by spoonfuls over mixture in pan. Using small metal spatula or knife, pull through the chocolates to create tiger stripes. Freeze about 1 hour or until firm. Remove from pan; peel off foil. Cut into 36 pieces. Refrigerate until ready to serve.

Makes 36 pieces

When melting chocolate for candies, cakes or cookies, be sure the utensils used for melting are completely dry. Moisture causes chocolate to become stiff and grainy. If this happens, add 1/2 teaspoon shortening (not butter) for each ounce of chocolate and stir until smooth. Also remember that chocolate scorches easily, especially when melted in a saucepan over direct heat, and once scorched it cannot be used.

Festive Popcorn Treats and Tiger Stripes

EASY LUSCIOUS FUDGE

2 cups (12 ounces) semisweet chocolate
   chips
¾ cup milk chocolate chips
2 squares (1 ounce each) unsweetened
   chocolate, coarsely chopped
1 can (14 ounces) sweetened condensed
   milk
1 cup mini marshmallows
½ cup chopped walnuts (optional)

Line 8-inch square pan with foil, extending
1-inch over ends of pan. Lightly grease foil.

Melt chocolates in medium saucepan over low
heat, stirring constantly. Remove from heat.
Stir in condensed milk; add marshmallows and
walnuts, if desired, stirring until combined.

Spread chocolate mixture evenly in prepared
pan. Score into 2-inch triangles by cutting
halfway through fudge with sharp knife while
fudge is still warm.

Refrigerate until firm. Remove from pan by
lifting fudge and foil. Place on cutting board;
cut along score lines into triangles. Remove
foil. Store in airtight container in refrigerator.

Makes about 3 dozen pieces

Variation: For Mint Fudge, substitute 1⅔
cups (10 ounces) mint chocolate chips for
semisweet chips and ½ cup chopped party
mints for walnuts.

CHOCOLATE TRUFFLES

3 cups powdered sugar
1 package (8 ounces) PHILADELPHIA®
   Cream Cheese, softened
1 package (12 ounces) BAKER'S® Semi-
   Sweet Real Chocolate Chips, melted
1 tablespoon coffee-flavored liqueur
1 tablespoon orange-flavored liqueur
1 tablespoon almond-flavored liqueur
   Ground nuts
   Powdered sugar
   Unsweetened cocoa

ADD 3 cups powdered sugar gradually to
cream cheese, beating with electric mixer on
medium speed until well blended. Add melted
chocolate; mix well.

DIVIDE mixture into thirds. Add different
flavor liqueur to each third; mix well.
Refrigerate several hours.

SHAPE mixture into 1-inch balls. Roll in nuts,
sugar or cocoa. Refrigerate.

Makes 5 dozen

Microwave Tip: Place chips in medium
microwavable bowl. Microwave on HIGH 1 to
2 minutes or until chips begins to melt, stirring
every minute. Remove from oven. Stir until
completely melted.

Prep Time: 20 minutes plus refrigerating

Easy Luscious Fudge

CASHEW MACADAMIA CRUNCH

2 cups (11.5 ounce package) HERSHEY'S Milk Chocolate Chips
¾ cup coarsely chopped salted or unsalted cashews
¾ cup coarsely chopped salted or unsalted macadamia nuts
½ cup (1 stick) butter, softened
½ cup sugar
2 tablespoons light corn syrup

1. Line 9-inch square pan with foil, extending foil over edges of pan. Butter foil. Cover bottom of prepared pan with chocolate chips.

2. Combine cashews, macadamia nuts, butter, sugar and corn syrup in large heavy skillet; cook over low heat, stirring constantly, until butter is melted and sugar is dissolved. Increase heat to medium; cook, stirring constantly, until mixture begins to cling together and turns golden brown.

3. Pour mixture over chocolate chips in pan, spreading evenly. Cool. Refrigerate until chocolate is firm. Remove from pan; peel off foil. Break into pieces. Store, tightly covered in cool, dry place.

Makes about 1½ pounds

Prep Time: 30 minutes
Cook Time: 10 minutes
Cool Time: 40 minutes
Chill Time: 3 hours

TRIPLE CHOCOLATE SQUARES

1½ cups BLUE DIAMOND® Blanched Almond Paste, divided
8 ounces semisweet chocolate, melted
¾ cup softened butter, divided
8 ounces milk chocolate, melted
8 ounces white chocolate, melted

Line bottom and sides of 8-inch square pan with aluminum foil. Beat ½ cup almond paste with semisweet chocolate. Beat in ¼ cup butter. Spread evenly in bottom of prepared pan. Chill to harden. Beat ½ cup almond paste with milk chocolate. Beat in ¼ cup butter. Spread mixture evenly over chilled semisweet chocolate layer. Chill to harden. Beat remaining ½ cup almond paste with white chocolate. Beat in remaining ¼ cup butter. Spread mixture evenly over chilled milk chocolate layer. Chill. Remove candy from pan by lifting edges of foil. Peel off foil and cut candy into 1-inch squares.

Makes 64 squares

Cashew Macadamia Crunch

FUDGY BANANA ROCKY ROAD CLUSTERS

1 package (12 ounces) semisweet
   chocolate chips (2 cups)
⅓ cup peanut butter
3 cups miniature marshmallows
1 cup unsalted peanuts
1 cup banana chips

Line baking sheets with waxed paper. Grease waxed paper.

Place chocolate chips and peanut butter in large microwave-safe bowl. Microwave at HIGH 2 minutes or until chips are melted and mixture is smooth, stirring twice.

Fold in marshmallows, peanuts and banana chips.

Drop rounded tablespoonfuls candy mixture onto prepared baking sheets; refrigerate until firm. Store in airtight container in refrigerator.

Makes 2½ to 3 dozen clusters

Tip: If you prefer more nuts, use chunky peanut butter when preparing Fudgy Banana Rocky Road Clusters.

WHITE COATED CHOCOLATE TRUFFLES

½ cup whipping cream
3 tablespoons butter
1 cup HERSHEY'S Semi-Sweet Chocolate
   Chips
1 teaspoon vanilla extract
   White Coating (recipe follows)

1. Combine whipping cream and butter in medium saucepan. Cook over medium heat, stirring constantly, just until mixture begins to boil; remove from heat. Add chocolate chips, stirring until completely melted; continue stirring until mixture cools and thickens slightly. Stir in vanilla. Pour into shallow glass dish. Cover; refrigerate until firm.

2. To form truffles, with spoon, scoop mixture; shape into 1-inch balls. Place on wax paper-lined tray. Cover; refrigerate until firm. Prepare White Coating. Dip truffles into coating; refrigerate. Serve well chilled. Store in tightly covered container in refrigerator.

Makes about 2 dozen truffles

White Coating: Combine 1⅔ cups (10-ounce package) HERSHEY'S Premier White Chips with 1 tablespoon shortening (do not use butter, margarine or oil) in small microwave-safe bowl. Microwave at HIGH (100%) 1 minute or just until chips are melted when stirred. (Coating works best for dipping between 85° and 90°F. If coating goes below 85°F, place bowl in larger bowl containing warm water; stir until temperature reaches 85°F. Be careful not to get any water into coating mixture.)

Prep Time: 1 hour
Cook Time: 3 minutes
Cool Time: 10 minutes
Chill Time: 5 hours

Fudgy Banana Rocky Road Clusters

Acknowledgments

The publishers would like to thank the companies and organizations listed below for the use of their recipes and photographs in this publication.

A.1.® Steak Sauce

American Lamb Council

BC-USA, Inc.

BelGioioso® Cheese, Inc.

Birds Eye®

Blue Diamond Growers®

Butterball® Turkey Company

California Olive Industry

California Tree Fruit Agreement

Campbell Soup Company

Chef Paul Prudhomme's Magic Seasoning Blends®

Del Monte Corporation

Delmarva Poultry Industry, Inc.

Dole Food Company, Inc.

Duncan Hines® brand is a registered trademark of Aurora Foods Inc.

Egg Beaters® Healthy Real Egg Substitute

Equal® sweetener

Filippo Berio Olive Oil

Florida Department of Agriculture and Consumer Services, Bureau of Seafood and Aquaculture

Golden Grain®

Grey Poupon® Mustard

Guiltless Gourmet®

Heinz U.S.A.

Hershey Foods Corporation

Hillshire Farm®

Hormel Foods Corporation

The HV Company

The J.M. Smucker Company

Kahlúa® Liqueur

Kellogg Company

Kikkoman International Inc.

The Kingsford Products Company

Kraft Foods, Inc.

Land O' Lakes, Inc.

Lawry's® Foods, Inc.

Lipton®

McIlhenny Company (TABASCO® brand Pepper Sauce)

MOTT'S® Inc., a division of Cadbury Beverages Inc.

National Chicken Council

National Cattlemen's Beef Association

National Fisheries Institute

Hebrew National®

National Honey Board

National Pasta Association

National Pork Producers Council

National Turkey Federation

Newman's Own, Inc.®

Norseland, Inc.

North Dakota Wheat Commission

The Procter & Gamble Company

The Quaker® Kitchens

Reckitt & Colman Inc.

RED STAR® Yeast & Products, A Division of Universal Foods Corporation

Riviana Foods Inc.

The Sugar Association, Inc.

Sunkist Growers

Uncle Ben's Inc.

USA Rice Federation

Walnut Marketing Board

Washington Apple Commission

Wisconsin Milk Marketing Board

Index

Y

Z

METRIC CONVERSION CHART

VOLUME MEASUREMENTS (dry)

$^1/_8$ teaspoon = 0.5 mL
$^1/_4$ teaspoon = 1 mL
$^1/_2$ teaspoon = 2 mL
$^3/_4$ teaspoon = 4 mL
1 teaspoon = 5 mL
1 tablespoon = 15 mL
2 tablespoons = 30 mL
$^1/_4$ cup = 60 mL
$^1/_3$ cup = 75 mL
$^1/_2$ cup = 125 mL
$^2/_3$ cup = 150 mL
$^3/_4$ cup = 175 mL
1 cup = 250 mL
2 cups = 1 pint = 500 mL
3 cups = 750 mL
4 cups = 1 quart = 1 L

VOLUME MEASUREMENTS (fluid)

1 fluid ounce (2 tablespoons) = 30 mL
4 fluid ounces ($^1/_2$ cup) = 125 mL
8 fluid ounces (1 cup) = 250 mL
12 fluid ounces (1$^1/_2$ cups) = 375 mL
16 fluid ounces (2 cups) = 500 mL

WEIGHTS (mass)

$^1/_2$ ounce = 15 g
1 ounce = 30 g
3 ounces = 90 g
4 ounces = 120 g
8 ounces = 225 g
10 ounces = 285 g
12 ounces = 360 g
16 ounces = 1 pound = 450 g

DIMENSIONS

$^1/_{16}$ inch = 2 mm
$^1/_8$ inch = 3 mm
$^1/_4$ inch = 6 mm
$^1/_2$ inch = 1.5 cm
$^3/_4$ inch = 2 cm
1 inch = 2.5 cm

OVEN TEMPERATURES

250°F = 120°C
275°F = 140°C
300°F = 150°C
325°F = 160°C
350°F = 180°C
375°F = 190°C
400°F = 200°C
425°F = 220°C
450°F = 230°C

BAKING PAN SIZES

Utensil	Size in Inches/Quarts	Metric Volume	Size in Centimeters
Baking or Cake Pan (square or rectangular)	8×8×2	2 L	20×20×5
	9×9×2	2.5 L	23×23×5
	12×8×2	3 L	30×20×5
	13×9×2	3.5 L	33×23×5
Loaf Pan	8×4×3	1.5 L	20×10×7
	9×5×3	2 L	23×13×7
Round Layer Cake Pan	8×1½	1.2 L	20×4
	9×1½	1.5 L	23×4
Pie Plate	8×1¼	750 mL	20×3
	9×1¼	1 L	23×3
Baking Dish or Casserole	1 quart	1 L	—
	1½ quart	1.5 L	—
	2 quart	2 L	—